Special Make-Up Effects

Special Make-Up Effects

Vincent J-R Kehoe

FOCAL PRESS

Boston • London

Library of Congress Cataloging-in-Publication Data

Kehoe, Vincent J-R
   Special make-up effects / Vincent J-R Kehoe.
     p. cm.
   Includes index.
   ISBN 0-240-80099-0 (pbk.)
   1. Film make-up. I. Title.
PN1995.9.M25K429   1991
791.43'027—dc20   90-3924
                                 CIP

British Library Cataloguing in Publication Data
Kehoe, Vincent J-R (Vincent Jeffré-Roux) 1921–
   Special make-up effects.
   1. Cinema films. Make-up. Techniques
   I. Title
   791.43027

   ISBN 0-240-80099-0

Butterworth–Heinemann
313 Washington Street
Newton, MA 02158–1626

10 9 8 7 6 5

Printed in the United States of America

Contents

Foreword

MAGIC MAKERS

As a child of 7 or 8, I was fascinated with monster movies. While other boys signed up for baseball or hockey, I preferred racing home to watch Chiller Theater's daily horror flick, usually a selection from Universal's timeless monster series of the '30s and '40s. I was captivated with the camera tricks of the day, how the mild-mannered Lon Chaney could transform into a hairy, bloodlusting werewolf right in front of my very eyes. The jaw-dropping first appearance of Boris Karloff as the Frankenstein Monster still gives me goosebumps till this day. I voraciously read the leading horror magazine of the day, *Famous Monsters of Filmland,* and fantasized about turning into werewolves and ape men.

Today, as the editor of *Famous Monsters'* descendent, *Fangoria,* I've become very familiar and in-synch with the dreams and goals of the new generation of horror fans. No longer do kids want to grow up to become the next Vincent Price or Boris Karloff. They're not interested in the monsters themselves anymore, but in the men who make the monsters. Countless *Fangoria* readers strive to be the next Rick Baker, or Dick Smith, or Tom Savini. The make-up FX artist has become the new horror star. In the 1980s, interest in make-up and special make-up effects increased tremendously, and the enthusiasm in this field continues to grow into the 1990s. All along there has been an insatiable desire to learn, "How'd they do that?"

In the past, make-up secrets were kept under wraps and in the dark by publicity-shy studios, who felt that explaining the process would take away from the creations' sense of mystery. Not so today. Modern fans and "technoheads" need to know everything, and the makeup creators feel honored to open up their workshops and scrapbooks to divulge the secrets of the trade. No one has done a better job of educating both layman and professional on the wonders of make-up than Vincent J-R Kehoe.

Vincent is the respected author of *The Technique of the Professional Make-up Artist for Film, Television, and Stage,* a revealing textbook that never leaves my reference shelf. He also lectures and teaches, publishes his own make-up newsletter and serves as president of the Research Council of Make-up Artists, Inc. In addition, he has written important articles on make-up safety for *Fangoria* and *Cinemagic Horror FX.* I can't imagine anyone with better credentials to write a book entitled *Special Make-Up Effects.* Here you'll get a perfect grasp on the world of the make-up artist, from the old techniques of live television to the latest fantasy wizardry featured in Oscar-winning films like *Beetlejuice.* Vincent's classes and writings have inspired countless people to careers in make-up and special make-up effects. With his latest work, Vincent continues to educate and encourage beginners and professionals alike on the magic of make-up.

Anthony Timpone

Anthony Timpone is the editor of *Fangoria, Gorezone,* and *Cinemagic Horror FX* magazines, as well as a respected horror expert and film consultant.

Preface

In 1931, Universal Pictures' release of the classic film *Frankenstein* with Boris Karloff as "The Monster" gave rise to a new era of cinemagic, and the *horror film* was born. Today, this art form has expanded in popularity to become a genre of its own. Advances in plastics technology and inventive mechanics adapted from other fields make possible a new approach to creating awesome characters and mutations almost beyond the scope of the imagination. Each time a new film or artist comes to the scene, fresh concepts are created that titillate the viewer with increasingly frightening, bizarre, or horrific effects. The key to this trend or direction, is *effect*, a word that has been loosely defined but is often the subject of controversy.

In *Webster's Dictionary, effect* has a number of meanings:

1. something that inevitably follows an antecedent (as a cause or agent).
2. a. PURPORT, INTENT
   b. basic meaning: ESSENCE
3. an outward sign: APPEARANCE
4. ACCOMPLISHMENT, FULFILLMENT
5. power to bring about a result: INFLUENCE
6. *pl:* movable property: GOODS (personal ---s)
7. a. a distinctive impression (the color gives the --- of being warm)
   b. the creation of a desired impression (her tears were purely for ---)
   c. something designed to produce a distinctive or desired impression (special lighting ---)
8. the quality or state of being operative: OPERATION (the law goes into --- next week)

Synonyms: EFFECT, RESULT, CONSEQUENCE, EVENT, ISSUE, OUTCOME,
shared meaning element: a condition or occurrence traceable to a cause.

How distinctively appropriate are the connotations and meanings of *effect* when the term is applied to the art of make-up! The adjective *special* modifies *effects*, referring to make-up in the sense of a different or unusual form of the art. Ordinarily, make-up is employed for beautification or enhancement of characterization; *special make-up effects* simply denotes the use of make-up products and materials to take us beyond the norm.

Special make-up effects can commence with simple exercises such as cuts, bruises, tears, scars, burns, and tattoos, and either progress to far more complicated designs or expand in new directions. Unfortunately, some controversies have occurred. When a make-up job is performed *on* the human face or body, there seems to be little dispute as to the make-up artist's responsibility. However, when the effect cannot possibly conform to the human form; is dangerous to it (usually due to chemical action); or crosses the lines of union contractual areas by requiring a simulation of the human form (such as a puppet), or an animal, vegetable, or even mineral figure; many consider that this extends beyond the art of make-up into another jurisdiction. Yet, on frequent professional occasions, those unions formerly responsible for the making of such figures no longer have the personnel competent to do the job of making the molds, casts, and items required by the production. Instead, *special effects make-up artists* have developed their own personal studios to accomplish this new and advanced work. Veritable factories are now turning out *effects, illusions, transmutations,* and *transformations* for the film and television industry.

As a result, although only a qualified make-up union member may be employed on the set (in unionized productions), the person in charge or the owner of the company that provides the effects employs many other technicians to manufacture the materials. In this way a new category in the field of make-up artistry has evolved for those who are solely interested in the creation and operation of special make-up effects.

In essence, *special make-up effects* are character work in make-up, but they belong to a highly specialized and specific market area. For the manufacture of the effects, talent is necessary in sculpturing, molding, and casting, as well as in making foamed and slush latex pieces, plastic appliances and forms, frame constructions for figures, manual and radio controls, and in painting and coloring the finished product. This work is not strictly *make-up, per se,* but rather, special effects manufacturing.

A new area of filmmaking has grown from the advances in special make-up effects technology. The categories of horror, splatter and gore, fantasy, extraterrestrial and science fiction are burgeoning and developing. Young hopefuls in a number of fields from fine arts to chemistry have taken to this trend with eagerness and avidity and are constantly entering the industry. Luckily, the openness of art has accommodated their efforts, and the availability of home television cameras has allowed them to produce videos in addition to still camera studies of their creations. These new artists provide a marvelous boost to the art of make-up by expanding the use of materials in novel ways.

In view of this trend, I have excerpted the relevant information from my professional book *The Technique of the Professional Make-up Artist* rather than write a less professional approach to the subject. New material has been added from Ve Neill and Steve LaPorte, who created the "Beetlejuice" character, played by Michael Keaton, as well as William Tuttle's Dr. Lao, played by Tony Randall. In addition, I have brought up to date all the information and methods in the sphere of make-up artistry.

Vincent J-R Kehoe

Acknowledgments

Make-up artists who contributed to this book:

Rick Baker	Craig Reardon
Gary Boham	Tom Savini
Tom Burman	Bob Schiffer
John Chambers	Dick Smith
Carl Fullerton	Terry Smith
Werner Keppler	Christopher Tucker
Steve LaPorte	Bill Tuttle
Ve Neill	Bud Westmore
Gus Norin	Stan Winston
Dana Nye	

Thanks to:

All the many chemical suppliers who so generously furnished samples and technical information for this work;

The many motion picture companies whose press departments furnished photos,

The many photographers who furnished photos,

The models who posed for photos and the performers in others,

The staff of the Editorial, Production, and Marketing departments of Butterworth–Heinemann for their work in producing and promoting this book,

And, finally, to my loving and patient wife who put up with my long stays at the typewriter, make-up lab, and constant research projects for this book.

Special Make-Up Effects

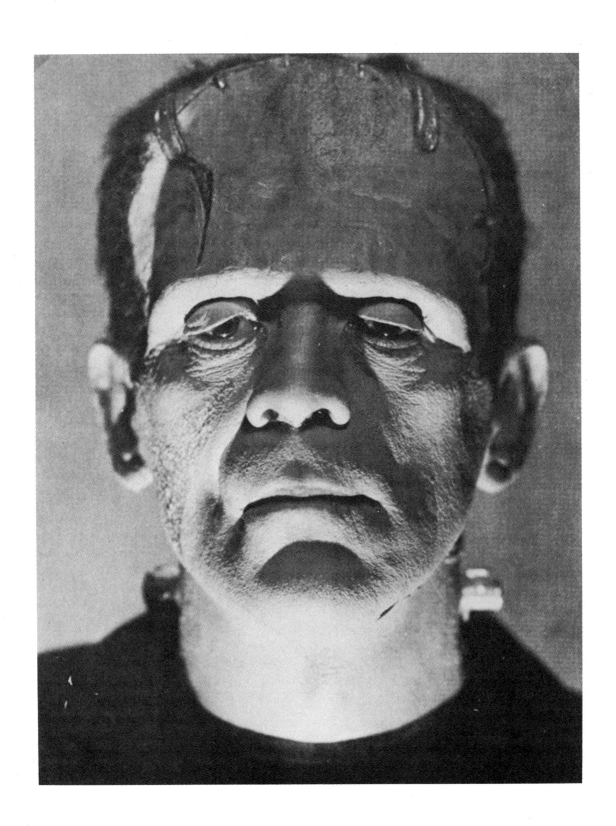

CHAPTER 1

Make-Up Products and the Kit

TODAY'S PROFESSIONAL MAKE-UP ARTISTS CARRY MANY more new and different items than they did some 10 or 15 years ago, so one can always tell the difference between an outmoded or amateur kit and that of the currently working professional. Products can be divided now into three basic categories: commercial, theatrical, and professional items.

Commercial products are generally sold in department or drug stores for street make-up to be self-applied, and fashion dictates govern their sale, variety, and promotion. They are often merchandized with voluminous advertising and sales promotion, with the buy-and-try adage being the main sales pitch. Competition between commercial cosmetic lines does not consist so much in product difference in the main but in how ostentatiously the item is packaged, how loudly the brand or product is touted with advertising, along with the invention of various phrases and semantics spiced with juicy brand names. Red is never just *red* but must be Witch's Blood, Roaring Red, or the like, and many directions are strongly overworked by the employment of terms such as *natural, organic,* and so forth, without more than a that's-what-sells attitude beneath it all.

Such products are designed not for use by professional make-up artists but as self-application items by the purchaser. Low-pigment liquid foundations (that provide little or no skin coverage), supposedly long-lasting (and possibly staining) lipsticks, soft pencil or cream-style eye make-ups (that smear but that are easily finger applied, nevertheless), lotions and skin care creams with exotic ingredients such as mink or turtle oil, fruit or vegetable additives (strawberries, cucumbers, and so on), and pH value ratings (with little or no real meaning of what they actually mean or why) are but a few of the directions of sales jargon and ingredients for commercial cosmetic products. In general, these are neither designed for coordinated use for screen or stage make-up nor really recommended as such by their manufacturers.

Theatrical make-up lines are mostly defined today as those advertised for sale in student kits or for amateur school and college use. They still have the archaic foundation names such as Juvenile Flesh, Sallow, Hero, and so forth, as well as many colored powders for the face, old nose putty, and such, all of which have seen little or no use for some years by make-up artists.

Professional make-up products, however, are manufactured for use by make-up artists and are not usually sold on a retail level (seldom, if ever, in department stores or the like). In the main, they are rather plainly packaged and designed to fit in the make-up artist's kit or in larger stock sizes. An enormous variety of products, sizes, special materials, and items are supplied in the professional category that may never be found in any of the commercial lines and are often more advanced products than those for similar use in the theatrical lines.

Note: Most of the cosmetics that are made in the United States are quite reliable overall (due to stringent pure food and drug rules that govern the ingredients), and reactions of an allergenic nature may occur only to the perfumes, stains, or to sensitivity to a particular ingredient by a particular person. However, all the theatrical and the professional make-up companies (not the commercial companies whose products are sold in department or drug stores) generally sell certain items that are not in general use by the public. For example, resin-based adhesives, vinyl-based sealers, plastic waxes, latices, or plastics that are in common, everyday use for character make-up by professional make-up artists are not sold except for this use. Since the solvents for these items may be alcohol, acetone, and such, there are possibilities that some performers will have a sensitivity to these products, resulting in an irritation factor. If the make-up artist finds that anyone does have a reaction to any such material, it should be removed and not further employed for that person. Such cases *are* rare because most human skin can stand more than is imagined. A face covered all day, for long hours, with a number of latex or plastic pieces will not breathe as well as one with just a coat of foundation, but such character make-up is necessary to the work of the professional make-up artist to create the necessary effects.

Many schools and colleges that have a make-up course as part of an audiovisual, television, film, or stage program or curriculum or that have drama clubs as extra activities for some years always purchased make-up products for the group and simply left them out on the make-up tables for use by the performers. As such, the destruction level of the products was high, and cleanup after one or two performances was minimal. Most often the make-up kit or box was a veritable mess. Only in those institutions or groups where one person (who was often more interested in make-up than in performing) had charge of the kit, show after show, was it kept in any semblance of cleanliness or completeness. Eventually, instructors of make-up classes found that small individual kits served the purpose better and were sold to the students or included in their lab fee. This may be fine for a performer level but is quite inadequate for one who wishes to study in make-up artistry or design. Here, a full make-up kit, on the level of the professional make-up artist, is really a necessity.

THE MAKE-UP KIT

Make-up materials consist of foundations, shadings and countershadings, cheekcolors, lipcolors, eyecolors, powders, pencils, mascaras, skin care products, tools of the trade, special materials (such as adhesives, sealers, latices, and plastics), cleansers, and many other additional items such as prostheses, hair goods, and so forth. The stock of the products in a professional make-up artist's kit changes as technological advances are made in the color response of film and television systems or advanced stage lighting techniques as well as when new products and materials become available through research. As such, the make-up kit should go through constant change and improvement.

The old theatrical make-up manufacturers originally serviced their foundations in paper tubes, and when films came into production use, a new form of soft paint in a metal squeeze tube was devised. This spread more easily and did not require an undercoating of cold cream to spread it properly. The next major advance was the introduction by Max Factor of a water-applied cake (Pan-Cake) make-up, which was basically a heavily pigmented mixture with clays and binders. This form applied very rapidly with a wet, natural sea sponge and was the mainstay of the make-up for black-and-white films and television production. As this type of foundation was often drying to some skins and appeared rather flat and dull looking on the face, a newer type of cream make-up in a swivel-up tube came next, then a creme-cake formula was introduced, both of which were applied with a dry, foamed sponge. Attempts were made at various times to produce a liquid or semifluid professional foundation, but they did not achieve acceptance. Today, the main foundation types are the creme cakes (in a variety of sizes) and the swivel-up in the 1/2-ounce size.

Since professional foundations produce the basic skin tone, they become the main criterion of film and TV make-up, and the carrying cases or kits of each artist are often made to contain either one or the other variety as a basic direction of design of the kit, with those employing the swivel-up foundations often using the

FIGURE 1.1   *Creme-cake foundations in various sizes.*

multidrawer variety with the top portion opening up to reveal a deep tray where the foundations are placed label side up for selection.

There are a number of varieties and styles of these kits, in wooden construction generally. A newer and quite efficient case of the accordion variety works very well with the flat, round, creme-cake foundations, and the top section will hold up to 30 of the 2/5-ounce size or 24 of the 1-ounce size in the same space, thus giving a variety of shades to choose from (Figure 1.1). Most make-up artists also have a *hair kit* (not to be confused with a hairdresser's kit), which normally consists of a soft canvas or leather bag in which are stored the items employed by the make-up artist for character work, plus extras such as tissues, towels, and other supplies for the make-up kit. For complete list of items recommended for make-up and hair kits, see Appendix B.

HISTORICAL PROGRESSION OF MODERN MAKE-UP

The first technical study of film make-up was published in the *Journal of the Society of Motion Picture Engineers* under the title of the "Standardization of Motion Picture Make-up," by Max Factor, in January 1937. It discussed in detail the tests and results of designing make-up bases or foundations for black-and-white film rather than using the old theater make-up shades. A basic series of shades, ranging from a light pink to a deep orange-tan and numbered from Panchromatic 21 to 31, became the standard for many years for all black-and-white screen use. This report discussed the history of the use of make-up on the stage and the evolution of film from the orthochromatic to the panchromatic types.

Some attempt was made in manufacturing the make-up shades so that psychologically the performers were not faced with highly unnatural colors; nevertheless, *panchromatic* make-up did appear rather yellowish to orange-tan in skin tone, and even though a cheek rouge of a very pale shade (Light Technicolor) was employed later to remove the flat look from the cheeks of women, the overall effect still had a made-up look offscreen. Incidentally, the cheek rouge was so light that it did not register on the black-and-white screen with any tonal difference and was solely for performer psychology. Unfortunately, for some years performers became so accustomed to seeing themselves in panchromatic shade make-up for films or television that they often attempted to employ it on stage—where they looked as if an advanced stage of jaundice had set in, especially in the men's shades, rather than the pink-ruddy-tan shades correct stage make-up required.

In the Max Factor tests, Lovibond tintometer determination was employed to carefully design the shades of make-up that would translate into comparative natural skin tones for performers in a black-and-white medium. Pan 25 and 26 became the women's shades, and Pan 28 and 29 were used for men, with a shade that was three numbers below the base shade (say, Pan 22 for women) employed to create *highlights* that would photograph three shades lighter on the gray scale, while one that was three numbers above (such as Pan 28) appeared as a *shading* that photographed three shades darker on the gray scale. All this information worked out perfectly well for black-and-white television too, but when film and television went to color, these principles became ineffective and basically incorrect.

The first technical paper on make-up for color mediums was published in the *Journal of the Society of Motion Picture and Television Engineers* under the title of "New Make-up Materials and Procedures for Color Mediums," by Vincent J-R Kehoe in November 1966, with a revision in the April 1970 issue and an entirely new set of recommendations in the November 1979 issue of this same journal. Here were set up the newest principles and methods, as well as new products, for color—all of which could be employed compatibly when a black-and-white print was made from a color film or a television colorcast was to be viewed on a black-and-white receiver. As such, a complete change of what the professional make-up artist should carry in his or her kit was made, and it became no longer necessary to carry any black-and-white or panchromatic shades.

Over the years, with the improvement in film types as well as the technological advances in color television, newer foundation shades were devised so that now, only one basic series of pink-beige to ruddy, natural tan that is very natural looking even offscreen or offstage is necessary for most professional use for Caucasoids. The design of this new series was made by the author after exhaustive comparative tests on stage and screen, with some of the leading film manufacturers and television stations acting as test areas.

FOUNDATION SYSTEMS

There are essentially four different *foundation systems,* each designed for its own mediums, along with some interim ideas and experiments in between. The old stage make-up system divided the shades of foundation or base color (with powders to match) into the skin tone effect required for the character to be portrayed:

Very Light Pink	Ivory	American
Pink	Juvenile	Indian
Deeper Pink	Gypsy	East Indian
Flesh	Othello	Negro
Deeper Flesh	Chinese	Mulatto
Cream	Japanese	Lavender
Sunburn	Arab	Vermilion
Sallow Old Age	Spanish	White
Robust Old Age	Mexican	Black

Next came the panchromatic or black-and-white television make-up that was numbered as Pan 21 to 31 and later, when some of the orange tone was removed, 1N to 11N. When color film make-up and later color television make-up was being experimented with and devised, much emphasis was placed on the development of this same type of rising skin tone value idea. However, later research proved that this was not the best manner in which to design color medium make-up since many of the in-between numbers saw no use at all.

It is interesting to note that during the 1930s to 1950s, when this era of professional make-up was taking place, commercial cosmetic companies seldom produced more than six shades of foundation in their lines, and most had a low percentage of pigment to the amount of vehicle in the formulations. However, many spoke of *color correcting* the natural skin with such products. For example, pinkish areas were said to be correctable with beige tones and sallow skins could be heightened with pink foundations. Some went as far as selling a green-tinted foundation to correct redness and a lilac-tinted one to correct sallowness. These were to be applied before the normal foundation but did little else but put a rather heavy coating on the face—all of which seldom, if ever, appeared compatible in color to the skin on the neck, producing a very masklike look.

For some years commercial companies also recommended three shades lighter for highlights and three shades darker for shading without having such colors in their lines. Erroneously, these principles were effective only for black-and-white mediums, while street make-up has always been a color medium. Certainly, shades such as Ivory, Beige, Peach, Natural, Rose, and Suntan did not lend themselves to this black-and-white theory, but being so lightly pigmented, little harm could be done—and little effect realized!

In 1962, the Research Council of Make-up Artists

(RCMA) was formed. This group devised the system known as *Color Process,* which provided a truly modern method of skin tone and undertone matching for professional foundation products. Ethnological studies showed that Caucasoid skins could be defined or separated by the terms *Northern European, Middle European,* and *Southern European* and as going from a pink to ruddy to an olive to olive-brown undertone value. Orientals or Mongoloids had a rather yellowish cast to their undertone value, while Negroids had a gray undertone. Skins could be divided into light, medium, and deep plus the value of the undertone color, and this rating better defined true skin tone. The make-up shades required then were light, medium, and deep with undertone values of pink, olive, yellow, and gray for both men and women. In addition, some suntan shades for Caucasoids could be added and a series of spectrum colors to change any foundation shade one way or another.

Compatibility to the various mediums (street, stage, and screen) then had to be taken into consideration, and the color response required for each film type, television system, or the stage and street had to be built into the shades finally selected. To achieve a natural skin color look, the foundations would have to be very highly pigmented so that a little, spread properly on the skin, gave it the appearance of a skin color rather than a coat of make-up.

To eliminate allergy problems, the foundations should not contain lanolin or perfume. Also, vegetable oils rather than mineral oil should be used as the vehicle to lessen facial shine and the constant retouching that was required with old greasepaints and swivel-sticks that used mineral oil in their formulations.

In the RCMA Color Process line, all the foundations, shadings, countershadings, and cheekcolors are made with the same vegetable oils and waxes with only the color pigments varied. Although most commercial brands of liquid make-up contain only 18 to 23 percent of pigment to vehicle and theatrical brands are in the 35 to 40 percent range, the RCMA shades are made with 50 percent pigment to vehicle, giving them a very high degree of coverage on the skin. Manufacturing controls of RCMA call for every batch to be skin tested so that no variance in color is allowable. Most commercial and theatrical batches have a tolerance of plus or minus 5 percent to up to 15 percent, but with lower pigmentation the difference on the skin may not be objectionable. Nevertheless, most professional studio make-up artists prefer their colors to remain constant.

William Tuttle's line of foundations has strict manufacturing controls as well, and he personally tests batches to standards to maintain accuracy of shade. In addition, good standardization has been noted in the Ben Nye professional line.

Color Matching

Matching a color or shade from one manufacturer to another is a very difficult procedure because of the infinite variety of shades that can be produced by the combination of the various earth colors available as well as the dilution of these colors with the waxes, oils, and tints of the colors that can be made by varying the amount of white. Exact shades are more difficult to reproduce in the light than in the dark skin shades since sometimes the deepness of the color will obscure some minor addition of a weaker color element.

As such, it is most generally accepted that one manufacturer's shade of olive and another manufacturer's olive, although semantically identical, may not only be a different concept of the shade but also, even though a match is intended, will show some variety when made in a professional foundation with a high percentage of color additives. In addition, to attempt to classify all the olives, reds, greens, and so forth into one master chart of everything made is a fool's paradise at best and a useless exercise in the least, due to the incompatibility of foundation materials such as waxes and oils from one manufacturer to another. For example, to say that the olive shade of one line is deeper in tone than that of another line, and so to number them as Olive #1 and Olive #2, implies that if one wants a deeper shade of Olive #1, then Olive #2 could be employed. However, Olive #1 may be a tube greasepaint with a mineral oil base, while Olive #2 may be a creme-cake variety with a purely vegetable oil and wax base, which on the skin may appear, as well as powder down, quite differently and not be at all compatible with other products used on the face from the same line of make-up. It is, therefore, considered good advice to select and employ the foundations, shadings, countershadings, and cheekcolors of a single manufacturer of professional products to complete this portion of a make-up so that they all accept powder with the same degree of absorption to make an even-surfaced skin texture. This advice is given, of course, with the premise in mind that all the named products such as the foundation, shading, countershading, and cheekcolor are made with the same wax-oil ingredient combination to insure compatibility on the skin.

Color Perception

It is essential that the make-up artist develop a keen sense of color perception and have a knowledge of the basic color ingredients that are utilized to manufacture the shades and colors of current make-up products. Color film and television systems today are extremely sensitive to nuances in the tonal values of foundations, lipcolors, cheekcolors, and so forth, so that identical batch matches during manufacture are essential for obtaining a correct color continuity from day to day on a performer. Basically, some eight earth colors are utilized for compounding skin tone shades to which are added white (titanium dioxide) and sometimes a bit of pink or red certified color to add a rosy tone. With careful combinations of these, professional make-up shades are manufactured.

The earth colors range from a light ochre, ochre, warm ochre, burnt sienna, red-brown, red oxide, burnt umber, to umber. Pure shades and dilutions in titanium dioxide can be seen in the RCMA Prosthetic Base Series 1 to 8, from A to C, in some 24 shades (three dilutions of each color) to show the effect of the white pigment on these basic colors. Note that judgment of color should always be made on the skin and never in the container since what appears to be the same shade may be quite different on the skin.

Foundation Shades

In the RCMA line the basic number shades are the F, KW, and KM series for Caucasoids, the KT series and Shinto for tan or yellow undertone skins, and the KN series for dark skins with gray undertones. Other special shades are sometimes named rather than numbered. The *shade* descriptions are given in the various lists for comparative purposes only because the key letter-number designations are all that are usually shown on the containers and that is generally how make-up artists delineate the shades.

In all cases in the foregoing lists, the light shades are listed first or with lower numbers, and the following ones increase the tonal value and color saturation in each particular series. Combination shade numbers are equal mixtures—for example, KW-36 is an equal compounding of KW-3 and KW-6 to produce the in-between shade.

In the basic shades, KW-1 to KW-4 show a cream to olive gradation, and KW-5 to KW-8 are a light to tan-pink for women. The men's shades, KM-1 to KM-3, are rising olive-tan tones, while the KM-4 to KM-6 are pink-tan to reddish tan and the KM-7 and KM-8 are red-brown skin tones:

WOMEN		MEN	
KW-1	Pale Cream	KM-1	Olive-Tan
KW-2	Beige	KM-2	Deeper Olive-Tan
KW-3	Warm Beige	KM-3	Dark Olive-Tan
KW-4	Olive-Beige		
KW-5	Light Pink	KM-4	Pink-Tan
KW-6	Warm Pink	KM-5	Reddish Tan
KW-7	Beige-Tan-Pink	KM-6	Dark Reddish Tan
KW-8	Tan-Pink	KM-7	Red-Brown
		KM-8	Deep Red-Brown

However, today's current recommendations for a basic series of foundation shades for screen and stage make-up are a combination of those mentioned here.

WOMEN		MEN	
KW-36	Light skin tone	KM-36	Lighter skin tone
KW-37	Normal or basic shade	KM-37	Normal or basic shade
KW-38	Deeper shade	KM-38	Deeper shade

For still photography and street make-up in general, the following shades are recommended for women (according to skin type):

PINK UNDERTONES		OLIVE UNDERTONES	
F-1	Very pale shade	F-2	Very light Cream shade
F-3	Pink Cream	F-4	Light Cream
KW-13	Medium (or basic shade)	KW-14	Medium (or basic shade)
		KW-24	Deep
KW-23	Deep	KW-34	Deeper
KW-67	Pink tone		

There is also a shade called Gena Beige that is a color sometimes used on light-blond women that have rather rosy skin undertones. This particular shade will mute the redness and even out the overall skintone.

NATURAL SUNTANS			
WARM TAN		YELLOW TAN	
KW4M2	Light	KT-1	Light yellow-tan
KW4M3	Medium	KT-2	Yellow-tan
KM-23	Deep	KT-3	Deep yellow-tan
		KT-34	Dark yellow-tan
		KT-4	Dark brown-tan (Tahitian)

Although the KT series is also suitable for warm tone oriental shades, another series, called *Shinto*, has a fully yellow undertone in four shades: Shinto I, Pale (yellow undertone); Shinto II, Medium Oriental; Shinto III, Deep Oriental; and Shinto IV, Dark Oriental.

A series for Negroid skins serves both men and women as there is no male-female undertone distinction as for Caucasoid skins, with some men being considerably lighter than some women and vice versa:

NEGRO SHADES (all with grayed undertones)			
KN-1	Very Pale Brown	KN-4	Deep Brown
KN-2	Pale Brown	KN-5	Dark Brown
KN-3	Brown		

Also

<table>
<tr><td colspan="2" align="center">(with gray-yellow undertones)</td></tr>
<tr><td>KN-6   Yellowed
Brown</td><td>KN-7   Deep Yellowed
Brown</td></tr>
<tr><td colspan="2" align="center">(with gray-blue undertones)</td></tr>
<tr><td>KN-8   Blued
Brown</td><td>KN-9   Deep Blued
Brown</td></tr>
</table>

while the KN series from 1 to 5 are ascending brown tones on the warm side, the KN-6 and KN-7 shades have a distinct yellowed brown tonality (suitable for some South Sea Island skin colors), while the KN-8 and KN-9 shades have a blue complement in their coloration (good for some of the people in India and Southern Asia).

In the Ben Nye line, there are the following series of shades. The L, M, N, T, and Y series are all designed for male and female Caucasoids.

NATURAL	LIGHTER VALUES	MEDIUM WARM BROWN TONES
N-1	L-1 Juvenile Female	M-1 Juvenile Male
N-2		M-2 Light Suntone
N-3	L-2 Light Beige	M-3 Medium Tan
N-4	L-3 Rose Beige	M-4 Deep Suntone
N-5	L-4 Medium Beige	M-5 Desert Tan
N-6	L-5 Tan-Rose	

NATURAL TANS	OLIVE SKIN TONES
T-1 Golden Tan	Y-3 Medium Olive
T-2 Bronze Tan	Y-5 Deep Olive Tan and Deep Olive

The 20 series includes rising tones for Asians, Latins, and Negroids:

22	Golden Beige	25	Amber Lite	28	Cinnamon
23	Fawn	26	Amber	29	Blush Sable
24	Honey	27	Coco Tan	30	Ebony

There are also some special shades:

AMERICAN INDIAN SERIES	MEXICAN SERIES: OLIVE BROWN TONES
I-1 Golden Copper	MX-1 Olive Brown
I-2 Bronze	MX-3 Ruddy Brown
I-3 Dark Bronze	

Other special shades include Black, White, Ultra Fair, Old Age, Bronzetone, and Dark Coco. Of course, as in all professional lines, the color series designations may be different from others, and individual color descriptions may vary.

Custom Color Cosmetics by William Tuttle are mostly designated by names, but some numbered shades are color copies of some of the old Max Factor and other shades that are no longer available in some areas or requested by some make-up artists:

Ivory	Warm Tan	Tawn-Shee
Truly Beige	Tan-del-Ann	Dark Beige
Fair and Warmer	Tawny Tan	Toasted Honey Tan
Light Peach	Fern Tan	Cafe Olé
Pink 'n Pretty	Bronze Tone	Rahma
Peach	Jan Tan	Natural Tan
Rose Medium	TNT	Chocolate Cream
Light Beige	Light-Medium Peach	Tan Tone
Light-Medium Beige	Deb Tan	CTV-8W
Medium Beige	Suntone	BT-5
Medium Dark Beige	Medium	BT-6
Bronze	Beige Tan II	BT-7
Tan	Shibui	K-1
Xtra Dark Tan	Deep Olive	Hi-Yeller
Hot Chocolate	Chinese I	Ebony
Sumatra	Chinese II	Desert Tan
N-1	Western Indian 11019 (Dark Tawny Tan)	
Natural Tan		

As the shades of the Tuttle make-up are not arranged in series, they are all listed here but not in any particular order.

Some make-up artists wish additional mixtures and shades for special or particular purposes, and these are often made available on order from some professional make-up manufacturers. Also, there are some RCMA foundations that will *minus* or *plus* the red content of facial coloration for certain corrective or character make-ups:

Minus Red   1667, a pale ochre; 1624 series, two shades of warm ochre.
Plus Red   6205, a russet tone.

When these are added over any regular RCMA foundation, they will change the appearance of the color from less red to more red content.

There is also a series of Color Wheel or Rainbow Colors:

Red	Midnite Green	Lilac
Maroon	Opal	Violet
Orange	Turquoise	Purple
Yellow	Ultrablue	Black
Lime	Blue	Superwhite
Green	Navy Blue	Light grey
		Dark grey

And there is a nonmetallic series (a combination of pearlescence and earth colors produce these colors) that includes gold, bronze, copper, pure pearl, and silver.

Foundation Thinner

RCMA makes a foundation thinner to dilute slightly any Color Process foundation to aid in spreading it on latex prosthetics or for rapid body make-up. There is another thinner for the (AF) Appliance Foundation series.

SHADING AND COUNTERSHADING

RCMA Color Process foundation base shades are limited to facial and body shades, and all *shadowing* and *highlighting* are done with shading and countershading colors, which are based on natural *grayed* or *counter-grayed* skin tones plus light-created shadows for *natural contouring* or special tones for character make-up.

SHADING COLORS

S-1	Grayed Tan	S-5	Brown
S-2	Blue Gray	S-6	Red-Brown
S-2W	Light Gray	S-7	Freckle Brown
S-13	Equal Mix of S-1 and S-3	S-8	Black-Brown
S-3	Browned Gray	S-9	(Light) Lake #1
S-14	Equal mix of S-1 and S-4	S-10	(Dark) Lake #2
S-4	Grayed Brown	S-11	(7-34 equiv.) Brown and Gray

COUNTERSHADING COLORS

CS-1	Light Skin	CS-3	Dark Skin
CS-2	Medium Skin		

BEARDCOVERS

The special problem of men's beardlines may be corrected or concealed with a spread foundation called *beardcover:*

BC-1 Pink Tone (used for black and white only)
BC-2 Orange Tone
BC-3 Orange-Tan (best for color mediums)

Ben Nye uses the following designations for countershading, shading, and beardcovers:

CREME HIGHLIGHT		CREME BROWN SHADOW	FIVE O'SHARP
Extra Lite	#40	Character (Purple-Brown)	Olive
Medium			Ruddy
Deep	#42	Medium (Brown)	
	#43	Dark (Warm Dark Brown)	
	#44	Extra Dark (Rich Dark Brown)	

In addition, a series of creme lining colors covers a number of uses, such as a Sunburn Stipple and a Beard Stipple, plus the brighter colors of Forest Green, Green, Yellow, Orange Fire Red, blood Red, Maroon, Misty Violet, Purple, Blue, Sky Blue, Blue-Gray, Gray, Black, and White. The following are some Ben Nye Pearl Sheen liners:

White	Shimmering	Copper
Green	Lilac	Mango
Turquoise	Ultra Violet	Rusty Rose
Royal Blue	Amethyst	Cabernet
Sapphire	Gold	Rose
Brown	Bronze	Charcoal
	Walnut	

William Tuttle recommends Special Hi-Lite for erasing circles under the eyes, and there is also Hi-Lite, while shading colors are Shadow I and Shadow II. For corrective contouring there is also Red-Out for erasing darkened areas or Sunburn Stipple for an outdoor look.

CHEEKCOLORS

Although cheek make-up has been made in both wet and dry forms for many years, currently the term *cheekcolor* denotes a compatible product to the foundation, while *dry blush* is applied as an additive color only after the foundation and other facial make-up has been powdered.

CHEEKCOLOR

Regular	Pink-Orange (similar to a Light Technicolor Blush)
Special	Muted shade of above (with a pinkish foundation)
Flame	Coral
Red	Stage red
Dark	Burnt Orange (similar to Dark Technicolor Blush)
Raspberry	Deep Pink (similar to old Natural Blush)
Lilac	Deep Lilac
Grape	Bright Grape
Grenacolor	Natural Pink (*Genacolor* is a trade name
Pink	of RCMA for natural cheek make-up colors.)
Grenacolor Rose	Natural Rose
Grenacolor Plum	Pale Plum
CTV	Brick Red

DRY BLUSH

Plum	Peach Pearl	Brown Pearl
Red	Bronze Pearl	Golden
Mocha	Rust Pearl	Brandy
Pink Pearl	Raspberry	Blush Pink
Candy Pink	Pearl	Flame
Garnet	Claret	Lilac

Cheekcolor and dry blush shades are added to, depending upon fashion dictates, but the Grenacolor Pink and Rose see the most use for studio production make-ups.

Ben Nye lists the following cheekcolors:

CREME CHEEK ROUGE	DRY CHEEK ROUGE	CHEEK BLUSHERS
Red	Red	Dusty Pink
Dusty Rose	Raspberry	Nectar Peach
Raspberry	Coral	Golden
Dark Tech	Dark Tech	Amber
Coral		
Blush Coral		

William Tuttle has Blusher, Tan Rouge, CTV Rouge, Mauve Blusher, Persimmon Piquant, and 007.

LIPCOLORS

Most commercial and theatrical lipsticks contain dibromo or tetrabromo fluorescein dye pigments (different from the more inert and nonstaining lipcolor pigments) to provide a long-lasting look to the lips. These act, however, to stain the lips (due to their reaction with the pH value of the saliva) with a pinkish hue, often destroying any color match with the wardrobe that may be red, peach, or orange colored. It was also stated in Edward Sagarin's comprehensive book, *Cosmetics—Science and Technology,* in an article by Sylvia Kramer, that "A possible increase in the incidence of reactions to lipsticks was noted with the introduction of the 'indelible type' lipsticks which use higher concentrations of these dyes than had been used previously" (p. 885). Although reactions to inorganic colors seem to be practically nonexistent, it was shown in a comparison chart in Sagarin's book that 48 percent of all cosmetic allergenic reactions were due to such dyes in lipsticks (p. 881).

RCMA designs and manufactures all their lip products including lipcolors, lipliners, and lipglosses without these dye stains to eliminate these problems. Although there are many shades of lipcolors, most make-up artists carry only a basic number of shades in their kits, varying them as fashion introduces new or revives an old color direction. In addition to the pigment colors, pearls, nonmetallic golds, bronzes, silvers, and coppers are employed for new color concepts (for a complete list, see Appendix A).

EYECOLORS

Years ago, brightly colored sticks called *liners* were used for eye make-up. On the advent of black-and-white film where colors became grays, the term *eye shadow* came into use to denote the application of a deep blue-gray or a deep brown paste employed to shadow the eye areas. The change to color film and color television brought back color into the make-up artist's vocabulary and kit, and once again bright colors were introduced for eye make-up, cheek make-up, and lip make-up, so the terms *eyecolor, cheekcolor,* and *lipcolor* described the placement effect with more exactness.

Eyecolors are now made in many forms including the following:

Pressed cake type, applied with a moistened flat brush;
Pressed cake type, applied with a dry soft brush or Q-Tip;
Liquid variety, brush applied, mostly in pearled colors;
Creme-cake style that requires powdering after application;
Large pencil or even some stick forms (similar in shape to old liners) of both hard and soft varieties;
Professional 7-inch pencils in bright colors.

The most efficient type for professional use is the water-applied cake variety because it is easy to blend and is long lasting. Most of the creme-cake, large pencil, or stick types are sold commercially and are easy to self-apply, but they run or gather into the folds around the eyes and therefore require constant attention to keep the area fresh appearing, unsmeared, and matching from shot to shot for any screen make-up.

PENCILS

The 7-inch, professional-type pencil comes in a variety of hair colors and bright colors, as well as lipcolor shades. They can be sharpened with a make-up pencil sharpener or a razor blade.

HAIR COLORS	BRIGHT COLORS	LIPLINER COLORS
Black	Blue	Light Red
Midnite Brown	Navy Blue	Red-Red
Dark Brown	Green	Dark Red
Medium Brown	Kelly Green	Maroon Lake
Light Brown	Gray Green	
Frosted Brown	Silver Green	
Auburn	Lilac	
Blonde (Silver Beige)	Turquoise	
Ash	Gold	
Deep Ash Gray	Silver	
Dark Silver Gray	White	

Just as with lipcolors, take care that only those pencils that do not contain dye colors should be used or they will stain the lip outline pinkish.

MASCARAS

Different forms of mascaras appear from time to time, but the most common varieties are the cake, which is applied with a wetted brush, and the semiliquid, which is in a tube with a wand applicator. Although they all come in a number of shades, the black and dark brown colors are the most useful and most natural. While the wand variety may be acceptable for personal use, make-up artists more often prefer the cake type as the brushes can be easily cleaned and sterilized between uses while the wand cannot.

FALSE LASHES

As an adjunct to or often combined with mascara are false eyelashes. These may be applied either singly or in strips. Most are supplied in black or brown, but colors are available on special orders from certain manufacturers. They are best adhered with a latex-type *eyelash adhesive* for the safest and easiest method. A type of strip lash with a transparent filament base is available when eyelining is to be kept to a minimum but when some emphasis is desired in the lash area. Take care in applying the single or tuft-type lashes (singles with three or four hairs attached) with any of the plastic glues or adhesives because these may cause damage to the natural lashes to which they must be attached.

POWDER

Years ago, paint and powder were the standbys of theatrical make-up, and in fact, early film make-up used the same system of a shade of powder for every shade of foundation color. With the advent of color film and color television, it was found that the heavily pigmented powders actually deepened the foundation shade and changed the make-up color on the face during the constant retouching required from early morning to late afternoon. For black-and-white film this change was not important since such tonal variations were not that apparent in the gray scale, but in color mediums, the effect was quite noticeable and undesirable. Therefore, a lightly pigmented *neutral* powder was first devised, and then later, a *translucent* (less filler and pigments) powder was recommended for all screen make-ups.

RCMA introduced a new concept of a transparent No-Color Powder for use with Color Process materials that did not change color on the face whatsoever, as it neither contained any pigments or fillers nor caked with constant use. As such, No-Color RCMA Powder can be applied to any shade of foundation, from the lightest to the darkest, with no color change or caking, so that only one powder need be carried in the make-up kit for general use. With RCMA Appliance Foundations a more heavily filtered (but not pigmented) powder called *AF Powder* provides a powder with more absorption power for these more heavily oiled foundations.

There are also some *overpowders* with gold and pearl pigments added, which are used for special facial and body shine effects (such as on the shoulders or cheeks). William Tuttle makes an Extra Fine Translucent Powder, while Ben Nye has Translucent, Coco Tan (for dark skins), and Special White (for clowns).

CLEANSERS

Because there are basically three types of skin conditions—namely, dry, oily, and normal—each requires a different variety of cleanser for best results. Dry skin needs a highly emollient and penetrating cleanser that has no drying aftereffect. A mineral oil-water lotion type like RCMA Deep Cleansing Lotion is recommended rather than the heavier solidified mineral oil creams.

Oily skin is best cleansed with a liquid that is nonsoapy but that has a foaming action so that it penetrates the make-up. It should not leave any oily residue or feel on the skin. This type is often preferred by men, and RCMA makes one called Actor's Special, which acts as a cleanser and a skin freshener with a slight lemon odor.

Normal or combination skins (with both dry and oily patches) may use one of the water-based cleansers that can be rinsed off after use with warm water. RCMA Hydrocleanser is one of this type.

Special Cleansers

RCMA Studio Make-up Remover and Studio Brush Cleaner are essentially the same product and are excellent for removing heavy make-up applications or for cleaning brushes after use.

Klenzer, RCMA's Appliance Foundation Remover, has been especially designed for removing RCMA AF make-ups or any other type of *rubber grease* foundations.

Mascara remover pads are oil-soaked cotton pads for removing mascara or other eye make-up without irritating the eyes. It is recommended that after removing make-up products from the face with a cleanser, a wash with warm water and a neutral soap (like Neutrogena) is best to clean the skin completely.

Ben Nye makes a make-up remover and a brush cleaner, while William Tuttle produces a more extensive cleanser and skin care line with:

Cleansing Lotion (for dry and normal skin),
Freshener (for dry and normal skin),
Oily Skin Cleanser,
Oily Skin Astringent,
Moisturizer (dry and normal skin),

Skin Conditioner (very dry skin),
Facial Scrub,
Sun Screen Moisturizing Lotion.

SKIN CARE PRODUCTS

Before applying any foundation to the skin, performers with dry skin should have a coating of RCMA Pre-foundation Moisture Lotion spread on the face with a dry foamed sponge. This emollient will sink into the skin and lubricate the surface of the face so that the foundation will apply more easily and smoothly. It is always best to use the same manufacturer's moisture lotion as foundation to ensure that they are compatible. Other brands may break up or clot when applied.

Oily skins often require the application of a freshener (with no more than 9 to 10 percent of alcohol) to eliminate some of the surface oil on the skin. Astringents or after-shave lotions often have up to 35 percent alcohol content and are quite strong for some skins—even though the skin is oily.

Hand and Body Lotion is recommended for use on the hands and body, if the skin is dry, prior to any make-up application. This product is especially designed for the body rather than the face area. For actresses with very dry skin, it is well to recommend proper skin care after removing make-up at the completion of the day on camera or stage by applying a coating of RCMA Overnight Skin Lotion or some similar product to combat skin dryness overnight. These are made with a high vegetable oil content and do not leave a greasy feeling on the face.

TOOLS AND EQUIPMENT

Only commercial cosmetic companies and amateurs advocate the application of any make-up product with the fingers for a beauty make-up. The professional make-up artist always employs the correct tools such as brushes, sponges, puffs, tweezers, Q-Tips, and so forth for applying make-up. Many application tools have changed over the years and, with advancing technology, will continue to do so.

Sponges

Foamed sponges are the mainstay of foundation application. However, it has come to the attention of dermatologists and skin specialists that certain *pseudo-cosmetic* reactions may cause skin irritations that are similar to an allergenic cosmetic reaction but not due to the cosmetics themselves. One of these is the use of foamed *rubber* or *latex* sponges for applying make-up. It has been discovered that a chemical employed in the manufacture of the foam, *mercaptobenzothiozole,* may produce a dermatitis effect on human skin. By using nonrubber sponges (such as polyurethane types), this condition or its possibility is completely avoided or alleviated. It is strongly recommended that only fine-foamed polyurethane sponges be employed for professional work and a new sponge be used on each person to ensure cleanliness and sterility.

There are also *stippling sponges* in both red rubber and foamed plastic with a variety of pores-per-inch styles that are utilized for applying various character effects. They should be cut into small pieces for facility in use.

Puffs

Three-inch, cotton-filled, velour powder puffs are best for applying powder. Note: Avoid using the so-called powder brushes as they are not only difficult to clean and sterilize, but also may streak the facial make-up.

Brushes

Brushes are made from many hair materials such as red sable (from the tails of the Kolinsky or Red Tartar marten); black sable (wood marten or stone marten); ox hair (from the ears of oxen); camel hair (from squirrels, ponies, or goats—not camels!); fitch hair (Russian fitch or skunks); badger hair (from Turkish or Russian badgers); goat hair (back and whisker hair); and many varieties of artificial hair made from plastic filaments. The best type for make-up brushes for most uses are those made from the best of the red sable hairs because they have better spring and workability (Figure 1.2).

Bristle brushes are different from hair in that hair has a single, individual natural point, while bristle has multiple natural tips or flags and also has a taper. This taper gives natural bristle brushes (such as those used for eyelash or eyebrow brushes) certain working qualities over any of the plastic bristle brushes. Bristle comes from hogs or boars, and the best comes from the back strip of older animals. Good real bristle brushes are difficult to find in today's plastic world.

Proper construction of a make-up brush from red sable hair for professional use is also important. The length-of-the-hair out of the ferrule (LOOF) must be combined by the best ferrule metal, and the hairs must be secured tightly in the ferrule. Handle length is also important so that brushes can be easily stored in a make-up kit. Although steel, copper, and aluminum are often used for making ferrules, seamless, nickle-plated brass is best because the hairs can be permanently heat sealed in a material known as Nylox, which is quite insoluble in solvents such as acetone, alcohol, and so forth. As such, the hairs stand up to repeated cleanings in RCMA Studio Brush Cleaner without falling out.

The length of the hair out of the ferrule controls the flexibility, snap, and painting quality of the brush that has been dipped in a material for use. Those for oil-wax products should be of shorter hair length, while those for spreading water-based products should be somewhat longer. A slight fraction of an inch too much

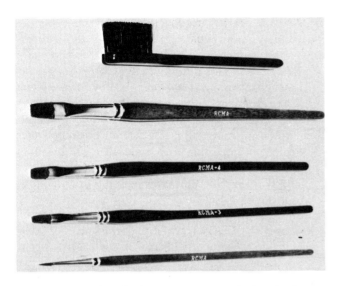

FIGURE 1.2 *Make-up brushes.* TOP TO BOTTOM: *Eyebrow brush; shading and countershading brush #7, flat; lipcolor brush #4, flat; eyecolor brush #3, flat; eyelining brush #1, round.*

out of the ferrule will make a lip brush too pliant or an eyecolor brush too stiff for best application.

Brushes designed for the fine arts where artists paint with heavy oils or with watercolors are not good for applying the waxy cremes or heavily concentrated wet or dry colors of make-up materials. A brush that is about 7 inches overall is best for make-up use and fit in the kit, and a walnut-finished handle adds to the professional look of the brush.

Both round and flat brush styles are used, and the following chart provides the brush sizes employed by many make-up people. Incidentally, the higher the number, the larger the brush size in number of hairs employed in its manufacture.

SIZE		USE	BEST LOOF
#1	Round	Eyelining	1/4 inch
#3	Round	Character lining	3/8 inch
#10	Round	Adhesives, sealers, and character work	11/16 inch
#3	Flat	Eyecolor application	9/32 inch
#4	Flat	Lipcolor application	1/4 inch
#7	Flat	Shading, countershading, blending	3/8 inch
#12	Flat	Blending	9/16 inch

The #10 round brush should have an unfinished wood handle so that it can be left standing in a bottle of adhesive or sealer without danger of the handle finish being removed by the solvent during use.

A camel hair brush for applying dry cheekcolors or powder to deep areas of prosthetic appliances with hairs about 7/8 inch out of ferrule and about 5½ to 6 inches in overall length is also useful.

Bristle: Natural or Plastic

Eyelash One row of seven tufts in a 4-inch handle is best. However, many artists cut off three rows nearest the hand-holding area to provide a smaller and more controllable applicator for mascara.

Eyebrow Two rows with a 4-inch handle.

Hair Whitening or Wig Cleaning Two rows in an unfinished bamboo handle.

Although artificial plastic bristle brushes (for brows and lashes) work almost as well as natural bristle brushes, the trend toward making application brushes from cheaper plastic fibers or filaments by some of the theatrical and commercial firms provides brushes that are less than suitable for fine blending or exacting professional work. There are also some foamed sponge tip applicators for eye products, but these are for personal use only and cannot be cleaned or sterilized for make-up artist service.

It is also well to avoid the large 1½- to 2-inch wide, long-handled soft camel hair brushes that are merchandized for dusting on blush or powder products. First, they are difficult to clean between uses, and next, a smaller brush for blush and a puff for powder are far better for control. Many pseudo-make-up personnel appear to be making fancy incantations and performing miracles with the flying camel hair dusters, but the overall effect in the end is minimal—often matching their talent.

Special Tools

Certain medical and dental tools have found use by make-up artists (Figure 1.3):

College Pliers Six-inch, stainless steel, curved tip dental pliers (large tweezers) are best for handling false lashes, small prostheses, and other items.

Dental Spatulas The stainless steel, 2½-inch blade spatula is excellent for mixing colors, stirring liquids (like stipples), taking a bit of make-up out of a container to be placed on a plastic tray or disposable butter chip for individual portions of lipcolor, and so on.

A variety of scissors are useful:

Hair Scissors Get the best available, keep them sharp, and cut *only* hair with them. The 3-inch barber's style is most useful.

Straight Scissors A good pair with short blades for cutting all other materials such as plastics, fabric, and so forth is best.

Curved Scissors Surgical, stainless steel with a 1½-inch blade length are best for cutting curves on latex or plastic appliances.

Pinking Shears A small pair of these for trimming lace on prepared hair goods should be part of a make-up artist's hair kit.

Comb An aluminum tail-comb with widespread, unserrated teeth for hair work.

Eyecare items would include *tweezers.* A good pair of slant-cut tweezers for brow care is important. Many complicated varieties of plucking tweezers are made as well.

Although some female performers like to curl their lashes, it is not a good practice to carry or offer an eyelash curler for general use. Not only are the rubber or plastic pads on their curlers hard to clean and sterilize, but also new research has shown that some individuals are allergic to the plating on the finish of some of the curlers when they are pressed on the eye area. Also, if the pads inadvertently slip or fall off, one can clip off all the lashes at the roots. This, of course, is not a pleasant prospect, but it has happened.

CHARACTER MAKE-UP MATERIALS

Many special materials that a make-up artist must have to do various character make-ups see little or no use for straight or ordinary corrective make-ups. These are listed here in alphabetical order rather than in importance, and their use is briefly explained. More information as to specific uses will be found in the chapters on character make-up. It is not necessary to carry all these items in the kit all the time, but in most cases, a bit of each that the artist may find important should be part of the everyday make-up kit.

We reiterate the statement that these are not ordinary materials and that some performers may have allergies to some of the products or solvents. If this occurs, discontinue their use on that particular performer.

ACETONE   A highly volatile liquid that is one of the main solvents of adhesives, sealers, and prosthetic plastics. Also used for cleaning the lace portion of hair goods after use.

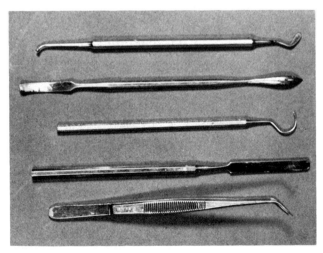

FIGURE 1.3   *Dental tools that make-up artists might find useful.* TOP TO BOTTOM: *A tool used for filling small indentations in a plaster mold; another tool for larger filling; a probe for picking up small items; a dental spatula for handling wax, and so on; and dental college pliers.*

ADHESIVE TAPE   Some new varieties of this old material are translucent and porous and have excellent adhesion. The 1-inch width is best.

ADHESIVES   This describes a very wide category of make-up materials and changes often as new items are researched and discovered. The original adhesive material for make-up was called *spirit gum,* which was nothing more than a solution of rosin in alcohol or other solvents (still made by many theatrical supply companies). Although it had fairly good adhesion, after a short while the dried gum took on an unwanted shine and, in the presence of excess perspiration, lost much of its adhesiveness and cracked off the skin. Today, although rosin is still one of the ingredients of most hair goods adhesives of that type, other materials have been added and combined in the manufacture to make an adhesive that not only has better stick but also does not have unwanted shine and, in some cases, stands up to the ravages of perspiration.

To disguise the lace portion of a hairpiece or beard, a firm bond must be made to the skin, and in most cases, old spirit gum darkened when any foundation make-up was placed on the lace or even close to it. A strong line of demarcation often occurred, necessitating removing the piece, cleaning it thoroughly, and re-adhering it. When the foundation to be applied was to be deeper than the color of the subject's skin, this presented a constant problem of maintenance. However, some of the new plastic adhesives have solved this problem (See "PMA Matte Lace Adhesive").

One way to take some of the shine out of spirit gum is to add some clay material (such as Kaolin or Attapulgus Clay) into it and stir thoroughly until the powder is well suspended in the gum. Although this will provide a gum with little shine, under some conditions it will whiten (or gray, depending on the shade of the clay) and therefore show—particularly on lace hair goods.

Matte, or nonshining spirit gum, was originally made by adding a very fine silica material to it and mechanically mixing the powder in. This produced a thicker gum and provided less shine but was not as flat as clay in matting. RCMA researched all these gums and matting materials and provides a series of matte adhesives for various uses and conditions.

RCMA MATTE ADHESIVE   This material was introduced in 1965 and is made by combining microsilica materials of various micron sizes with the resin mix under high shear. In this way, the smaller-sized silica particles hold the larger ones (the latter provide better matting) in solution and, at the same time, adds considerably more adhesion to the final mix due to the molecular structure of the finished material. RCMA Matte Adhesive can be employed both as an adhesive for hair goods or lace to the skin as well as a skin sealer with residual tack.

RCMA MATTE ADHESIVE #16   A superstick adhesive for hair goods that contains additional solids plus a plastic material to aid adhesion even when a subject perspires more than usual.

RCMA MATTE PLASTICIZED ADHESIVE   An adhesive designed for use with latex appliances that provides more all-ways stretch capability and the tackiness required for holding slush cast or foamed appliances to the skin.

RCMA SPECIAL ADHESIVE #1   Specifically designed to adhere any lace goods or hair to plastic bald caps. Normally, the bald plastic cap or front is attached to the subject with RCMA Matte Plasticized Adhesive or one of RCMA's Prosthetic Adhesives and then the hair goods are attached. Special Adhesive #1 is a very fast-drying heavily matted adhesive/sealer that will form a film that incorporates itself into the plastic bald cap while adhering the hair or lace to it. The product must be thoroughly shaken before use and applied *over* the lace as the hairpiece is held in place. Foundation make-up may be applied directly over RCMA Special Adhesive #1 without darkening the surface of the lace (also see page 000).

RCMA SPECIAL ADHESIVE #2   A neoprene-based adhesive for attaching velcro or other items to appliances.

RCMA PROSTHETIC ADHESIVES   These are adhesives from the medical profession that have found various uses by make-up artists.

Prosthetic Adhesive A   This is a solvent-based, clear, quick-setting contact adhesive that has a very low irritation factor to the skin. It is less affected by perspiration and water than other adhesives, so it can be used for scenes in the rain or water. Diluted with Prosthetic Adhesive A Thinner, it can be sprayed on body surfaces to attach large appliances or hair goods (also see page 000).

Prosthetic Adhesive B   This is a water-based, milky white (but dries clear) acrylic emulsion adhesive that sets less rapidly than Prosthetic Adhesive A and also has a low irritant factor because it does not contain any strong solvents. Although the dried film is insoluble in water, the liquid can be diluted with a few drops of a mixture of isopropyl alcohol and water.

A word of caution: Take great care in testing or using some of the new superadhesives made for industrial use as they are extremely difficult to remove from the human skin without serious damage.

Ben Nye, Stein's, and some of the other theatrical make-up manufacturers produce various adhesives of the spirit gum style but do not furnish any matte type of sealers or adhesives. They also have stage bloods, nose and scar waxes, and so on for character stage work. Also see Appendix A for full listing of these and other items of a similar nature.

Adhesive Remover   RCMA makes a cleanser that will dissolve and remove from the skin any type of plastic sealer, adhesive, scar material, or such made for make-up use, leaving the skin soft and lubricated. It is not for use in cleaning adhesives from lace goods or in cleansing the face *before* applying hair goods as it contains a moisturizing agent that prevents proper adhesion.

Alcohol   Ordinary drug store rubbing alcohol is only a 70 percent type and is not a suitable solvent for make-up use. A 99 percent isopropyl alcohol should be stocked because many adhesives and sealers have a mixture of 60 percent acetone and 40 percent isopropyl alcohol as solvents. Alcohol is also a good sterilizing agent to clean tools and table tops.

Artificial Bloods   The search for realistic-appearing human blood has led to many products from casein paints to food-colored syrups. RCMA makes the following types:

COLOR PROCESS TYPE A   A water-washable material that is very realistic in appearance and flow. It is nontoxic and does not cake and dry but appears fresh looking for some time.

COLOR PROCESS TYPE B   A resin plastic formulation designed for use where a blood effect must remain in place and not run during a long scene. It is solvent based and sets quickly, remaining shiny and fresh flowing in appearance. It is removed with RCMA Adhesive Remover.

COLOR PROCESS TYPE C   A soft creme variety serviced in a tube to make bloody areas for an effect where the blood does not have to run.

COLOR PROCESS TYPE D   A rapid-drying liquid suspension of a brownish tone employed to simulate dried blood on bandages. Not for any fresh blood effect or skin use.

Artificial Tears and Perspiration   A clear liquid that can be used to simulate tears when placed in the corner of the eye. It can also be stippled or sprayed on the skin to simulate perspiration.

Beard-setting Spray   A solvent-based artificial latex material that is used to set pre-made laid hair beards on forms. Not for facial use as a spray.

Gelatin Capsules   These capsules are obtainable in various sizes from most drug stores. They can be filled with RCMA Color Process Type A Blood and then crushed with the fingers or in the mouth for blood flow effects. Don't prefill these for future use because the artificial bloods will soften them too much.

Hair Whiteners   RCMA makes four shades of cream-style hair whiteners: HW-1, Grayed White; HW-2, Pinked White; HW-3, Ochre White; and HW-4, Yellow White. In addition, there is a Superwhite that can be used for highlighting. These are for small areas of whitening only, and full head graying or whitening should be done with sprays of liquid for this use. Nestle-LaMaur Company makes the following shades of liquid sprays in cans: White, Beige, Silver, and Gray. It also makes other hair colors such as Brown, Black, Blonde, Auburn, Light Brown, and Gold as well as Pink and Green for special effects. Very realistic hair changes can be done with these sprays.

Latex   There are many grades of latices for specific uses:

PURE GUM LATEX   An unfilled pure gum rubber that air dries to a tough elastic coating. It is not suitable for casting but is excellent for making inflatable bladders (see pages 93 and 97).

CASTING LATEX   A latex compound employed for slush or paint-in appliance making. Can be tinted to any shade with colors (see page 93). Casting Filler can be added to this product to control buildup density and stiffness of the finished item.

FOAM LATEX   A three- or four-part combination of materials used to produce foamed latex appliances, the actual latex portion being a heavy gum mixture.

EYELASH ADHESIVE   A special latex form that has excellent adhesive qualities for attaching strip and individual lashes as well as for an edge stipple for latex appliances.

RCMA OLD AGE STIPPLE   A compound containing latex made specifically for wrinkling the skin. Not just any latex material will act in the same manner. RCMA Old Age Stipple is made in four regular shades: KW-2, KW-4, KM-2, and KN-5, and special colors are available on order.

PMA Molding Material   PMA (Professional Make-up Artist) materials are made by RCMA for professional use and encompass some interesting new special materials. PMA Molding Material is a paint-in type of plastic for making small or flat appliances. It dries rapidly and builds up well. It is supplied in three shades: Light (KW), Deep (KM), and Dark (KN) colors (also see pages 110–111).

Plastic Cap Material   The lightly tinted variety is used for making plastic bald caps and fronts. It is also available in Clear for coating plastalene sculpture (see pages 77, 110–111).

PMA Press Molding Material   A clear, heavy liquid employed to make press molded appliances (see pages 111–113).

Appliance Foundations   RCMA makes a series of Appliance Foundations (AF series) for use with latex or plastic foamed or non-foamed appliances in a number of shades (see page 128).

Scar Material   A slightly matte scar-making material with a tinge of pink color that dries on application to form very realistic incised scars. Can be removed with RCMA Adhesive Remover (see pages 61–62).

Scar- or Blister-Making Material   A molding plastic type that can be formed into scar tissue or dropped on the skin to simulate second degree burns or other blister effects (see pages 60–62). Serviced in a tube for easy application.

Sealers   One of the first sealers used by make-up artists was flexible collodion that was gun-cotton dissolved in ether with castor oil as a plasticizer. Employing build-ups on the face with successive layers of spirit gum, cotton batting, and a cover of collodion was the method employed by Jack Pierce to do the first Frankenstein Monster on Boris Karloff. This was a laborious method and did not guarantee a fully controllable surface or buildup. Most theatrical make-up books employed this procedure for many years, and unfortunately, some actors still thought it was the only way to change features. The resultant film over the cotton did not have much flexibility and hardened as the day went on. The surface could also be easily marred if pressed.

Next came the vinyl plastics, one of which was called *Sealskin,* a medical sealer made from a polyvinyl butyral that was too slow in drying. A similar type, but faster drying, was George Bau's Sealer #225. Unfortunately, both these sealers (and many of this type on the market) dry with a glossy, objectionably shiny surface, and foundation make-up slides off it easily.

The RCMA sealers combined various varieties of polyvinyls and added matting materials to produce sealers that had not only good adhesion and no shine but also sufficient tooth to hold make-up foundations better.

RCMA MATTE PLASTIC SEALER   Can be employed both as a surface sealer for wax buildups or as an adhesive for lifts (see page 59). It can also be used in conjunction with other materials to cover eyebrows and seal latex pieces and wherever a film former is required.

PMA MATTE MOLDING SEALER   A sealer for the edges of appliances made from PMA Molding Material. Dries matte.

PMA MATTE LACE ADHESIVE   A sealer/adhesive that is very fast drying and suitable for use with hairpieces, blocking brows, and so forth.

Toupee Tape   A number of varieties are available but a product called *Secure* is a colorless, two-sided, very sticky tape that is excellent for holding down toupee tops.

Waxes

DENTAL WAXES   (See page 60.)

Black Carding Wax   Useful for blocking out teeth for a toothless effect,

Red   For simulating gum tissue,

Ivory   A hard wax that can be used to form temporary teeth.

MOLDING WAXES   Although some grades of mortician's wax may see some make-up use, old nose putty is seldom used today. A new type of micro-synthetic-wax material is made by RCMA and comes in various shades and is less affected by body warmth than the mortician variety (see page 59).

RCMA PMA PLASTIC WAX MATERIAL

Light	Pale shade
Women	KW-3 color
Men	KT-3 color
Negro	KN-5 color
No-Color	A clear wax that can be tinted with RCMA Color Process foundations.
Violet	Matches RCMA Color Process Violet and is used to make raised bruises.

In addition to RCMA's regular Color Process foundations (which can be employed with foundation thinner for foamed appliances), RCMA makes an Appliance Foundation series and an Appliance Paint series especially for appliances of all kinds.

DRESS AND APPEARANCE OF MAKE-UP ARTISTS

Most make-up departments do not set any dress standards, and the white wraparound barber's or lab coat is seldom seen except for make-up lab people who may use one to protect their clothing. In the main, a clean, professional look—hands washed, nails clean, breath fresh, no overuse of strong perfumes, colognes, or after-shave lotions—presents to a performer a pleasant and appealing look. The female make-up artist must be especially careful to be attractive and not over-make-up or look like a washerwoman. The female performer is apt to think, "Will I look like *that* when she finishes my make-up?" Dress on locations must often bow to the weather, but cleanliness of appearance must be paramount.

KIT MAINTENANCE

Just like the person, the make-up kit reflects the artist in many ways. Clean brushes, fresh sponges, sharpened pencils, and so forth are always necessary. Take time during lulls in work to keep the kit clean. Wipe off the tops and sides of foundation containers, and keep everything neatly labeled. Every once in a while, empty out the entire kit and clean and restock it. Do the same for the hair kit, and you'll always be proud to show off your working tools.

CHAPTER 2

Special and Popular Characters

MYTHOLOGY, MODERN AS WELL AS ANCIENT, HAS INFUSED a myriad of popular conceptions and fantasies into human thought. Some are stylized, popular, and happy characters that have become part of our life as well as entertainment, while others have drawn upon our dark imaginations and hidden fears to instill a different element to which many are drawn out of curiosity and desire to see the unknown.

HORROR CHARACTERS

Perhaps the misty world of spirits and demons offers the greatest scope for the imagination, and make-up

FIGURE 2.1 *Lon Chaney, Sr., in* The Phantom of the Opera *in a make-up that inspired many young make-up artists of the 1940s to attempt to copy. This was a classic horror make-up done with old nose putty, facial distortion, false teeth, a bald front wig, and strong highlights and shadows. (Universal Pictures.)*

artists' conceptions have opened avenues of thought, sometimes heretofore inconceivable in frightening aspects and elements. Certainly, advancing technology and research in the field have produced more realistic and startling effects and creatures year after year, and it seems that the public not only dotes on these imaginative films but also supports the trend by contributing huge box office returns to the producers. Motion pictures have expanded the scope and depth of the horror style of entertainment far beyond what was possible on any stage in the past. Today, and in the future, we will see even more thrillingly terrifying films with the use of electronic and other spectacular tools of the engineers as well as the visual creations of the make-up artist. Special effects have entered many fields including not only make-up but also lighting, filmic superimposition, musical accompaniment, and other related crafts and arts.

Silent films introduced Lon Chaney and his many characterizations and special make-ups (Figure 2.1). Lon Chaney, Jr. told the story that his father kept his make-up/dressing room closed to everybody, and when he had to make repairs or changes, filming stopped and he went alone into his sanctum, emerging only when he was satisfied that his appearance was as he wanted it to be. Father passed no secrets down to son, and much of his art and craft died with him.

By the 1930s, studios had formed make-up departments that were mainly concerned with beautifying the performers until Jack Pierce of Universal Studios was faced with creating a Monster for the film *Frankenstein* (Figures 2.2 to 2.5). His creation commenced a trend that still leads the box office: the fantasy-horror film.

Although the early "horror" make-ups were done laboriously with old-time materials, later re-creations employed latex pieces that are far easier on the performer and can be pre-prepared for use. For example, *The Mummy* make-up had a complicated cloth wrapping on the body covered with a glue and dusted with Fuller's Earth to simulate a decaying body, while the same effect was later created with a grayed latex base paint covering a pre-made costume.

Other horror style make-ups such as *Dracula* were done with a gray-green foundation, very dark red lips and the eyes outlined to appear deep and penetrating

FIGURE 2.2   *Mild-mannered, gentlemanly Boris Karloff became the newest screen sensation in 1931, not as the Englishman he was but as the fearsome Monster in the Universal Studios film,* Frankenstein. *(Universal Pictures.)*

FIGURE 2.3   *Universal's make-up artist Jack Pierce created the make-up with a headpiece made of cloth, cotton batting, spirit gum, and collodion. (Universal Pictures.)*

FIGURE 2.4   *So strong was Karloff's portrayal that audiences began to call the Monster "Frankenstein" rather than the evil doctor who created the creature in the film! (Universal Pictures.)*

(Figure 2.6). *Mr. Hyde,* the alter ego of Dr. Jekyll, has gone through many phases from the John Barrymore one, to that of Frederic March, Spencer Tracy, and Louis Heyward; and to the more modern ones often seen in revived productions today (Figure 2.7).

Two of Rick Baker's horror make-ups include the decaying corpse sequence in *An American Werewolf in London,* which was done with foamed latex appliances on the actor (Jack Stave), showing the destruction on the side of the face and neck by the claws of the

 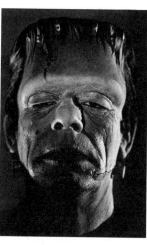

FIGURE 2.5   *The evolution of the Monster make-up from the Pierce-Karloff cotton and collodion head (*LEFT*) to the easier-to-apply and wear latex one evolved for Glenn Strange (*RIGHT*) when he took the role in the 1940s. (Universal Pictures.)*

werewolf that had attacked him (Figure 2.8). The slush molded latex mask made for the same film for one of the Nazi demons shows the detail of the sculpture to demonstrate the decay the mask was supposed to convey (Figure 2.9).

Although not really in the horror make-up category, distortions of the human body that are startling to the eye, such as the recreation of the terribly disfiguring disease known as neurofibromatosis that afflicted a man named Jon Merrick during the last part of the nineteenth century, can be grouped in this classification. When Merrick died at age 27, his body and face were so distorted by the ravages of the illness that he was quite unrecognizable as a human being.

To create this effect for the Paramount Pictures film *The Elephant Man* starring John Hurt, Christopher Tucker studied the actual photos and even a cast taken of the head and shoulders of Merrick that are the property of the London Hospital. It was found, however, that the actual distortions of the jaw and cheek lines were so radical that if the prostheses that he would make for the actor were to match the actual features, they would be impossible to apply on a normal face. Tucker therefore produced distortions so that the actor could still articulate his lines, and yet retain the patheticism that was required for the audience to have sympathy for the poor creature rather than be just horrified by the effect.

In designing the project, Tucker had to break down the make-up appliances into sections. Due to the thickness required in some facial areas where joins are normally made, he designed the make-up in two levels. That is, he had appliances that were *under* the outer ones.

On a face cast of the actor, he first sculpted his concept of the completed Elephant Man. Then, on a separate facial cast, he modelled the underlying sections, made molds, and cast these in silicone rubber.

Outer sections were molded separately, overlapping each to match the skin texture. The head was made in two sections, the face in fifteen, and the right arm was made in three—hand and wrist, elbow joint, and the upper arm. The upper torso was built in nine sections, some of them being up to four inches thick in places. Due to the exigencies of the shooting schedule, the molds were made in triplicate, and so it took long hours for eight weeks to prepare them.

Although most of the appliances were made of

FIGURE 2.6   *Other famous make-ups were those created by Jack Dawn: (A) Dracula for Bela Lugosi; (B) The Mummy and (C) The Wolfman, both for Lon Chaney's son (who hated to be called "junior" after his father died!), all in films for Universal Studios, which seemed to monopolize the horror film field at that time. (Universal Pictures.)*

  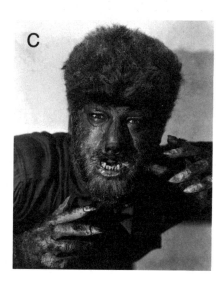

FIGURE 2.7   *Frederic March as Mr. Hyde in the Paramount Pictures production (1932) of* Dr. Jekyll and Mr. Hyde, *the most exciting version of this much filmed story. Note the painted nostrils, overpainted mouth, false teeth, and shadows and highlights make-up along with extra brows and a low-browed hairpiece. (Paramount Pictures.)*

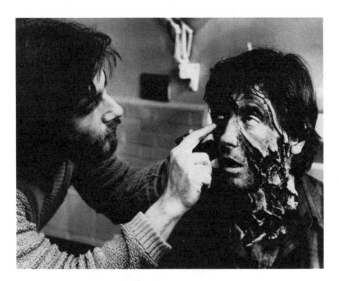

FIGURE 2.8   *Rick Baker's horror make-up for the decaying corpse sequence in* An American Werewolf in London. *(Polygram Pictures, 1980.)*

foamed latex, the two head sections were made of polyurethane foam with a latex skin into which hair was inserted, hair by hair, and, being more durable, were used a number of times (see Figure 2.10). A urethane foam made by Dow Corning was employed for a number of the sections.

The make-up took some six hours to apply during the production, and due to the long make-up time as well as the long shooting day, John Hurt worked only every other day. The actor's patience as well as the make-up artist's skill resulted in a classic make-up and a remembered film. The point was made once more that regardless of how skilled a performer may be, unless the actor "looks" the part, the audience loses much of its empathy for the character being portrayed (see Figure 2.11).

SKULLS AND SUPERNATURAL CHARACTERS

Always related to horror is the fear of necromancy, demons, and devils that pervades all cultures to some degree. Bones and skulls induce the fear of death and

FIGURE 2.9   *A slush molded latex mask made for one of the Nazi demons in* An American Werewolf in London. *(Rick Baker photo.)*

FIGURE 2.10 *Christopher Tucker applying the prostheses on John Hurt for* The Elephant Man *(Paramount Pictures).*

skull cap provides a standard effect as do the pointed ears. Facial colors range from red to green or even a natural shade.

Witches are weird, mysterious, not-quite-human women that are portrayed in many ways in films and television (Figures 2.14 and 2.15). Shakespeare's Three Witches in *Macbeth* are classic examples of these creatures that make excellent study vehicles, and make-up artists should always attempt to make them as different as possible. Such have long hooked or flat, shapeless noses and chins; thin, wrinkled, or overly distended lips; missing or blackened teeth; straggly brows and hair; and the skin from a dull yellow or greenish tone to possibly purplish color often covered with moles, hair, or dirt. Cracked and blackened or long, curved, sharp fingernails on thin, bony, ugly hands with large knuckles are generally in order.

The beautiful variety of witches or those portraying the evil women in Dracula's castle should be cold but exotic, forbidding yet compulsively exciting, and always sensual to the point of which no one can refuse whatever they desire of one (Figure 2.16). Blood-red lips set in pale, translucent skin with green or purple eye make-up and long hair can add to their filmy costumes and gliding walk.

Mephistopheles, in Gounod's opera *Faust,* is one of the most popular conceptions of the devil character. He has been portrayed in many different ways and with various foundation colors—such as greenish tones,

destruction, and the image of the Devil might take many forms, but all of them are basically evil. Figure 2.12 shows a skull make-up done with black-and-white foundations in a carefully drawn replica of the human skull on the face. A black, hooded costume completes the overall effect.

Figure 2.13 shows conventional devil make-up with horns, small moustache and pointed goatlike beard, and upturned eyebrows and eyes. The hairstyle or a

FIGURE 2.11 *(a) and (b) John Hurt, before and after make-up. (Photos courtesy Christopher Tucker.)*

A

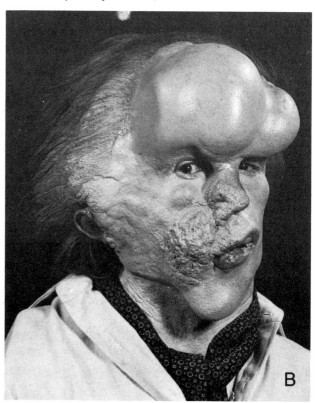

B

red, or even a fluorescent make-up have been used. The overall feeling of the make-up should display a diabolical intent and extreme maliciousness unless the script calls for these qualities to be hidden until the moment of exposure. Hands may have long nails in black or green, with the color being the same as the face. They might be shadowed and highlighted to appear long and delicately bony. Human nature is steeped in the lore that devils and witches are evil in intent, and the make-ups may be asked to reflect this.

ANIMAL-PEOPLE CREATURES

Some of these creatures are created to be horrible, like the Wolfman of Jack Pierce, while others are the benign Lion created by Jack Dawn on Bert Lahr for the MGM production of *The Wizard of Oz* (Figure 2.17). One of the first major uses of foamed latex for appliances, the make-ups in this film have become works of enduring excellence. Also see page 32.

Bob O'Bradovich designed the make-up on Richard Burton, shown in Figure 2.18, for the NBC TV production of *The Tempest*. The clip-on fangs were never used because they impeded the actor's speech. See section on Tooth Plastics for tooth casts and construction.

FIGURE 2.13   *Devil make-up.*

FIGURE 2.14   *Witches. Three witches with make-up by the author on three older actresses. The facial effect was enhanced by asking them to remove their dental plates. (Carl Fischer Studios/make-up by the author.)*

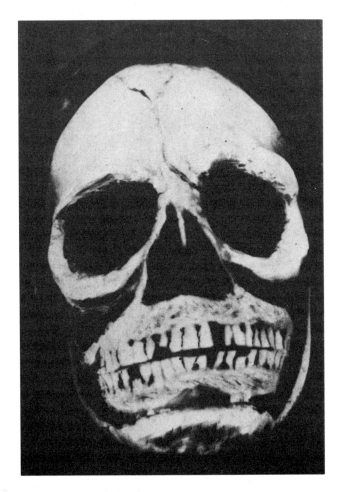

FIGURE 2.12   *A skull make-up.*

FIGURE 2.15   *Witches. The hooked, warted nose and chin, straggly hair and brows, wrinkled features and discolored skin typify the concept of the ugly witch. The eyes can be bleary and bloodshot or small and piercing. Blackened teeth also help.*

FIGURE 2.16 *Witches. Beautiful witches also have their place in fantasy films and can have the over red lips and uptilted brows of those shown, to the less stylized form of just straight make-up.*

FIGURE 2.17 *The Cowardly Lion of Bert Lahr in MGM's* Wizard of Oz. *(Courtesy MGM Pictures.)*

John Chambers's make-ups in *The Planet of the Apes* made an unusual script idea into a spectacular production with his chimpanzee, gorilla, and orangutan creatures (Figure 2.19). Although the extras had slush molded heads, the principles and *speaking* apes had foam latex pieces that consisted of sections for the upper face, lower lip, chin, and so on. Many of the pieces were precolored before application, and foundation was used to blend in the edges. Much facial hair and head hair also aided in disguising the edge of the appliances. The performers' faces had their own teeth and lip areas blackened out, and many had false teeth (of the ape creatures) inserted into the appliances. This was a first in making performers into truly believable animal creatures, and what could have been a laughable B-grade picture, turned out to be a film classic solely due to the design of the appliances to allow the performers a means of making expressions that were almost human on animal features. A foamed latex from the Goodyear Rubber Company was used in making the pieces on many of the characters.

However, the man who carried the ideas of making a man to animal to unusual dimensions is Rick Baker. As a very young man, he was obsessed with the idea of producing a gorilla creature that was completely believable and ended up in the animal suit himself to make the characterization complete. He even played the most famous gorilla in screen history in the color film version of *King Kong* as well as many other commercial and feature films.

Before the project of making a full ape culture for the film *Greystoke,* for which enormous undertaking he had a complete lab-workshop-studio built in En-

FIGURE 2.18 *Richard Burton as Caliban in* The Tempest.

gland—a project that took him two years of incessant work to complete, aided and encouraged by ex-wife Elaine (who ran all his foamed latex for him)—he had

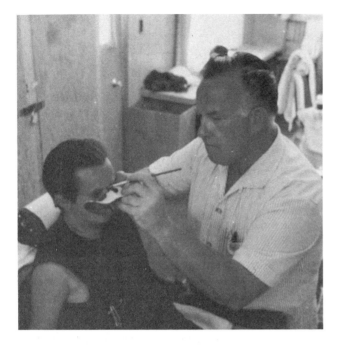 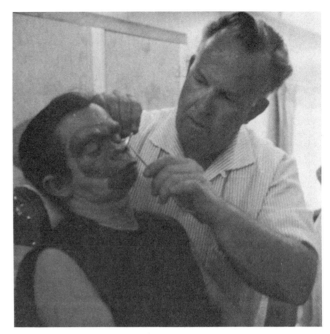

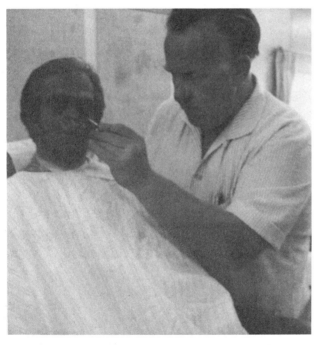 

FIGURE 2.19 *John Chambers's extraordinary make-up for* The Planet of the Apes *(20th Century Fox—1967) gained him a special Academy Award for making the apes so lifelike and completely practical in use for the performers to create characters the audience could believe fully. Without this credibility, the effect could have been ludicrous. (Courtesy John Chambers.)*

accumulated a vast knowledge of the primates and other animal creatures and won the first regular Academy Award for make-up for his spectacular *An American Werewolf in London* (see Figures 2.8 and 2.9). One of the projects that worked out many of the methods for producing facial expressions on oversize heads and body conformations and ease in replacing fragile parts for the suits of hair was for the film *The Incredible Shrinking Woman*—again, with Rick playing the gorilla and his wife pulling the strings (Figures 2.20 and 2.21).

The operation of the facial expressions in the gorilla mask were far beyond what a performer could do with his own face pressing against any part of the mask, so a series of devices was required to activate these. Again, it becomes evident that even though a performer ac-

tually does the role *in make-up* (even though it is a full or partial covering of the face at times), if mechanical devices improve the performance, are they not a part of the *make-up?*

In *The Incredible Shrinking Woman,* Rick played the gorilla Sidney and we see in Figure 2.20 the complexity of the costume he constructed. In the center is the knotted hair suit with its sponge rubber chest. The heads in front of this are the close-up head, the "hoot" head, and the "roar" head—designed to form the various expressions that gorillas employ—while to the left is a slush molded head, and above it a fake fur suit for stunt men to wear. In the boxes are the dextrous mechanical extension hands (four pairs in case of damage to the hands during filming), while surrounding are various hand and foot positions to be exchanged on the suit for various attitudes of the appendages. Extra heads, hands, and feet for replacements are also seen as are various simian skulls in the upper left that were used for research to sculpture.

For *Greystoke,* Rick improved the simian suits to an amazing degree of reality (Figure 2.22). First, he drew sketches of the apes, giving each its own facial features and personality traits distinguishable from each other. Next, sculptures were done over the performers' life masks to follow the sketches. Note the similarity of

FIGURE 2.20   *Complexity of costumes constructed by Rick Baker for* The Incredible Shrinking Woman. *(Courtesy Universal City Studios, 1980.)*

FIGURE 2.21   *On set with wife Elaine and special effects technician Guy Faria, Rick is in the Sidney suit with the close-up head. Note the multiple cables that produce the movements in the headpiece. As the feet were not being filmed here, Rick wore comfortable shoes! (Courtesy Universal City Studios and Rick Baker.)*

the drawing of the character Figs with the sculpture at the lower left.

For the film, these ape characters were developed extraordinarily by Rick Baker, as can be seen in the ape Silverbeard (played by Peter Elliot) as he first appears and then later in the film showing an aged character (Figure 2.23). This is an unusual instance where make-up has been employed to age an animal character played by an actor.

Each ape character in *Greystoke* had four heads: a close-up head that was cable operated and capable of changing expressions from, for example, eating to licking lips (however, the performers supplied the jaw movements and the eyes were covered with full scleral lenses); a "roar" head to snarl and show teeth activated by the performers' movements; a "hoot" head that made a pursed lip expression; and a stunt head of slush latex filled with polyfoam (Figure 2.24). The suits were hand knotted onto a lycra spandex base body stocking that was stretched over a muscle suite made of lycra spandex with varying densities of foam muscle formation, rib cages, and other bone structures. As well, there were various hands and feet that were interchangeable (Figure 2.25).

Once again, the art of make-up and the genius of those who can achieve the likenesses of both humans and animals becomes the entire point—of the plot, the story, the script, the action, the characters, and direction of that portion of the film. Without the make-up, it would make so much dumb show by competent performers—and no one has union-organized simians as yet to perform quite as such!

Not to be outdone in the animal-men gender, Stan Winston came up with his "Manimal" transformation for the television series of the same name (Figure 2.26). His unusual method of going beyond the simple facial cast of a performer to sculpting a full head in plastalene of the expression he wants to depict demonstrates his artistic ability and desire to make his creations as lifelike as possible. Working with a series of close-up photographs and measurements in addition to a life

FIGURE 2.22   LEFT: *Drawing of character "Figs."* RIGHT: *Clay sculptures of characters. "Figs" lower left. (Photos courtesy Warner Bros. Pictures and Rick Baker.)*

FIGURE 2.23 *The aging of the ape Silverbeard, played by Peter Elliot, as he first appears in the film,* left, *and then later,* right, *showing an aged character.*

mask, he inserts teeth and eyes into the sculpture to visualize his conceptions. In the case of the "Manimal," this snarling expression is seen reflected in all the stages of the transmutation from man to black panther (Figure 2.27).

FANTASY TYPES

Fairies, elves, sprites, nymphs, and other fanciful characters can be done in an impressionistic style. Fairies can be made up straight and pretty in light shades of foundation, while elves, sprites, and the like should be done in light shades of brown or green to resemble forest colors. They can have small pointed noses and ears. Somewhat similar are leprechauns, although the foundation shade can be normal while the ears and nose can be pointed. Upturned brows and a small unkempt wig will add to the effect (Figure 2.28).

Within the fantasy types one can include such makeups as might be found in *Alice in Wonderland* (Figure 2.29), Shakespeare's *A Midsummer Night's Dream, The Wizard of Oz* (Figures 2.30 and 2.31), and similar productions on stage or for the screen (Figures 2.32, 2.33, 2.34, and 2.35). Again, foamed latex or urethane appliances will see wide use to depict the characters.

Also related to fantasy types might be included humanoid robot creations like the one Stan Winston devised and made for the film *Heartbeeps,* with Bernadette Peters and Andy Kaufman playing the two characters (Figure 2.36). To achieve the necessary translucence and artificiality and to produce a new look for the

make-up, Stan Winston employed a gelatin mixture for the appliances and intrinsically colored them with gold for Aqua, the female, and bronze for Val, the male robot. The latter had 12 separate pieces, and Aqua had 6. The coloration was delicately and carefully done using silver as highlights, so no extrinsic color or foundation was required on the appliance, only on the exposed skin areas. Matte adhesive was used to

FIGURE 2.24 *White Eyes is shown with his roar head, showing the fine detail in the facial portion of the foamed latex head, the teeth in the mask, and the scleral contact lenses on the actor's eyes.*

FIGURE 2.25   *Figs on set in the foreground with Kala, Tarzan's ape-mother, and on the left, a tiny latex rubber Tarzan. The other apes are background characters whose suits and heads are as carefully made as the principles' costumes. Figs is seen with his relaxed-mode feet and dextrous mechanical arms that extended the performer's arm proportions but still allowed him to manipulate the fingers and pick up things.*

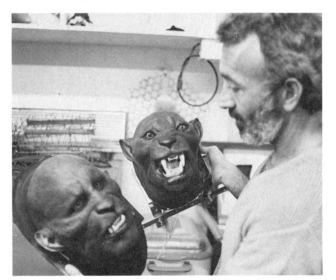

FIGURE 2.26   *Stan Winston, sculpting the Manimal progressions from man to black panther. Final sculptures are on right.*

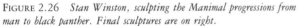

adhere the pieces, but being the material they were, they required constant attention. The make-ups were nominated for the Academy Award as being innovative and unusual in concept.

DOLLS, TOYS, AND TIN SOLDIERS

Within the range of fantasy and children's stories are found playthings come to life (Figure 2.37). Light shades of foundation, with stylized cheekcolor circles, drawn red lips, accented eyelash make-up, and drawn brows are suitable here. Any make-up done for chil-

dren's stories should avoid any effect that might be frightening and should induce children to cuddle the toy rather than be afraid of it.

STATUARY

A marble effect can be obtained by first covering the skin with a white foundation and then carefully giving the skin reflectivity with a pearl foundation. A plastic or latex cap is used over the hair or a very stiff wig, sprayed with white and the same pearl for translucence.

Gold or bronzed statuary can be simulated with

FIGURE 2.27 *Stan Winston's* Manimal *sculpture of the commencing facial expression of Simon MacCorkindale taken from the photo below it on the left, and a stage in the transformation with make-up appliances on the right showing the progression of the idea and the expression. The on-screen transformations included the use of various bladder inflation effects and film superimposition as well as make-up changes in tight close-up from man to black panther.*

FIGURE 2.28 *Roddy MacDowall as a leprechaun in CBC-TV General Electric Theatre. (Make-up by the author.)*

FIGURE 2.29 *Bobby Clark as the Duchess in NBC-TV's* Alice in Wonderland *with a complete foam latex face by Dick Smith.*

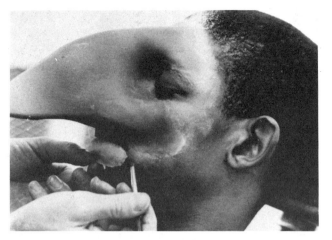

FIGURE 2.30   *Ray Bolger as the Scarecrow in MGM's classic* The Wizard of Oz, *with make-up created by Jack Dawn. Although the face appears to be covered with cloth, it is actually a latex skin with a cloth impression. (Courtesy MGM Pictures.)*

FIGURE 2.32   *Two of Stan Winston's make-ups for the film,* The Wiz, *showing the application of a stylized beak-nose prosthesis, and the completed Lion make-up, showing a different concept from that of the earlier* Wizard of Oz *film (Universal/Motown, 1978).*

FIGURE 2.31   *Jack Haley as the Tin Man in the same film. Although much of the effect is costume, the silver painted face and spout nose was very effective along with the head and chin pieces. (Courtesy MGM Pictures.)*

FIGURE 2.33 *Maurice Manson's "Santa Claus" or "Jolly Old St. Nicholas" is a plump, happy, old elf with pure white hair and whiskers in abundance. Red cheeks, a round, red nose, and laughing eyes complete the picture.*

FIGURE 2.34 *"Old Father Time" is another fanciful character that must be far more decrepit than "Santa Claus." Long, white hair, a drawn face, and a long, whispy beard typify this make-up.*

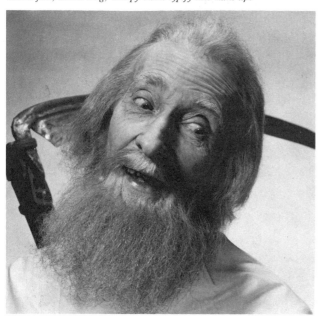

gold, bronze, or copper foundations. Gold, white, and other colored hairsprays (Nestle) can also be used on the skin, or the old method is to use a mixture of gold or bronze bronzing powder, with glycerin, water, and alcohol as a vehicle. This is then applied with a large silk sponge in a thin coat on the body. Care should be taken with the latter as it can block the skin pores, so the entire body should not be covered to allow breathing space for the skin.

SURREALISTIC MAKE-UPS

The world of surrealism is wide and varied, and many different aspects and directions can be taken with make-ups to express the craft and imagination of the artist. Some employ flower petals around the eyes, others use sequins, while some design with color.

Rock singers sometimes employ such fantastic make-ups as contributory to the imagery they wish to convey. Originality in application, design, and placement of colors on the face or hair gives free reign to the imagination. However, once the concept is established, it becomes an intrinsic part of the singer or group, and to copy such exactly by another person or persons is often considered to be a breach of theatrical etiquette—just as it is for specific clown make-ups in the circus. Nevertheless, certain forms exist that seem to establish a framework or create a style indigenous to the person or group.

FIGURE 2.35 *Bob Schiffer of Walt Disney Studios created this pumpkin head on Jonathan Winters for a Disney Halloween Special with a slush and paint-in molded head in two sections with the inside fit made of polyurethane foam.*

FIGURE 2.36   *From the film* Heartbeeps. LEFT: *Bernadette Peters as* "*Aqua.*" RIGHT: *Andy Kaufman as* "*Val.*"

FIGURE 2.37   *Toy soldier.*

FIGURE 2.38   *Barton MacLane in RKO Pictures,* The Spanish Main (1945) *in a typical pirate make-up. Note the scars on the cheek and forehead, the unshaven beard effect, and the added drawing of the eyebrows along with the period wig.*

PIRATES

Most pirates should be dark, swarthy characters who seldom shave and often have scars on their faces to add to their ferocity (Figure 2.38). KM-8, KT-3, KT-4, or K-3 are foundations that may be used. Eye patches, hairy arms and bodies, and straggly, unkempt hair are typical. The pirate crew should always be interspersed with Negroid and Mongoloid types, and appropriate foundations should be used.

CLOWNS

Basically, professional clowns divide their make-ups into the *whiteface* and the *tramp*. The typical whiteface uses a clown white or Super White that is powdered with a white powder or prosthetic base powder (Figure 2.39). Red, blue, green, and black shades are used to create the designs and accentuate the features. Many clowns employ ordinary china marking pencils for the colors as these are easy to sharpen by unraveling the paper covering. Copying the face or special markings by another clown is considered to be a serious breach in circus etiquette, so unless one is copying a specific clown character, new designs are always called for in design.

Facial hair is seldom used—unless just painted on for Keystone Kops or beard effects. A skull cap can be made from a white stocking and pulled over the head. Earholes can be cut when the cap is centered. Wigs with bald fronts and red hair are often seen. Red latex noses (slush molded, usually) are special clown features and can be made in various shapes.

The tramp clown variety can be made happy or sad, depending upon the turndown or turnup of the mouth drawing. Here the unshaven beard effect is almost always used, and the face can be made up with light to medium shades of foundation to set it off. Mouths

FIGURE 2.39   ABOVE: *Tramp clowns.* BELOW: *Various whiteface clowns.*

can be white or red. The costume is always of the old clothes variety, seldom fitting anywhere and exaggerated whenever possible.

There have been many famous clowns from the Barnum and Bailey Circus; among them were Emmett Kelly and Paul Jerome as tramps and, in whiteface, Felix Adler, who always wore a rhinestone on the end of his nose (he called it an Irish Diamond, or a shamrock) and always led a baby pig on a string for his walkaround (Figure 2.40). Other famous whiteface

FIGURE 2.40   *Whiteface and tramp clowns.* LEFT: *Felix Adler in the whiteface make-up he made famous.* CENTER: *Paul Jerome as The Tramp.* RIGHT: *A classic whiteface clown, Jackie Le Claire.*

clowns include Jackie LeClaire, Al White, Ernie Burch, Al Bruce, Arnie Honkola, and many others.

Another phase of this type of make-up is practiced by mimes. However, this is mainly a white face with few other markings, and the neck is seldom painted, leaving a rather masklike look to the make-up.

FIRST SPECIAL ACADEMY AWARD FOR MAKE-UP—1964

A landmark in make-up artistry was established when William Tuttle, then head of the MGM make-up department, won the Academy Award for make-up artistry for the Galaxy-Scarus/MGM film, *The Seven Faces of Dr. Lao*. Combining every form of character make-up procedure, along with foamed appliances, special hair and head dresses, and the coordinated costumes for each character, these multiple make-ups on a single face will forever remain a goal for other artists to accomplish.

A pre-make-up photo of Tony Randall (Figure 2.41) serves to enforce and delineate these changes in the characters portrayed. The first test of the *Dr. Lao* old oriental was done with a plastic bald cap, but as this is a time-consuming and annoying daily procedure (to the actor as well as the make-up artist), and as Dr. Lao was a main character, Tony agreed to shave his head. All the other parts required various wigs anyway (Figure 2.42).

Dr. Lao required foamed latex appliances over and under the eyes to produce the epicanthic fold of oriental eyes. An appliance was also added to the nose to broaden it. Hairlace brows, moustache and beard, and small frame glasses added to the effect. Additional aging was done with stipple and painting.

Making the facial structure of one race appear to be that of another must take into careful consideration the structural appearances of the performer and what must be added, or subtracted, to produce the desired effect. Bill had the experience of producing the Asian lid make-up on Marlon Brando for *Teahouse of the August Moon* for MGM in 1956, and employed the same technique for converting an African-American woman to a Geisha. This latter make-up was done during the period of filming of the *Teahouse*. *Ebony Magazine* had requested (for a special article) that he do an unusual transformation on the woman. Rather than do an old age make-up as suggested, and having the Geisha wigs and costumes available from the film, he was inspired to do this spectacular transformation. It proved to be so convincing that she was accepted as a visitor from Japan when she visited the *Teahouse* set (Figures 2.43–2.44).

Continuing on the *Dr. Lao* make-ups, the character

FIGURE 2.41 *Tony Randall, no make-up.*

FIGURE 2.42 *Tony Randall as Dr. Lao.*

FIGURE 2.43 *Marlon Brando in* Teahouse of the August Moon.

"Pan" was done with a new nose, new eye make-up, brows, moustache and beard, and a wig with balsa wood horns along with a dark make-up base (Figure 2.45).

"Appolonius of Tyana" consisted of again a different nose, beard, moustache, brow, and wig with a light-colored make-up foundation along with blue corneal lenses for the eyes (Figure 2.46).

"Merlin the Magician" called for more nose and hair changes, deep aging with make-up and stipple effects, and pale blue corneal lenses to accent the age level (Figure 2.47).

"Medusa" had foamed appliances over the eyes. To produce a smooth facial appearance, appliances were made to fill in Mr. Randall's facial structure. Both upper and lower lips of foamed latex produced a more feminine appearance. Lips were painted green and green corneal lenses were used on the eyes. The MGM Special Effects Department made and animated the snakes in the hair piece (Figure 2.48).

"The Abominable Snowman" make-up was a large foamed prosthesis with balsa wood teeth. The skin was made a pinkish hue and dark circles were painted around the eyes. The tongue of the actor was painted with powdered charcoal for an effect. Although the body suit was made of synthetic fur, the wig was made of the skins from Colobus monkeys, using only the white portion of the fur (Figure 2.49).

FIGURE 2.44 *Before and after Geisha make-up.*

FIGURE 2.45   *Tony Randall as Pan.*

FIGURE 2.47   *Tony Randall as Merlin the Magician.*

FIGURE 2.46   *Tony Randall as Appolonius.*

FIGURE 2.48   *Tony Randall as Medusa.*

FIGURE 2.49 *Tony Randall as The Abominable Snowman.*

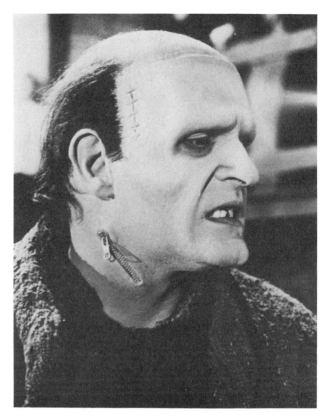

FIGURE 2.50 *Peter Boyle as the Frankenstein monster.*

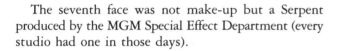

The seventh face was not make-up but a Serpent produced by the MGM Special Effect Department (every studio had one in those days).

WILLIAM TUTTLE'S FRANKENSTEIN "MONSTER"

As everyone who does make-up "wants" to do a Frankenstein "Monster", Bill Tuttle did this make-up on Peter Boyle in MGM's hilarious spoof with Gene Wilder in 1974 (Figure 2.50). Although foam rubber was utilized on the forehead and the housing of the zipper on the neck, along with hairlace side pieces, most of the make-up effect was done with highlighting and shading procedures. Mel Brooks, the director, had heard that the original "Monster" make-ups done by Jack Pierce at Universal Studios had employed a greenish foundation, so he asked Bill to do the same for the make-up (even though it was to be shot in B&W film). Bill obliged and did the shadows in dark green and the highlighting with yellowish-green. The missing tooth was done with black tooth enamel.

CHAPTER 3

Special Effects

SINCE THE 1950s WHEN SOME NEW AND DIFFERENT TEXtures and effects were introduced in *The Technique of Film and Television Make-up* (Focal Press, London, 1958), the advances and research into the complicated field of make-up special effects has expanded in many and various directions and is only bound by human imagination. Entire make-up laboratories, far advanced from those previously envisioned, have become the spawning places of more blood and guts, monsters, and extraterrestrial creatures through the talents of a small band of make-up artists that has gone far beyond the usual. To anyone interested in this field, the workshops of Dick Smith, Stan Winston, Tom Burman, Rick Baker, Rob Botin, and others are wondrous places indeed where the illusions of these artists come to life for the screen.

Although the Special Effects Departments and personnel of the old Hollywood studios performed marvels of the time, an increasing trend toward the transition from the human face and form to what might be termed *puppets,* whose actions are controlled by wires or cables, both manual and motorized, bladders of air, and other means of manipulation, has bridged the visual imagery in seemingly magic ways to lead the audience down the path of deception and false impression when combined by clever editing of film or tape. The demands of directors have spurred the almost overreaching thoughts of these special effects make-up artists into creating a new form of entertainment that combines the talents of the make-up artist with that of magician or creators of visual illusions. This trend has brought forth a number of magazines (with very high-quality color pages) such as *Cinefantastique, Fangoria,* and *Cinemagic,* which are distributed worldwide to the enthusiasts of this genus and are contributed to and enriched by the work of these artists in careful coverage of their films.

The combination of make-up skills with those of sculpture, casting, latex and plastics, painting, and making mechanicals produce the learning level (and all in this area will agree that they are constantly researching and learning) that pervades in their results. All the good artists are ready to share their knowledge with others in the field as one person or one laboratory or workshop cannot experiment with or discover everything that might be the best for the job. Gone are the secret rooms that Lon Chaney or Jack Pierce locked themselves into to create their make-ups, and an opening of sincere talent and sharing makes the effects grow. Granted, like all artists who are immersed in a project, make-up artists seek closed facilities to focus their concentration, but with their peers and workers, such is respected and understood because they wish the same for themselves. Here are a series of special effects make-ups that go from the human body or face to exact image counterparts (when the human form could not stand the distortion or materials required for the effect), showing the details and directions that served in each case.

BIDDING ON A PRODUCTION

Films that entail mostly straight make-ups have their expenses in make-up covered under personnel and production costs for supplies. However, when the entire premise, scope, and effectiveness of the film depends strongly on its make-up effects, such as in the *Planet of the Apes* series by John Chambers, Rick Baker's *American Werewolf in London,* Dick Smith's *Exorcist* and *Altered States,* Tom Burman's *Invasion of the Body Snatchers,* Tom Savini's *Creepshow,* and many others, then the budgetary factors related to make-up begin to soar.

With the many private laboratories for creating these effects concentrated mostly in the Los Angeles area, it makes it easy for producers and directors of this type of film to begin to shop around for someone to do the very special make-up that is often required. They seek bids on the projects, and like everything else done on that basis, the lowest bid may not be the truest. More and more, this is *not* due to competition between the labs but because the production people start changing their minds as to the effects as each bid is received along with a composite breakdown of the project as explained and discussed with one lab.

As the concepts change, and with the variance of effects directions vacillating, the unions start to place obstacles of craft crossovers, the writers begin to alter their ideas of story direction, the directors get brainstorms injected by the input of fresh elements, and what was minor becomes major. Whereas a bid of $150,000 for the make-up might be the lowest as compared to another of $200,000 or more, the over-budget ideas can climb to $400,000 just as easily unless a strong hand controls the artistic flights of fancy often indulged in by production people sometimes unfamiliar with the creative minds of the make-up artist when they are let loose to produce an effect. Terry Smith once said to a producer who was beginning to allow his mind to wander beyond the agreed-upon concept of an effect allowed for within the budget, "Sure, I can change it. You pay for it and I'll make anything you want. It only costs money. But don't expect it to be contained within the present budget, because it's not there!"

There are other factors that also occur after the filming is in progress. First, the production can have personality problems and the director is taken off the picture or quits. The new one hired has an entirely different idea of what direction the make-up should take and changes everything. The budget goes out the window in this act. Make-up labs have a mound of canceled molds, casts, effects, and so on and make many trips to the dump to clear their storage space for the next foolish change.

Next (and this is often the worst) is the performer who decides to be uncooperative and does not want to wear the make-up in which he or she was hired to perform. When a make-up artist has a professional performer to work with who is cooperative, he or she is more than pleased. Tom Burman said of Michael Ironside, "Michael was absolutely the perfect actor to support the make-up. It made me feel good to be instrumental in making this part possible and in making it come alive."

Finally, there are cinematographers who will not change their camera angles or lighting to aid the aspect and effectiveness of the make-up. This adds to the difficulties of producing the best appearance for the screen and sometimes seriously detracts from the illusion. As one can readily see, only with sincere coordinative efforts can any special make-up effect be at its optimum all around.

In this regard and because of past disappointments, Stan Winston now often insists upon directing and editing any so-called special make-up effects, illusions, or *transformations* (as he calls them) that he feels require his guiding hand to achieve the result that he has envisioned—and has been hired to deliver! In this way, the proof of the effectiveness of the make-up or illusion is in the audience reaction, and its reflection is the satisfaction of the creator.

Due to the horizontal work structure of some unions in opposition to the creative singularity of some lab technician/make-up artists, the majority of make-up labs is off-premises to the film studios where union jurisdiction and control are contractual. Most of those who have these outside make-up labs are free to hire and train their own specialists at this time, but only the future holds the answers to the controversy of whether or not the special effects that are being designed and executed in the make-up labs come under the union job descriptions and contracts of the myriad of directions that are being taken to produce these illusions and transformations today. It would have been sad to have unions disputing whether Leonardo da Vinci was an art director, scene painter, plasterer, construction grip, or such while completing his work in the Sistine Chapel. Present-day make-up art must remain unfettered by organizational politics and restrictions and our Leonardos allowed full rein in their quest for viable and exciting ideas and their fruition. Openmindedness in art is mandatory for the human spirit.

The following are just a few examples of the varied use of special materials by a few of the make-up artists engaged in this very creative and challenging work.

RICK BAKER

Make-up artists who love to do character work are always fascinated with on-screen, progressive, facial and body changes because they offer a different type of challenge and require a variety of approaches to achieve the effects. In recent years, the most outstanding transformation on-screen was the one devised and executed by Rick Baker and his company of talented technicians for the Polygram Pictures production, *An American Werewolf in London,* by the use of special devices that went beyond the physiological functions of the human body to make the change from man to wolf-creature. He called his body parts "Change-Os" to define them from static reality. The first spectacular effect was two stages of a Change-O-Hand made from Smooth-On PMC-724 with hair imbedded in the arms (Figures 3.1 and 3.2).

The Change-O-Heads used for the facial progressions were also made of PMC-724 (about 1/4 inch thick) over a mechanically controlled skull section made of fibreglass and dental acrylics that was operated by technicians to achieve the facial extensions so graphically portrayed in the film (Figure 3.3). Rick used a series of appliances on David Naughton to effect the commencement of the transformation and brought the make-up up to the stage of the first Change-O-Head (Figures 3.4 to 3.6).

The Change-O-Back effect again demonstrates the number of technicians required for this change (Figure 3.7). A number of bladders and syringes that acted as pneumatic rams for the effect were employed to ripple the spinal cord.

There are a number of ways that camera work aids effects:

1. A special camera can be employed that runs at high speed to give a slow motion effect when played back at normal projection speed.

FIGURE 3.1   *Rick holds Change-O-Hand #1 that shows the metal rod extension that controlled the wrist movement. In his other hand is the device that controlled the individual finger movements, and the tubing connected to the pneumatic rams controlled with air pressure to extend the hand in the palm area. (Photos courtesy Rick Baker for Polygram Pictures.)*

FIGURE 3.2   TOP: *In Change-O-Hand #2, the palm extension was continued further with the action of the pneumatics as the palm section was fluctuated with bladders controlled with plastic tubing and a syringe. All the hair was added as the filming progressed and was laid by hand on the arm and the chest (as the actor, David Naughton, had little chest hair). A small appliance nose commences the facial transformation that was the next progression in the make-up.* BOTTOM: *Due to camera framing, as the actor looked at the hand (seemingly his own), the changes occurred and he reacted to them. (Photos courtesy Rick Baker for Polygram Pictures.)*

2. This process can be reversed and the camera run more slowly, which speeds up the screen action.
3. The action is performed in reverse for a normal camera run and a print made that again reverses *that* action. For example, a section of skin (made from PMC-724 or a similar product or even a foamed one) can have long hairs implanted. As the camera is running, these hairs, attached to a material under the false skin, are withdrawn until the skin is smooth. The reverse printing makes the hair appear to grow from the skin in the proper pattern.
4. A diffusion disc or filter can sometimes be employed to soften certain effects, or sometimes colored filters can add to an effect. Proper lighting to *see* the effect is essential!

A thorough discussion of all special effects in a film by department heads will aid the final concept as sometimes a minor contribution to an idea will make it work better. However, a make-up artist who does these special make-up transformations or effects should have a thorough knowledge of what the film camera can do as well as be familiar with all the new advances in electronic techniques or special effects. Of the latter, make-up artists should be aware that some directors get carried away with the sight of electronic changes and employ them to superimpose over make-ups. This may add to the overall visual effect or, in the case of some overuse of such, destroy the make-up concept. Films like *Altered States* displayed an excess of electronics or light-created effects *over* a splendid concept designed by Dick Smith for the transformations. The creative illusions of the make-up artist can be *aided* at times with such visuals but should not overpower them with their inherent artificiality.

Editing also plays an enormous role in creating visual effects. For example, if one videotapes a film and then plays it back frame after frame, the methodology

FIGURE 3.3   *The skulls, shown here in (top) frontal and (bottom) profile views, show the jaw and teeth portions that could be extended out, along with an acrylic nose section. Space was left in the forehead area for another acrylic section that could extend the movement. Ear movement was controlled by the tubing devices seen on the sides of the skull, and the cheekbone extensions were being constructed (see frontal view). (Photos courtesy Rick Baker for Polygram Pictures.)*

FIGURE 3.4   *Sequence photos of Change-O-Head #1, showing facial distortion activated by the devices of the skull that stretched the outer plastic skin in the mouth, nose, cheekbone, and forehead areas. Facial hair was individually embedded in the face mask and a wig added to complete the effect. The body hair also increased during the sequence. (Photo courtesy Rick Baker for Polygram Pictures.)*

FIGURE 3.5 *During the filming on set, note the various cables, tubes, connectors, boards, and other devices operated by the technicians activating the Change-O-Head devices. (Photo courtesy Rick Baker for Polygram Pictures.)*

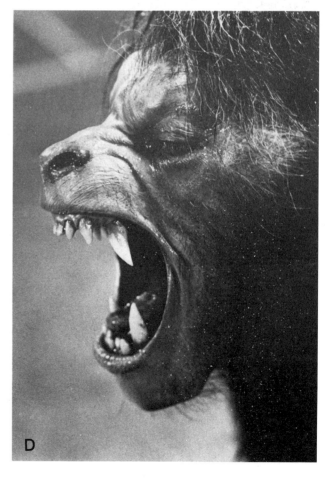

FIGURE 3.6 *With Change-O-Head #2, Rick made the sculpture asymmetrical, with the mask's left side more human and in pain while the right side is more wolflike. (Photos courtesy Rick Baker for Polygram Pictures.) (A) A test with the head, note areas where teeth will be set. (B–D) The extensions continue and the face becomes more and more animalistic during the change. Note that the eyes remained closed during the Change-O-Head sequences so no false eyes were required.*

FIGURE 3.7   *The Change-O-Back photo shows the number of technicians required for the change to activate a number of bladders to ripple the spinal cord by means of various syringes that acted as pneumatic rams for the effect. The hands, made of slush molded latex and mounted on long sticks, were moved on each side by technicians. With the camera shooting downward, the hands were in their proper place in the frame. (Photos courtesy Rick Baker for Polygram Pictures.)*

the various Change-O effects. In these, first the actor's face is made up with various appliances (during cutaways), then the first Change-O-Head is used to its full extension, another cutaway to another part of the body changing, and then back to the face that is now Change-O-Head #2 that is starting its extension at the point that Change-O-Head #1 left off.

Body positioning to show just the head and neck, with the rest of the body a simulation, is sometimes used, as with Tom Savini's arrow-through-the-throat effect. Here only the head of the actor is seen through a pillow, but the neck and shoulders are an appliance. In *Werewolf*, Rick Baker used this same type of effect when the wolf-body transformation is taking place, by having the actor's upper torso showing through a hole in a false floor, and the wolf body attached (which, due to its conformation, could not possibly be done on a human body) is a dummy simulation.

Within the framework of these cooperative illusionary visuals the audience is fooled into believing what they *think* they see on the screen. The mind connects these illusions into a pattern of thought that shows the effect but is deceived by the camera work and the film editing during the sequence of the transformation, change, or final result in addition to whatever bladders or mechanical devices are utilized in the make-up to produce the changes.

of the sequence is revealed. Take for example Tom Savini's throat-cutting sequence in *Friday the 13th.* One sees a frightened girl up against a tree and the back of a figure approaching with a knife. We see the knife gleam on the left side of the frame and sweep toward the girl. As it does, the figure effectively blocks out the scene for a few frames. Here the cutting of the film takes place. Then we see the girl lift up her head, revealing a cleverly concealed throat-cut appliance, the blood pumps out as the knife gleams on the right side of the screen, appearing to be a continuation of the slash. For safety, even the knife blade was a rubber copy made by Savini to look realistic. In this momentary film cut, the audience is fooled by a visual illusion of a continued action.

This same type of illusion of continued action is also accomplished by cutaways. In the case of the *Werewolf* transformation sequence, reaction shots of the actor's face are intercut with changes of appliances for

CARL FULLERTON

Although in the production of Paramount's *Friday the 13th: Part II* much of the gore and effects that Carl Fullerton made for the film were cut in the final editing due to a clamp-down on explicit grisly make-up effects, there remained some good foam latex appliances. The character of Jason from the original film *Friday the 13th* has grown up into a deformed, retarded youth so Carl constructed a foamed latex head, along with false eyes, upper and lower dentures, and laid-on brows and beardline to go on the actor's face (Figure 3.8).

The decapitated head of another character from the earlier film is also shown, and this is a prop made with an epoxy substrate and covered with a skin of a slush molded latex (Figure 3.9). Epoxy eyes along with a set of acrylic teeth, a wig, and some dried blood effect all add to the realistic figure. The coloration was done with acrylic paints.

In *The Hunger,* which Carl worked on with his mentor, Dick Smith, he made a number of mummified figures. One of them, seen in Figure 3.10 with Carl, was a very tall and very thin man for which a full body suit (that zipped up the back) was made. Various latex products were employed to construct the suit.

Those mummies that had to crumble into bones and dust were largely made of a fragile wax compound with a very friable polyurethane foam as an interior

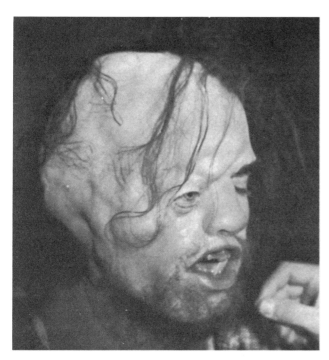

FIGURE 3.8   *Jason from* Friday the 13th: Part 2 *(Georgetown Productions, 1981).*

FIGURE 3.10   *Carl with one of his mummified figures.*

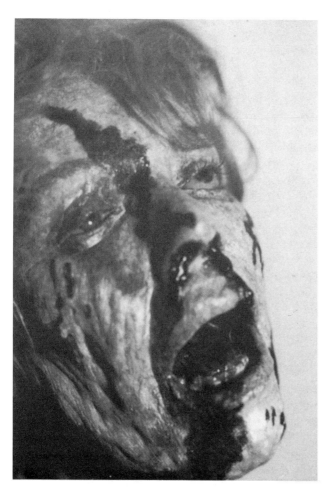

FIGURE 3.9   *A prop decapitated head by Carl Fullerton.*

FIGURE 3.11   *Two mummies that were cast from human figures and constructed in the wax material that crumbled with very little agitation.*

support medium. Figures 3.10 and 3.11 show two examples of figures, one an appliance bodysuit make-up on a performer, and the other, puppets or props of similar characters, and both were designed and executed by the make-up department for the film to give continuity to the overall concept.

SPASMS BY DICK SMITH

In July 1981, producer John Newton and Bill Fruit of Toronto came to my studio in Larchmont to talk to me about their film, *Death Bite* (later retitled *Spasms*). Earlier I had agreed to help Canadian special effects make-up artist Stephen Dupuis with an arm inflation effect for the film. Now Newton and Fruit had written a more elaborate effect into their modest film about a supersnake and wanted something special.

In their new scene, the bad guy is bitten by the monster and dies slowly and spectacularly. They knew about bladder effects (which I had developed for *Altered States*), but asked if I didn't have something new and exciting that hadn't been used before. I started to lecture them that much time and effort had to be expended to come up with such an effect when an idea floated into my consciousness. Years before I had used trichloroethane (a cleaning fluid) to raise weltlike letters on Linda Blair's foam latex stomach in the *Exorcist*. Recently, friends of mine, Steve Laporte and David Miller, inspired by the *Exorcist* effect, had used trichloroethane together with air bladders to change a lady into a grotesque hag. These associations pointed to an ideal solution because the swelling and distortion trichloroethane produces in foam latex resembles that of a poison.

I excitedly led Newton and Fruit to my basement where I demonstrated the effect on a scrap piece of foam. I knew from experience that the fluid would attack tears in the foam more extremely, so I made some in the foam piece. At first invisible, these tears became gaping wounds as their edges swelled up. It occurred to me that the trichloroethane could probably be colored, enhancing the illusion. We all agreed that the potential was excellent. Later, it was decided that in the first part of the scene, air bladders under a foam skin on the actor's face would cause it to swell up grotesquely. Then the camera would move to his arm, which would also swell. When it cut back to his face, a dummy would be substituted which would take the face to further stages of ghastliness through the use of trichloroethane and mechanics.

There were also a number of other make-up effects including the swelling arm of a sailor who is the first to be bitten, so Carl Fullerton joined Stephan Dupuis and myself on the project. We started by molding the head and arm of the bad guy, Al Waxman (Figure 3.12). On his life mask, an asymmetrical mass of lumps was sculpted in plastalene as a means of designing the shapes and arrangement of the bladders. From this, patterns for the various inflatables were drawn on the plaster head as the clay models were removed. The patterns were transferred to flat plexiglass sheets on which the bladders were made of Smooth-On PMC-724.

Meanwhile, thin foam latex appliances were sculpted, molded, and processed to cover the bladders and restore Al Waxman's face to its normal appearance. A set of bladders was glued to his plaster head with the foam latex skin over them. Then on another Waxman head (made of wax), I sculpted a copy of how the first head looked when I inflated the bladders. This sculpture was for the head-and-shoulders dummy that would display the trichloroethane effect.

Next, an Ultracal 30 negative in two halves was made of the dummy sculpture. After removing the wax and plastalene, I modelled a thick layer of plastalene back into the negative, making it thickest in the large facial swellings. A positive core was now cast of Ultracal. After opening the mold and cleaning off the plastalene, a flexible urethane negative was made of the core. In this negative, a fibreglass "skull" about 3/16 inch thick was formed and removed, and the jaw was cut and hinged.

I had decided to increase the horror of the effect head by having the eyeballs bulge and the tongue protrude and swell up. The eyes were rigged to have side-to-side motion and move forward one inch. The tongue was a thick balloonlike structure that was moved forward on a hidden cradle. The head also had ample mouth and neck movement.

The main engineering problem was devising a plumbing system that would pump the trichloroethane through 15 small tubes into the inner surface of the thick foam latex mask that covered the fibreglass skull. Eventually, we used a painter's pressure pot, various mainfold switches, and thick-walled vinyl tubing to do the job.

Assembling the head for a take took hours. The mass of tubes had to be fed through the proper holes in the skull and connected to the manifolds and switches. The working of each small tube had to have a deflector on it so that no stream would squirt right through a mask wound. At each swollen bump on the mask, the foam had to be carefully torn clean through in an irregular, natural-looking way. The insides of these tears were painted bloody with watercolor (not affected by the trichloroethane). Then each tube was hot glued into the back end of the appropriate tear wound. Getting the mask onto the skull was a nightmare; so was the adjustment of the torn foam latex so the tears wouldn't show. Finally, the wig and eyebrows and final touches of make-up had to be applied. A partial test was made with one unpainted mask using an incomplete pumping system. It looked promising.

Finally the time came for a complete test of all systems. The pressure pot (5 gallon) resembles a pressure cooker, and compressed air goes in from an air line. The liquid in the pot is driven out a hose (usually leading to paint spray guns). Our hose led to a manifold that divided the liquid into four smaller tubes, each of which could be switched off. These tubes in turn were divided into four to six smaller tubes attached to the dummy face. We had found that uni-

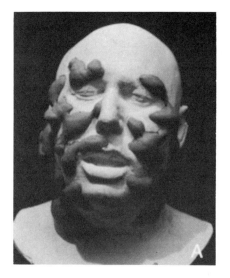

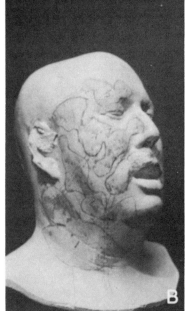

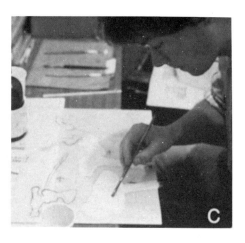

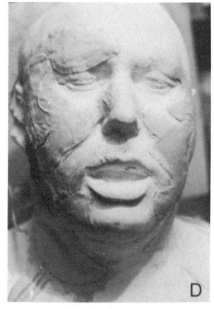

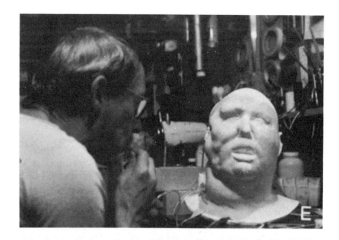

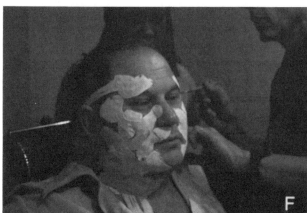

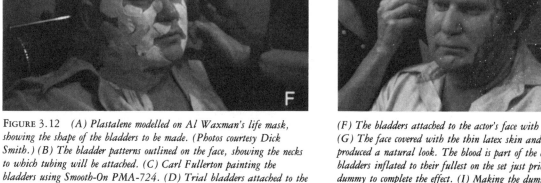

FIGURE 3.12   (A) *Plastalene modelled on Al Waxman's life mask, showing the shape of the bladders to be made. (Photos courtesy Dick Smith.) (B) The bladder patterns outlined on the face, showing the necks to which tubing will be attached. (C) Carl Fullerton painting the bladders using Smooth-On PMA-724. (D) Trial bladders attached to the life mask for a test. (E) A thin, foamed latex face was made to cover the face and attached over the bladders. Dick tested the inflation of the bladders on one side of the face by blowing into the attached tubing.*

(F) *The bladders attached to the actor's face with Prosthetic Adhesive A. (G) The face covered with the thin latex skin and make-up applied produced a natural look. The blood is part of the effect. (H) The facial bladders inflated to their fullest on the set just prior to switching to a dummy to complete the effect. (I) Making the dummy head for the effect (next 11 photos). A plastalene sculpture on the life mask showing the extent of the inflated bladders at the end of the live sequence.*

FIGURE 3.12 (cont). *(J) A two-piece Ultracal 30 mold of the head is finished with a Surform tool. (K) The two-piece mold is taken apart, the head and sculpture removed, and plastalene is added on each side. A core can now be made so a foam latex skin can be made to fit on the dummy. (L) Adding coarse weave burlap to strengthen the core of the dummy head. Note that the mold is strapped together firmly around the face portion. (M) The core. A polysulfide rubber mold is made of this to form the skull. (N) The skull or inside of the dummy head, showing the eyes and acrylic teeth inserted. Note the holes drilled for the plastic tubing.*

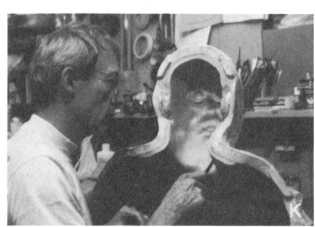

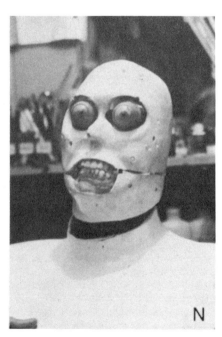

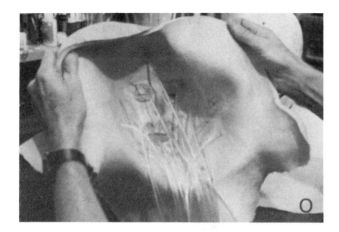

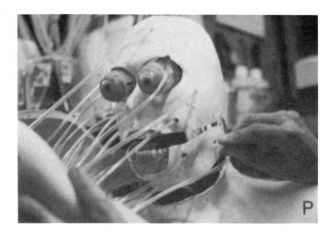

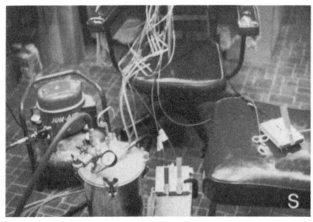

FIGURE 3.12 (cont).   (O) *Tubes for the trichloroethane attached to the inside of the dummy head's latex skin. (P) Fitting the tubes and skin over the dummy skull. This had to be redone a number of times to make the tests, with a new foamed latex mask made and fitted for each sequence. (Q) The first test with trichloroethane pumped into the lower part of the dummy head. (R) The dummy head fully assembled with all the apparatus for a film test. (S) The compressor and paint pot containing the trichloroethane, showing the switches, manifolds, and tubing.*

versal colorant would give the trichloroethane a sickly green color. We knew that the solvent could swell out tubing but hoped the effect would be all over before that became a problem. We had no idea how long it would take for the effect to work, so we set everything to pump as much trichloroethane into the foam latex as possible. To cover our test, we set up a 16mm camera and a still camera.

It was incredible—shocking! It all happened so fast that we could hardly believe it. In 20 to 30 seconds, the bumps swelled, burst open, kept swelling until the whole face was a mass of discolored shaking blobs. The bulging eyes and tongue were activated too late and hardly showed. Some of the wound tears looked too straight and artificial, but we were delighted with the general effect.

As a result of our test, I suggested that the film be overcranked when we shot the effect in Canada. At the same time, we slowed down our pumping. Unfortunately, the combination was too much and problems were had in editing. Also in our on-the-set tension,

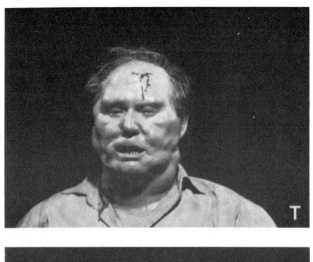

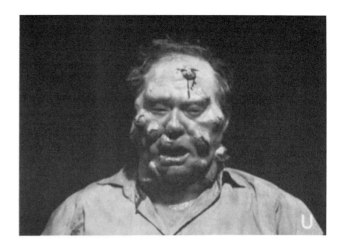

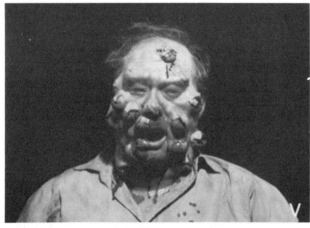

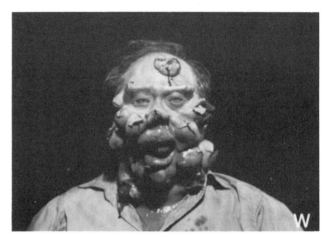

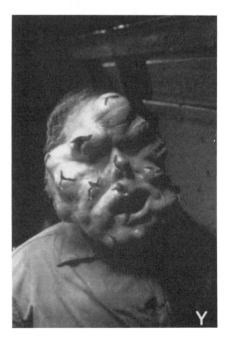

FIGURE 3.12 (cont).   (T–X) *The effect in sequence. The test sequence showing the action of the trichloroethane on the foam latex skin in a very effective and grotesque manner. Obviously, this particular effect could never be done on a human face with this solvent, and the logical progression is only possible with a dummy figure or puppet. The final result of the test was spectacular—to say the least! (Y) The final effect as it was seen on screen.*

we forgot to shake up the color in the pressure pot just before shooting so no green color came out. Nevertheless, the effect looked so good to the eye that it was not shot a second time.

I suspect this is not the last time that the effect of a hydrocarbon on foam latex will be used. Actually, it all started with a story I heard many years ago from a make-up artist who worked on *The Wizard of Oz*. The MGM make-up department had a diffident apprentice who was supposed to clean the Munchkins' foam latex appliances at the end of each day in a pail of acetone. Some older wags in the lab put carbon tetrachloride in the acetone supply can, and when the apprentice dumped his load of appliances into the carbon tet, they practically exploded out of the pail, to a chorus of feigned dismay and "Boy, are *you* in trouble!" and "Wait until Jack Dawn [department head] hears about this!" When I heard the story, I tried out the effect, and years later I remembered it—but this time used it to advantage!

The special bladders made for *Spasms* were constructed from four-part Smooth-On PMC-724 (also see page 72). First, the outline of the bladders was made in pencil on a sheet of plexiglass, and then two coats of the PMC-724 were painted on, which extended about 1/4 inch beyond the line. Next, a separating coat of plastic cap material was painted on just up to the line but not over the extension. Two coats of Smooth-On Sonite Wax separator were then added. On the long narrow neck made to attach the tubes for inflation, a piece of latex rubber coated with silicone grease was laid down. Then two thin coats of PMC-724 were brushed on, carrying the coating over the previously painted-on extension to seal the bladder edges. The formula for painting the bladders was 50 grams of 724 Part B combined with 15 drops of Part D. Then 5 grams of 724 Part C and 5.4 grams of Part A were added along with the tip-of-a-spatula amount of Monsanto Modaflow to control the flow qualities of the mix.

CHRISTOPHER TUCKER

Christopher Tucker, the leading British make-up artist, resides and works in an elegant manor house in Pangbourn, England, that combines the high ceilings, marble staircases, ornate carved-wood walls and furniture, and spaciousness of the houses of the Elizabethan through Georgian periods, with a complete series of workshops in many rooms, which provide him with a "factory" second to none in the world of make-up special effects. He has rooms to construct mechanicals—radio controlled and manual—a full stillphoto studio, laboratory areas for mixing foam, sculpture rooms, chemical laboratories, a huge conference room, and make-up rooms for applying the finished products. Distinctive in his approach to make-up conceptions, he enjoys creating a different avenue and resultant to achieving a make-up effect.

One of his recent films is *A Company of Wolves* (Cannon Films) for which he created a number of transformations of humans to wolves in various sequence forms. Rather than follow the usual path of humans

FIGURE 3.13 TOP: *The wolf's head, covered with real wolf's fur, emerging from the puppet head.* BOTTOM: *The wolf's head snarling. The elongation of the foamed latex required special foam construction as well as a lubrication so that it would not split during the action. (Courtesy of Palace Pictures.)*

to werewolves, his character changes were designed to show humans believably changing into wolves rather than wolf-like creatures. Some of the concepts were quite bizarre, such as the head of the wolf emerging from the open mouth of a dummy figure (see Figure 3.13).

This effect was achieved by making a life-sized head of the actor, Micha Borgese, with a foamed latex skin over a hard plastic form. The mouth of the head was lubricated so that a wolf's head could emerge, pneumatically forced through the mouth opening, open its mouth, and snarl. The eyes, neck, and head movements were controlled by cables.

Another metamorphosis was produced as a human went through a series of changes by first peeling off its human skin to show the underlying muscle structure. The features then began to elongate into lupine form as its body assumed an all-fours position to finally become a hairy wolf (see Figures 3.14–3.20).

An underlying appliance with a surface structure of muscle tissue covered by a thin foamed latex prosthesis resembling the actor's own face was applied for the first sequence in which he tears away his outer skin to reveal the muscle·tissue beneath it. A skull cap was used to cover the actor's hair and during the sequence, a pair of yellow contact lenses were inserted into his eyes. A skeletal, muscular arm was used in conjunction with the actor's movements, and it was operated by two puppeteers.

From here, Tucker switched to dummy figures or puppets to complete the sequence, and named the first transmogrifications, Bert 1, 2, and 3.

The Berts were constructed of latex, foamed latex, silicone, and polyurethane foams, polyester resins, fibreglass and BJB's Skinflex. The mechanics were made at the same time as the fibreglass skeleton, and pneumatic air rams employing compressed nitrogen operated the movements. Jointly, a system of cables activated the head motions, and the eyes were radio controlled using micro servos. In addition, the eyelids worked, the teeth grew and changed their anatomy, the tongue articulated, the temples pulsated, and tiny tubes were inserted in the inner corners of the eyes so that tears could be simulated. Bert 1 had separate head and neck movements and the neck could also twist laterally and the jaw could open; a very versatilely constructed figure.

FIGURE 3.15 *The outer skin on Stephen Rea's face being torn away by the articulated mechanical skeletal arm. Note that portions of the face and body have been torn off. (Courtesy Palace Pictures.)*

After Bert 1 had been through his routine of changing as far as it was possible for him to do so, the entire torso was made to tilt forward and the head to come backwards, so that it would approximate the position of a wolf when standing normally. At this point the camera cut to Bert 2, which was designed so that the neck would grow and the shoulders would pulsate and rearrange their anatomy. This was done primarily with air bladders, although the neck extensions were produced by pushing the head and back through the shoulders manually.

Bert 3 had ears and a nose that would grow pneumatically. He also had radio-controlled eyes, a tongue that worked, and full neck movements. Although Berts 1 through 3 were constructed life-size, the next phase where the figure becomes a wolf was made 25% larger to accommodate the inner works. As the audience had no idea of scale, due to camera angles, the size difference did not affect the overall completed effect.

These figures were named Rover 1 and 2 and also had radio-controlled eyes, a working nose that could be raised and snarled together with the lips, the tongue worked and the mouth was capable of frothing. The figure could lunge forward and his flanks had built-in inflatable "lungs." Rover was constructed of latex and foamed latex and required ten people to work him in all his movements. The Berts needed up to fifteen operators as there were so many functions that had to occur simultaneously.

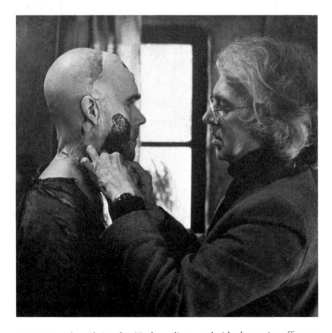

FIGURE 3.14 *Christopher Tucker adjusts and aids the tearing effect on Stephen Rea's face showing the outer skin and underlying muscle tissue structure. (Courtesy Palace Pictures.)*

FIGURE 3.16 *The next stage with the Bert 1 head showing the rig control box with its many operators and controls. (Courtesy Palace Pictures.)*

FIGURE 3.17 *Bert 1 undergoing the pneumatical transformation. (Courtesy Palace Pictures.)*

After this plethora of transformations, it will be hard to do another werewolf picture with new effects— but you can be sure someone will try to challenge this!

STAN WINSTON

Two effects by Stan Winston using fibreglass resin underheads or skulls for puppet substitutions are shown in Figure 3.21.

A decapitation effect for the film *The Exterminator* starts with a fibreglass resin body, arms, and skull controlled by various cables (Figure 3.22). A Moto-

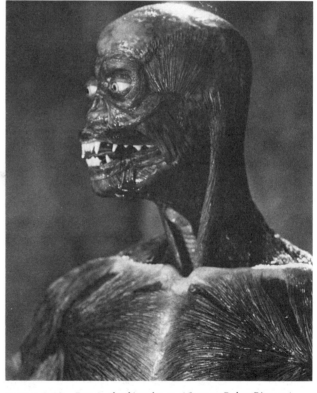

FIGURE 3.18 *Bert 1, the skinned man. (Courtesy Palace Pictures.)*

FIGURE 3.19   *Bert 3 with the elongated jaw, teeth and head motion.*
(Courtesy Palace Pictures.)

tool was used to drill the various holes needed for
mechanical fitments, and the head was rigged to fall
to the side during the action.

Foamed latex head, arms, and body appliances were
fitted over the fibreglass forms. With hair and eyelashes added, a set of acrylic teeth and a natural make-
up, the puppet is ready to perform. Once again, we
have the substitution of a realistic dummy for an effect
that was not possible with a human performer (Figure
3.23).

FIGURE 3.20   *Rover 1, the wolflike effect being completed. (Courtesy*
Palace Pictures.)

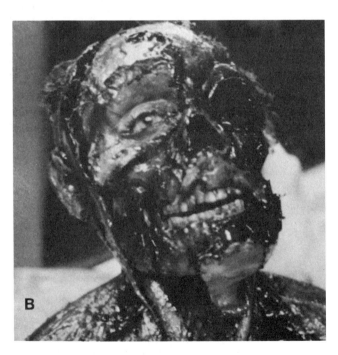

FIGURE 3.21   *(A) From the film,* Dead and Buried, *Stan Winston's*
basic plastalene sculpture was the basis for making a head that was
covered with a foamed latex skin. (B) A burn effect created with gelatin
appliances, gelatin blood, and various acrylic paints as well as the foam
latex skin, false eye, and acrylic teeth. (Photos courtesy of Stan Winston.)

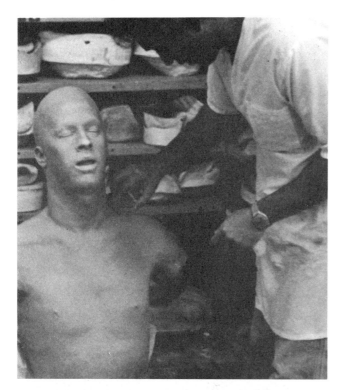

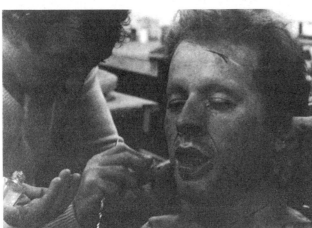

FIGURE 3.22   TOP: *The foam head and body fitted over the fiberglass inner body.* BOTTOM: *Note the decapitation line on the neck where the head of the dummy joins the dummy body. (Photo courtesy Stan Winston.)*

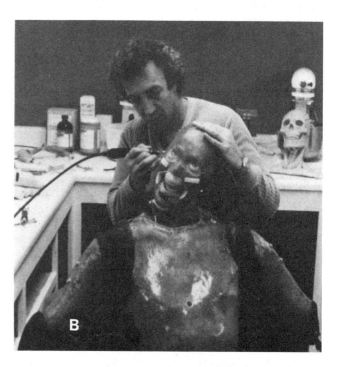

FIGURE 3.23   *(A) Stan fitting controls on the skull. (B) On the bench are the latex arms and face that will be fitted over the skull section. (Photo courtesy Stan Winston.)*

BEETLEJUICE

Ve Neill and Steve LaPorte created the "Beetlejuice" character for the Geffen Co./Warner Bros. film of the same name on actor Michael Keaton. It was billed as "the ultimate creature from the after life," winning an Academy Award for Make-Up in 1988.

A rubber bald cap was first applied and two small foam appliances were added to the bridge of the nose. The bald cap was stippled with a mixture of PA-B and pigment, and then an appliance foundation (yellow-gray tone) was applied. Dark brown and grayed-brown shadings were painted and blended in the eye circle areas, then three shades of greens, olive, mustard and emerald, were stippled from the hairline down toward the face, and powdered (Figures 3.25, 3.26).

The wig was applied and a combination of textures, consisting of spanish moss, cotton fibres, and a shredded foam mixture, were adhered with PA-A and toned with colored hair sprays. This latter mix was also utilized on the hands along with jagged acrylic fingernails. Finally, dentures appropriate to the character were inserted. Ve commented very favorably on the on-set conscientiousness and care taken by Michael Keaton with the make-up (always an important point in the success of any complicated character make-up) (Figures 3.27, 3.28).

New techniques by Dennis Hoey of Starmist of airbrushing cosmetic colors on the skin were employed on some of the other characters in the film. This was accomplished by first spraying on a pale, fair shade of liquid base and then varying the effect with other colors. RCMA "No-Color" Powder was pressed on between coats of color so that the shades did not run

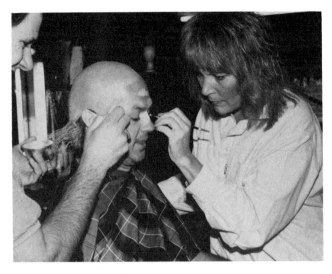

FIGURE 3.25   *Steve and Ve attaching cap and appliances.*

FIGURE 3.26   *Appliance foundation added.*

FIGURE 3.24   *Michael Keaton, no make-up.*

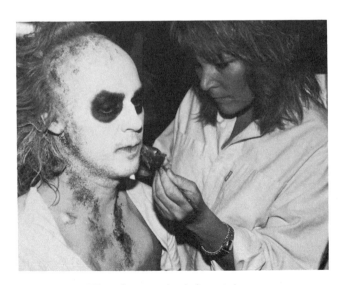

FIGURE 3.27   *Wig and textures plus dark eye circles.*

FIGURE 3.28 *Completed* Beetlejuice *character with dentures.*

together. Details were added by hand around the eyes with brushes. Up to six other make-up artists were employed each day of the filming due to the many special characters called for in the script.

BASIC MAKE-UP EFFECTS

A number of basic make-up effects are called for on many occasions, while others often depend upon the ingenuity of the individual artist. Cuts, bruises, burns, tattoos, scars, sunburns, perspiration, tears, and such are simple make-up effects that come under this category. In the make-up artists' examination procedures for union membership, these effects are always called for under the heading of exercises, and most techniques for them can all be accomplished out of the kit that every make-up artist should carry.

Waxes

Of all the effects materials for the make-up artist, wax is one of the oldest and still most useful for temporary use. Old nose putty was a resin-wax mixture that required some manipulation with the fingers to get it soft enough to work with. Being a somewhat heavy material, it often slipped out of place or distorted easily in warm weather. It is seldom, if ever, used in films or television. Related to this is mortician's wax, which is softer than nose putty but manufactured to be employed by morticians on cold bodies. It softens readily in the heat and has been replaced for professional use by the microwax materials. RCMA makes an excellent plastic wax material that holds its shape better and is far more adhesive than the former outmoded waxes. It comes in No-Color, Light, KW-3, KT-3, KN-5, and Violet shades.

Plastic Wax Material

The No-Color variety can be colored by melting it with a small amount of any Color Process foundation. However, the tinted varieties will suffice for most skins and effects.

One of the basic uses of Plastic Wax Material (PWM) is to make a change in nasal bone structure. First, coat the area to be built up by the PWM with a thin application of Matte Adhesive, and tack with the finger until set. Powder with No-Color Powder. Next, add a small piece of the PWM with a dental spatula to the area, and begin to smooth out and shape the desired nose change. When almost complete, the final shaping and poring can be done with a fine polyurethane stipple sponge or a red rubber one. Blend the edges carefully, and give the surface and just slightly beyond three coats of Matte Plastic Sealer, drying between coats with a hand-held hair dryer. Additional stippling can be done over this sealer coating to finish the nose. Color Process foundation can then be applied with a sponge in a stippling motion or with a brush. Powder with No-Color Powder. Moles, wound areas, or small build-ups can be done the same way.

Very realistic cuts can be made with a dull tool or a dulled knife blade right through a Plastic Wax Material build-up made in the preceding manner. If a small blood tube is rigged on the knife with a rubber syringe of blood held in the palm of the hand, a good cut effect can be done. In addition to the PWM materials, a gelatin appliance can be used in the same way (see page 115 for gelatin formulas). For other uses of Plastic Wax Material, see the following sections on bruises, burns, and scars.

Dental Waxes

A number of grades of dental wax are useful. One is a soft pink shade used for simulating gum tissue. Dental inlay wax is used to create teeth on a form or to fill a prominent space in the teeth. This is done by warming the wax with a dental spatula in a flame and placing the wax on a dry tooth. As soon as the wax hardens it may be carved with dental tools to the desired shape. A cotton swab can be used to buff the wax to give it a natural shine. This inlay wax is supplied in a number of light shades.

Black carding wax is excellent for the quick creation of missing or broken teeth. Simply cut out a small piece from the sheet of wax and press it over and around a previously dried tooth area. Don't get too much wax on the inside of the teeth as it might make it difficult to talk.

Wax for Molding

Suppliers of sculpture materials can also furnish various waxes for either carving or pouring into a form for certain effects. Breakaway heads can be made with some of these waxes as well as other body parts.

Glycerin

Glycerin can be used to create perspiration and is applied with a stipple sponge or a manual spray bottle. Placed in the corner of the eye (not *in* the eye), it will run and simulate tears. A very heavy grade of this product is furnished by RCMA, called *Tears and Perspiration.*

Burns

There are three categories of burns. First-degree burns redden the skin, second-degree burns blister the skin as well as redden it, and third-degree burns show charred flesh, with bleeding, blisters, and considerable reddening.

Most first-degree burn effects can be done with red foundation and raspberry cheekcolor, using a polyurethane sponge for application. Don't make the edges too even or the color too bright. Powder with No-Color Powder to avoid a shiny surface.

Second-degree burn blisters can be made with RCMA Scar or Blister Making Material (in the tube) for temporary effects or with the gelatin molding material (see page 115) warmed up and added to the desired area with a small spoon in large drops. One of the older ways was to place a blob of petroleum jelly on a piece of fishskin and invert it on to the area and blend off the edges. This technique can also be done with a film wrap (Saran Wrap) in small pieces. Broken blister effects can be made by laying down a coat of pure gum latex or eyelash adhesive, drying it, and lifting the center of the area with a small dental spatula. Always surround second-degree burns with the reddening of the first-degree burn.

Third-degree burns exhibit charred and broken tissue that can be created with Plastic Wax Material or an appliance in latex or plastic, and deep burn areas can be blackened with black foundation. For the broken and cracked tissue, use the raspberry and red colors, and add some RCMA Type C tube Blood as well. A slight run of blood from the cracks can be done with RCMA Type A or Type B Blood. Surround with second-degree blisters and first-degree reddening. RCMA makes a Burn Kit with four colors in one container.

Bruises

Realistic bruises can be simulated with RCMA Color Wheel Violet applied with a brush or sponge. Older bruises should have a surrounding of Color Wheel Bruise Yellow. Bruise areas can be made deeper with a bit of black added to the violet or lighter with some red. RCMA makes a four-color Bruise Kit with these shades. Raised bruises can be made with Plastic Wax Material in the violet shade for temporary buildups or with foamed latex or Plastic Molding Material and covered with the violet foundation.

Blood Effects

There are many forms of blood effects and many materials that appear as blood for production work. Some show the free flow of blood for active bleeding, while others must hold a static effect when the scene takes a while to shoot and the blood must appear in the same place all the time.

Flowing Blood Types

RCMA makes a Blood Type A, which is a liquid that will flow very much like real blood and is easily washed off with water. Similar types have been made with Karo or other corn syrups that have been tinted with vegetable coloration. Some make-up artists use a thin gelatin mixture with color for this effect. The 1-ounce RCMA squeeze bottle is handy as the blood effect can be applied by the drop or in a stream for running blood. The cap effectively seals the plastic bottle, which fits well in the kit.

This variety of blood effect can also be put into clear plastic bags and placed over small explosive charges such as those employed by the special effects personnel to simulate a bullet hit. Take care that they are not overused as the effect will appear ridiculous if the blood bursts out of an area where the bullet hits. Often, it is better to see the exit of the imaginary bullet when using the explosive charge and the blood bags.

Appliances can be made of PMA Molding Material, foamed latex, or similar materials to cover an area of the body in a thin coating under which is imbedded a small polyethylene plastic tube that leads to a syringe full of Blood Type A. At the proper time, a cut can be simulated by passing a dull knife over a precut area or a small precut plug pulled with an invisible nylon thread from a simulated bullet hole and, with pressure on the syringe, the blood made to appear to flow from the wound. There are many variations of this method that can also be done with the knife blade having the small tube taped to it and a rubber ear syringe held in the palm on the other end of the tube. When the cut is made, the hand squeezes the syringe at the same time and the blood flows from the filled syringe through the small plastic tube and down the knife blade. For safety's sake, the knife blade should always be dulled and rounded smooth so it will never create an injury. Tom Savini makes many such weapons out of rubber and then paints them in a very realistic fashion to simulate the real thing.

Nonflowing Blood Types

The first nonflowing blood type is a thin plastic style that is useful for long scenes as it will dry in place wherever it is applied in a very short time but still appears to be fresh and running (RCMA Blood Type B). Another variety is the soft creme one that comes in a tube and can be used for smeared effects or for quick wound applications. It does not dry out and stays fresh looking (RCMA Blood Type C).

Dried human blood is reddish brown in color, and RCMA Blood Type D is a liquid that dries rapidly and leaves an effect similar to dried blood. It can be used on bandages and wardrobe.

Scabs or clotted blood on wounds can be made by mixing a dark wood flour (such as walnut or mahogany dust from a sander) with RCMA Prosthetic Adhesive A. First, dampen the wood flour with a few drops of Prosthetic Adhesive-A Thinner, then mix in some adhesive until the flour is the consistency of peanut butter. Apply directly to the skin (as it will dry rapidly) in the shapes desired. This mixture will hold to the skin very well, even when wet. It is removed with RCMA Adhesive Remover. These scabs can also be premade on a glass plate and then attached to the skin with Prosthetic Adhesive-A.

Scars

Raised scars can be made with latex or plastic appliances or for temporary use with Plastic Wax Material (Figures 3.29 to 3.31). They can also be formed with

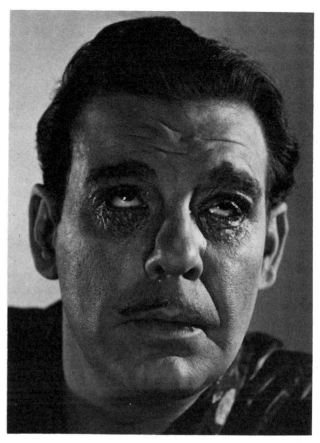

FIGURE 3.30 *Lon Chaney with deep scars under his eyes for the 1944 film,* Dead Man's Eyes *(Universal Pictures).*

FIGURE 3.29 *Ray Codi with a long and deep scar. The eye is pulled downward by the shrinking action of the scar material.*

FIGURE 3.31 *Raised cicatrix scarring on the character Queequeeg in* Moby Dick. *(Warner Bros./Moulin, 1956.)*

the tube variety of RCMA Scar or Blister Making Material by squeezing out some plastic from the tube and forming it with a dental spatula. Thickened latex (see page 95) can also be used to form raised scars. When the surface has set slightly, it can be dried with a hand-held hair dryer to form a skin and then be colored with foundation.

Indented or deeply serrated scars can be made with RCMA Scar Material, which dries semimatte with a slightly pinked tone. Simply apply with a brush on the skin in a line or roughly outlined area, and allow to air dry. The dried scar will pucker the skin and can be slightly colored with red and white foundation to accent it. Cotton batting built up in successive layers with Matte Plastic Sealer and then colored with foundation can also be used for scar tissue.

Nonflexible collodion was formerly used to create incised scars, but it dried with a high shine that was hard to tone down, and the edges often came loose as it dried quite hard on the skin. Most scars for production use are now made with foamed latex or with Plastic Molding Material preformed in molds and attached to the skin in the usual manner.

Tattoos

Temporary tattoos can be made with blue ball-point pens, filling the area with a red lip-lining pencil (Figure 3.32). For a matching tattoo each day, rubber stamps can be made and applied to the skin. The inner parts of the outline can then be filled with a red lip-liner.

To get a perspective for a full body tattoo, it is a good idea to sketch out the planned drawings on a store dummy using fine felt-tipped pens before doing the actual work on the body (Figure 3.33). Tattoo

FIGURE 3.32 *Various tattoo designs.*

FIGURE 15.27 *Various tattoo designs.*

FIGURE 3.33 *Tattoo designs by Ben Lane on a dummy for a film test.*

artists generally use some form of transfer paper to delineate their designs with holes punched through them and a powder applied to transfer the design.

Reel Creations, a firm formed by two make-up artists in California, Fred Blau and Mike Hancock, has produced a kit for professional body art that consists of colors, transfer designs, brushes, and full instructions on their use. They perfected the method doing

the make-up for the film, *Tattoo,* and with a little care, the application will last several days. For this long-lasting effect, no oils or lotions should be applied to the body art area, and although one can shower, rubbing with a wash cloth should be avoided. The body can be powdered with talc or No-Color Powder before retiring to absorb any possible body oils. Faded designs can be touched up by reapplication of the colors. Removal can be made with their developer or isopropyl alcohol, followed by soap and water.

Application of the designs with the body art materials is simple (Figure 3.34).

VOLATILE SOLVENTS

A list of some of the volatile solvents is useful for differentiating them. Many are *not* used in the manufacture of any professional make-up products, and most should be only used when proper ventilation is available as some produce fumes that are absorbed by certain human organs and will cause serious internal disorders from prolonged breathing.

ALCOHOLS	ESTERS
Ethanol	Ethyl lactate
Methanol	Ethyl acetate
Propanol	Sec butyl acetate
Isopropanol	ETHERS
Butanol	Ethyl ether
Sec-butanol	Methyl ether
Amyl alcohol	Ethyl vinyl ether
2-ethyl 1-hexanol	Isobutyl vinyl ether
Cyclohexanol	Dioxane

FIGURE 3.34 *Application of tattoos. (A) Cleanse skin area where transfer is to be located with special developer/remover to remove all excess body oil or debris. (B) Pre-moisten velour puff with developer. Just enough to dampen. Not dripping wet. Place transfer face down on skin. Press puff on transfer taking care not to move transfer (to prevent smudging). Transfer should be complete in about 20 seconds. Peel off transfer smoothly. (C) Powder your finished transfer design with talc. (Use any talc, body powder, etc.) The transfer design is now set. If at this point the outline is not uniform you may outline with the black paint. Or, if lightly smudged, clean the smudge off with cotton swab and developer/remover. (D) Select the colors you wish for your design (be sure to shake colors thoroughly) and begin painting, working each area selected. When total design is finished powder again and then gently wipe off powder with water and your creation is completed. Note: Powder is not necessary. It only acts to set and dry the artwork quickly.*

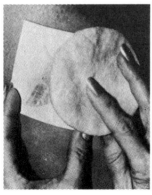

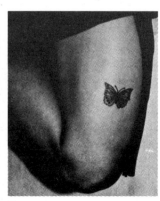

A   B   C   D

HYDROCARBONS
  Petroleum ether
Hexane
Stoddard solvent
Cyclohexane
Methycyclohexane
Tetralin (DuPont)

CHLORINATED
  HYDROCARBONS
  Chloroform
Ethylene dichloride
Methylene dichloride
Carbon tetrachloride
Chlorobenzene

POLYHYDRIC ALCOHOLS
Glycerol or glycerin
Propylene glycol
Polyethylene glycol
Sorbitol
Polyoxyethylene
  sorbitol

ETHER ALCOHOLS
  GAF Gafcol glycol
  ether
Diethylene glycol
Triethylene glycol
Hexamethylene glycol
Polyethylene glycol
  400
2.2 thiodiethanol

KETONES
  Acetone
Methyl ethyl ketone
  (MEK)
Methylcyclohexanone
2 butanone

ALIPHATIC AMINES
  Ethylene diamine
Diethylenetriamine

AROMATIC
  HYDROCARBONS
  Toluene
Xylene
Benzene

ALIPHATIC
  HYDROCARBONS
  Naphtha
Heptane
Kerosene (refined)
Mineral spirits
Di-isobutylene
Mineral oil

Solvents may also be listed under the headings of nonpolar, or non-H-bonding, medium polar, or high polar:

NONPOLAR	MEDIUM POLAR	HIGH POLAR
Benzene	Linseed oil	Ethanol
Toluene	Dioctyl	Methanol
Xylene	phthalate	Propanol
Turpentine	Cellosolve	Butanol
Mineral spirits	Polyglycols	Ethyl acetate
Naphtha	Polyester resins	Ethylene glycol
Hexane	Epoxy resins	Butyl acetate
Heptane	Alkalyd resins	Glycerol
Mineral Oil	Polyurethane	Acetone
Carbon	resins	Methyl ethyl
tetrachloride		ketone
		(MEK)

The main solvents employed in special materials for make-up purposes are isopropanol (isopropyl alcohol), acetone, MEK, refined kerosene, and trichlorotrifluoroethane. Of these, only MEK has a really pungent residual odor as it is slower drying than acetone (which is the fastest of the solvents to evaporate, with TCTFE not too far behind). These solvents are part of the formulations of most adhesives and sealers and are relatively safe for use (MEK is not recommended for any skin use). Again, always use with proper ventilation. Many of the hydrocarbon products should be used only with extreme care.

THICKENING AGENTS

Dow Chemical makes a number of grades of *Methocel* (methyl cellulose) that are film-forming, thickening agents for water solutions. The standard solution is 2 percent Methocel, first dispersed in about one-third of the amount required of hot water. When the powder is completely wetted, the other two-thirds of the water (cold) can be added. The mixture should then be stirred until smooth.

Carbopol 934 (B.F. Goodrich Chemical Co.) is a water-soluble resin with thixotropic qualities. A 0.5 percent solution mixed in a high shear blender is neutralized (mixing pH is about 3) with 10 percent sodium hydroxide solution. This will produce a stiff gel that may be diluted with water.

Cab-O-Sil is useful in thickening petroleum products and oils in addition to its other uses. A 5 percent dispersion produces a very stiff gel.

Wyoming Bentonite is a colloidal montmorillonite clay that will absorb many times its weight in water, swelling to several times its original volume and forming a thixotropic gel. A mud is prepared by sifting the clay into water while mixing under high shear. These thickening materials and gels can be employed for various effects where inert jellylike substances are called for. Samples for research and developmental use can be obtained from most manufacturers along with technical information and specifications. Also see latex thickening agents on page 95.

REMOVING CHARACTER OR SPECIAL MAKE-UP EFFECTS

Most regular foundation make-up can be removed from the skin using RCMA Deep Cleansing Lotion. However, Appliance Foundations (AF) are best cleansed with RCMA KLENZER, as it is a deep-penetrating oil variety. All Adhesives and Sealers made by RCMA can be removed with RCMA Adhesive Remover, using a brush to loosen the blending edge of an appliance or hair goods. An exception to the above is RCMA Old Age Stipple, which should never be taken off with an oil or liquid cleanser. It is best removed from the skin with a towel that has been moistened with rather hot water and allowed to remain on the face for a short time. The Stipple will then peel free without any other cleanser. Stubborn edges should be soaked further and gently rubbed off. Adhesives employed under RCMA Old Age Stipple (due to loose edges, etc.) can then be removed with RCMA Adhesive Remover. Use a brush to apply the Remover and gently dissolve the Adhesive with a circular motion.

CHAPTER 4

Casting and Molding

MANY YEARS AGO, ALL THE WORK TO BE ACCOMPLISHED on a performer's face had to be done on the face for that performance only. Products such as spirit gum, cotton batting, adhesive tape, collodion (both flexible and nonflexible), nose putty, mortician's waxes, thread, and other materials were employed. However, the make-up artist now can premake several of a needed appliance out of rubber and synthetic latices, plastics in a great variety, gelatins, and other prosthetic materials so that a fresh appliance with a finely blendable edge is available whenever required. The clarity of the image structure of the screen and the closeness of the audience in small theaters require this excellence.

To achieve this, the first step is to make a duplicate positive casting of the performer's face or the body part required with a permanent material such as plaster or stone. From this casting, the make-up concept can be sculpted in modeling clay called *plastalene* and a negative made of the newly sculpted features. Then, by various methods, a copy of the sculpture is made, called an *appliance*, or *prosthesis*, in a skinlike, flexible material that is attached to the performer to delineate a character

for a specific part. Impression and duplicating materials for molding and casting can be quite varied and different, and each is employed to accomplish a particular purpose.

Although make-up laboratory work and knowledge are not part of the requirements of various make-up unions' entrance tests, the developments and principles form the modern extension of character make-up. Even those make-up artists who have no particular desire or even skill in the lab should know, as part of their complete knowledge of the present field, the language and techniques of this advanced branch of the profession. We shall try to survey briefly the salient points here for reference.

LABORATORY TECHNIQUES

To begin with, the work area of the make-up lab should be separate from the make-up room due to the fact that the procedures of the lab often require the use of materials that create considerably more debris and mess, and at the same time the equipment and products employed are different, requiring their own work and storage space (Figure 4.1–4.3). The lab room should be well lit and ventilated (with a fan-exhaust hood if possible) and should have some strong work

FIGURE 4.1 *The author's small appliance laboratory. It illustrates the water arrangement with a 5-gallon bottle siphoning water through glass and plastic tubing to a small sink with a rubber hose drain to a 5-gallon bucket. In this way, no insoluble plaster goes down the regular plumbing, yet sufficient water is available for most molding and casting.*

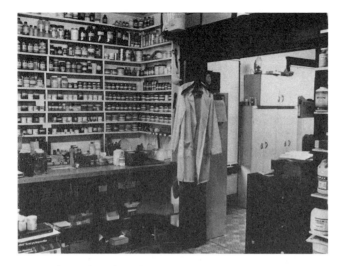

FIGURE 4.2   *The author's developmental lab.*

FIGURE 4.3   *Three views of Tom Burman's Studio where "monsters are made" from molds and casts by the ton.*

tables for both sitting and standing work levels, a linoleum-covered floor, plenty of electrical outlets, and substantial shelves for books, molds, casts, storage, and so forth. Great care must be taken to clean sinks so the drains do not become clogged with plaster or other residue. For a small lab, a safe way is to use a siphon or spigot system on a 5-gallon water container to a small sink whose drain is simply a rubber hose that leads to a 5-gallon bucket. The latter can be emptied carefully when the residues settle in the bottom, and water can be separated from the solid masses (which can then be thrown in the trash bucket). Large labs sometimes have special filter systems built in to their sinks.

As for personnel, one will find that there are always many neophytes interested almost solely in sculpting, mold making, prosthesis making, experimenting with new items, and doing make-up research rather than the (to them!) more mundane daily straight make-up application that takes up at least 80 percent of the make-up artist's normal career. Almost all the new make-up labs in California (where the bulk of the work is done in this field) have a stream of young hopefuls who want to work in that area of make-up, but competition—and talent—is quite fierce and extensive. Certain specialists have evolved whose work has been outstanding, but there is always more room for the best. Almost every procedure in lab work is enhanced and aided in time and effort by more than one person doing the particular job, so a crew system has been developed, and therefore, the finished product may be a blend of the work of many hands and minds.

As in all cases where enormous talent has affected the output, there are those in the production field who have no concept of the time, energy, and effort that must be put in to produce a laboratory creation. Many directors and producers have never understood or even taken the time to see the involved procedures that may

be necessary to devise a prosthetic appliance, special make-up effect, or such and thus often set time frames for completion of lab work that is unrealistic. The more complicated and the more innovative make-up effects become, the more competition for exciting and new visual results will be asked for—almost as a matter of course.

However, in today's rapidly advancing technologies, it does not seem that a day goes by without some new laboratory method, material, technique, or discovery being made that improves and adds to our knowledge of make-up magic. As such, make-up artists are closely akin to magicians and illusionists in the sense that once a new trick is invented or produced, someone is bound to improve upon it.

It should be borne in mind that the products and tools mentioned herein are the author's recommended ones solely because they have been found to achieve the purpose he has desired. There are, no doubt, other methods and procedures as well as products and items that will accomplish similar techniques or parallel ones so one should always look for other ways to do the job. Artists who rest on old methods, regardless of their tried-and-true qualities, will more likely than not be left behind by those willing to research and test further to improve any make-up procedure or item. Look for both the unusual *and* the commonplace when searching because, as with any concept or working method, both innovation and adaptation will solve most problems. As well, every make-up lab technician has run into problems, breakage, and disasters, so plan every phase carefully and follow directions closely, but don't be discouraged if something goes wrong. Redo it, and most times, whatever you do will be better.

Appendices A and B provide listings of many equivalent products in addition to addresses of suppliers and manufacturers of special items.

IMPRESSION MATERIALS

Impression materials are used in taking casts and making molds of a *positive,* or original, item by making a *negative* into which plaster or stone can be poured to form a *duplicate positive* (Figure 4.4).

There are rigid types of impression materials such as plaster, Ultracal, and dental or tool stones, and there are flexible varieties such as the thermoplastic, reversible types of *moulages,* and the nonreversible *alginates.* Each material is rather specific in use and is

FIGURE 4.4 *Tom Burman explains the complications of a special mold to Gena Kehoe.*

best suited for certain purposes. No one material will do the work as well as a combination of methods and applications.

Rigid Impression Materials

Materials that harden and form a nonflexible cast or mold include the various plasters and stones. Although there are many varieties of these, we limit our selection to a few for ease in operation and suitability for make-up work.

Dental Plaster

This is a quick-setting (3 to 4 minutes from liquid to hard) material for use when speed of casting and setting is important. It is the weakest of the rigid materials, so it should not be used where strength of the cast or mold is a prime requisite.

To mix, add the plaster to cold water, making small mixes because the setting time is so rapid that a set will occur before a large mixture can be spatulated properly. A thin mix will take longer to set than a thick mix but will be weaker in tensile strength. Keep adding plaster to the water until the surface of the water is covered. Then immediately mix by spatulation until a smooth creme is obtained. Generally, 10 to 15 seconds is taken for mixing with water, so this leaves about 2 minutes for application to the subject before setting time is reached.

Dental plaster can be used to take small impressions of parts such as noses, chins, eye sockets, or fingers and for repair of casting plaster molds where speed and not strength is required. It makes an excellent waste mold material because it breaks away easily. It is generally sold in 10-pound cans.

#1 Casting Plaster

The U.S. Gypsum Company makes most of the casting plasters and stones, and they can be readily purchased from large building supply companies in 100-pound bags. They should be stored in a dry place in plastic covered trash cans placed on a wheeled platform for ease in handling.

Casting plaster is a white material that sets in about 20 to 25 minutes and is the standard type of plaster used in making many casts. It is not suitable, however, for pressure molds or for those that require any heat curing. It is the best for any slush or paint-in latex molds as it has good absorptive qualities. To hasten the setting time when taking casts of faces or other body parts, add a teaspoonful of sodium chloride (common table salt) to each quart of water used in the mix. In this book, we shall refer to casting plaster only as *plaster.*

Hydrocal and Ultracal

These are low expansion gypsums that are considerably harder than plaster and can be used for pressure- or heat-cured molds. Although there are varieties such as Hydrocal A-11 and B-11 (two setting grades), the Ultracal 30 is most used by the make-up lab technician because it is a superstrength product. It is recommended where extreme accuracy and additional surface hardness are required, and it is harder and stronger than Hydrocal A-11 or B-11. It also has the lowest coefficient of expansion rate of any gypsum cement available, but its very gradual set and ample plasticity make it ideal for the splash casting that this work requires. It dries with a grayish color so as to distinguish casts and molds made of this material from plaster. Ultracal 60 is similar in all respects except that it has a set of about 1 hour and is designed for very large models where additional working time and the highest possible degree of accuracy are required.

Dental or Tool Stones

This is one of the hardest of the casting materials and is a somewhat heavier material than other rigid types. It has low absorption qualities so is not suitable for slush latex molding. Its setting time is similar to that of Ultracal 30, and most of the professional lab technicians are split between these two excellent materials for any foamed latex or urethane molds.

Although dental stones come in a variety of colors, they are more expensive than pink tool stone (made by Kerr), which is a similar if not identical stone. It is best purchased, therefore, from a jewelry manufacturing supply house than a dental supply for reasons of price. Both Ultracal and stones become quite hot as they harden and so should not be used to take facial or body casts.

The mixing procedures for plaster, Ultracal, and stone are similar, and the strength, hardness, and density of the cast depends upon the amount of water used in the mixing. With all mixes, a thin mixture sets more slowly than a thick one. Small quantities can be prepared in flexible rubber or plastic bowls that dental technicians use, or large mixes can be done in polyethylene kitchen wash bowls (which are available in most department stores in kitchen wares).

Before use, always loosen up the surface of the gypsum material so it will not have any lumps. Then place the desired amount of water in the container. This can only be judged by experience, but remember that gypsum materials are cheap and it is better to have too much than too little when casting. The gypsum can then be added a little at a time with a large spoon or ladle, sifting the material in so that it does not enter the water in lumps. To make a regular mix, keep adding the gypsum material into the water until the surface of the water is completely covered with *dry* material. Then allow this mix to soak undisturbed for about 2 minutes, when the surface of the material will take on the appearance of a dried river bed. Now stir with a spoon or a nonflexible spatula until a cremey

mix is obtained. It is then ready for immediate use. If one wants a thin mix to make a splash coating in the mold, put less gypsum material in the water and stir right away to remove any lumps. Dental technicians often use a very stiff mix of dental stone for making positive casts of teeth or for imbedding the casting in a tray. Such requires vigorous spatulation in the bowl to get the mix smooth and workable.

A number of methods can be used to further strengthen Ultracal or stone molds, and they vary from expert to expert. As usual, you will find that whatever works best for *you* is what you will settle upon. Basic strengthening of the mold is done by Werner Keppler and Terry Smith with wet hemp fiber applied in layers. Gus Norin always used spun glass, but this material is difficult to handle. Dick Smith uses a 5-ounce burlap in strips, which he says is easier to handle than the loose fiber and can be guided more readily into the areas that require the most strengthening. He also uses a wire cloth for strengthening the outer surface of small molds. John Chambers sometimes employs an acrylic latex cement hardener from the Wilhold Company, while Dick Smith uses Acryl 60 to reinforce the strength of Ultracal 30, employing 100 cubic centimeters of Acryl 60 with 100 cubic centimeters of water and then adding 660 grams of Ultracal 30 for a sample mix. Sources for these supplies are given in Appendix B. It should be noted that these strengtheners may be found to be an aid to the longevity of molds that require baking or for pressure molds to prevent cracking. Also, the heavier and thicker the mold is, the longer the baking time will be for foamed latex.

Flexible Impression Materials

Moulage

Years ago there was only one flexible impression product, known as *moulage* (one trade name was Negocoll). This was a reversible material that had to be heated up in a double boiler and brushed on to the part of the body to be cast while it was rather hot. It did not have much tensile strength, so a heavy coating was necessary along with a *mother mold* of plaster to hold the correct shape and act as a retaining form. It could be reused many times as long as the water content was kept to the correct level. Still, it was a tricky material to use and required much preparation and care afterward.

Alginates

Today we have a number of impression materials, called *alginates,* that are simple to prepare, are easy to apply, require no heating, and form a considerably stronger gel than moulage. Dental alginates have a normal setting time of about 3 minutes, so a technician must work quite rapidly if he or she wishes to take an impression. However, these alginates have been used with considerable success by many make-up artists.

Recently the Teledyne-Getz Company, one of the major producers of the dental alginate, has introduced a Prosthetic Grade Cream (PGC), which is a colorless, odorless, fine-grade, slow-setting alginate impression material. Normally, PGC sets in 4.5 ± .5 minutes, but a retarder may be added to allow as much as 16 minutes of use before setting. This PGC has a long shelf life of up to 5 years when stored at room temperature in a sealed container.

The Mid-America Dental Company also makes a prosthetic grade alginate product that has a 5-minute set time. Their directions state that warmer water than 70°F hastens the gel while colder water slows it, and up to 25 percent more water can be used for easier mixing. They also recommend to maintain the gelled alginate on the subject for about 3 minutes beyond the gel time because the material gains strength during this period. Otherwise, the directions and material are similar to PGC by Teledyne.

In use, all alginates should be shaken in the container to fluff up the powder and ensure uniformity. They come with two small measures, one for water and one for the powder. The faster setting types are affected by temperature, and warm, humid weather will hasten the setting time. Some workers use ice water to extend the setting time. PGC is rated for use between 70° to 77° F and from 40% to 60% relative humidity, so it has a wide latitude for use. Alginates of all grades are measured quite similarly, with two scoops of powder for one full vial of water—that is 17.7 grams of powder to 50 cubic centimeters of water.

To mix, measure out the desired amount of water into a mixing bowl, and add the powder. Immediately spatulate for about 45 seconds, and transfer directly to the portion being cast. Once gelation takes place, a second coat of alginate will not adhere to the first unless the area is brushed with a solution of sodium carbonate (monohydrate) in water (a teaspoon of powder in 6 ounces of hot water and dissolve). This will make the surface tacky; then additional alginate mix may be added. A retarder can be made with a solution of tri-sodium phosphate or may be obtained from Teledyne-Getz (PGC Retarder) or Mid-America.

This material will take deep undercuts and can be applied in a far thinner application than the moulage. It must, however, be supported by a mother mold for most applications, and impressions made with alginates must be used to make positive casts immediately as they commence to dry out very fast. Many people submerge the finished alginate impression in water while they are mixing the positive casting material, but if two are taking the cast, one can have the positive material immediately ready for use when the alginate impression is removed from the original (face, arm, and so on). As PGC has less than 3 percent defor-

mation, very accurate casts can be made with it. However, with the use of any extra retarder, the physical properties of PGC are reduced in value. The retarder is not recommended for the standard dental alginates as they will become lumpy and fail to set properly.

DUPLICATING MATERIALS

Duplicating materials differ from impression materials in that the latter are generally used to take primary or original casts of the subject, while the former are used in making duplicates of the original positive by making a permanent negative mold suitable for this operation.

Formerly, heavy concentration and thickened natural latex compounds were utilized for duplication as well as a heat-melt synthetic material called Koroseal. However, we now have a series of cold molding compounds in polysulfide rubber, silicon rubbers, and polyurethane synthetic rubbers that serve as very fine duplicating materials and exhibit great flexibility as well as have a variety of hardnesses to duplicate many varied materials.

Cold Molding Compounds

Although a number of firms make cold molding compounds, the Perma-Flex Mold Company and the Smooth-On Corporation make a number of flexible compounds that are used in the make-up lab for duplicating purposes. Perma-Flex CMC Blak-Tufy, Blak-Stretchy, Gra-Tufy, and UNH are polysulfide liquid molding materials cured at room temperature by means of catalysts. They are available in three- and two-component systems, and while the two-part systems are fast and produce good duplicates, the three-part systems are indefinitely stable while the others have a shorter finished product shelf life.

Blak-Stretchy is the most elastic of the types, with a 9 to 1 elongation and a durometer hardness of between 12 and 15. It has a working time of 20 to 30 minutes. The first coats can be applied free flowing, then Cab-o-Sil M-5 can be added to the mix to thicken it so it can be spatulated on. It is a two-part system so has a cast storage life of about 4 months of shape retention. Its weight is about 12 pounds to the gallon, and like other black materials, it is reinforced with carbon black. Curing time is 20 hours at 80° F.

Blak-Tufy is a three-part system that cures in 16 hours at 80° F and has a durometer hardness of 23 to 25. In-between hardnesses can be produced by mixing Blak-Stretchy and Blak-Tufy.

Gra-Tufy is a similar product to Blak-Tufy except that it has a zinc oxide reinforcement pigment instead of the black. It is useful when snow-white plaster casts are necessary in reproduction. Elongation is similar to Blak-Tufy at 4 to 1. Its weight is 15 pounds to the gallon.

UNH is similar to Gra-Tufy except that the set time makes an extremely fast cure possible. The setting time is 5 to 10 minutes, with usable molds available in less than an hour at 80° F. This is a three-part system and has a hardness of 20 to 22 on the durometer.

Regular CMC carries no reinforcing pigments or filler and is considered to be the most dimensional of the cold molding compounds. The base A polymer is a clear viscous liquid cured by additions of B and C curatives in various proportions to get work life and setting time from 1 hour to overnight. Regular is the least viscous of all the cold molding compounds and is often used as a safe thinner for any of the other polysulfide cold molding compounds. Durometer hardness is 14 to 15. Directions for use of these polysulfide materials are available with the products from the Perma-Flex Company.

Perma-Flex makes another type of cold molding compound that deserves experimentation, the *P-60* and *P-60-S* series. These are two-component systems. They are amine polysulfides whose shelf life extends to a year or more. The item to be cast can be given a two-coat layer, then a layer of open weave fibreglass cloth and another layer of compound. This will provide a strong but lightweight mold. In use, as these are all flexible molding materials, a mother mold of plaster is recommended to hold the shape of the cold molding compound. The compound needs to be properly keyed into the plaster to set correctly for duplicating. Open weave burlap can also be used for a reinforcing material.

To duplicate a plaster positive, it must be first given a couple of thin coats of orange shellac. Then it is coated with a silicon mold release for ease in separation.

Another type of duplicating material is Perma-Flex CMC *Blu-Sil,* which is a room-temperature-set two-component system consisting of a white silicone type fluid base A, and a blue-colored modified silicone catalyst B. It is designed to be mixed at the time of use into a fluid that will set to a flexible rubbery solid about 30 on the durometer. It is often used when a duplicate is to be made of a very delicate positive. Few or no parting agents are required. However, its cost is double that of most polysulfides.

Another variety of elastomer (rubberlike substance) for making molds is Smooth-On Corporation's *PMC-724,* which is a polyurethane and polysulfide synthetic rubber compound. Part A is a brown thin liquid, and Part B is a white syrup that remains pourable for at least 20 minutes when mixed. At a mix ratio of 10 A to 100 B, it has a durometer hardness of about 40. Sonite Seal Release Wax or petroleum jelly are suitable release agents, and shellac can be used to seal porous casts before duplicating with PMC-724. A Part C is available to achieve varying degrees of durometer hardness down to 6, and a Part D can be added to produce varying viscosities in the mixed uncured rubber. Con-

sistencies can range from a thin latex paint to a grease-like putty that can be buttered on to vertical surfaces. Up to 80 parts of Part C can be added to make the softest mold, and only 2 parts of Part D need be added to make the mix very heavy. PMC-724 remains usable for at least six months from shipment date in unopened containers stored in a cool, dry location. None of these duplicating elastomers is suitable for skin use, and none has a long shelf life so order what you need when you need it rather than stocking it in the lab. Also see page 000 for its use as a prosthetic material.

SEPARATORS

Separating mediums are also known as parting agents, mold lubes, or releasing compounds and serve to ensure that two materials, similar or dissimilar, can be easily withdrawn from each other when desired. Some separating mediums are more versatile than others, and some are for a specific purpose or material.

In addition to preventing adhesion, separators must provide upon the faces of the model or mold a continuous, non-water-soluble, and smooth film that possesses little or no frictional resistance to movement across its surface. A properly selected sealer-separator combination prevents penetration of moisture from the fluid gypsum material into the pores of the mold or hair on the body. It also allows free movement of the set gypsum as it expands. The basic requirements of a satisfactory separation medium are that it:

1. Prevents adhesion of the cast;
2. Protects and lubricates the surface of the mold;
3. Spreads easily and uniformly in a thin, continuous insoluble film;
4. Will not react destructively with the gypsum surface or with the mold surface.

One of the most versatile separators in general use is petroleum jelly. This can be used to separate any gypsum material from any other during casting procedures. It is also used to coat facial or body hair when taking a cast with either a rigid or a flexible impression material. It can be used full strength or diluted with two parts of RCMA Studio Make-up Remover for a thinner mix.

Many varieties of liquid alginate dental separators can be adapted for make-up use. These are heavy liquids that can be painted on a gypsum cast and that form a film when dry (also see pages 89–90 on transferring plastalene). These separators are excellent for use with tooth plastics to gypsum (see pages 113–115). Dental technicians also employ thin sheets of wet cellophane for separation and to obtain a glossy surface on acrylic teeth in the mold. Dental supply houses carry these items as does RCMA on their Special Materials list.

Silicons are also good release agents and PMA Silicon

Mold Release or Dow Corning Compound DC-7 are excellent for coating any gypsum material to separate many plastic compounds such as RCMA Molding Material, Plastic Cap Material and others. It can be used full strength or can be diluted with methylene chloride or MEK.

It is well to keep separate brushes for use with the above two separators so that they can just be wiped clean after use rather than cleaned each time in a strong solvent.

Many sculptors use a separator made from 120 grams of stearic acid and 540 cubic centimeters of kerosene. However, to avoid the odor of the kerosene, Studio Make-up Remover can be substituted for the solvent. The stearic acid is melted and the SMR carefully added by stirring after the melt has been removed from the heat.

Another favorite sculpture separator is one made by dissolving shavings of Ivory Soap in hot water to form a saturated solution. Both the stearic acid and the soap separators are brushed into the molds until the surface appears glazed.

Alginates and plastalene do not require separators from gypsum materials. However, if the plastalene is coated with Plastic Cap Material, some technicians use a very thin coating of the silicon type mold release over the surface of the positive so that the cap material does not stick to the negative when it is separated after casting.

Sealers

Many technicians coat their porous plaster or stone face casts with thin orange shellac (dissolved only in alcohol) to protect them from the oils in the plastalene and to make separation easier. Polyurethane lacquers are used to coat molds for use with some foam latices or for those employed for flexible urethane castings.

CAST OF THE FACE

The face is the basic body area for which most appliances are made, and the *life mask* is a primary tool for the make-up lab technician. To prepare for taking the impression in PGC, sit the subject in a comfortable chair with a headrest (Figure 4.5). Make certain that the head is not in a completely horizontal position as otherwise the chin and neckline will be distorted in the cast. Some workers prefer a 45° angle while others will cast with the head almost erect. If just a limited front section is to be cast, the hair can be covered with a shower cap, but if a more extensive cast is desired, a rubber or plastic bald cap can be attached. Any hair showing—brows, lashes, moustaches, or head hair— must be coated with petroleum jelly in a liberal fashion. As well, the entire face can be given a very thin coat of petroleum jelly or mineral oil. Of course, all women's street make-up should be removed. Cover the clothing of the subject with a plastic make-up cape.

If just the upper part of the face, such as the eye and forehead area, is to be taken, the nostrils can be filled with cotton batting and covered with petroleum jelly, with the subject breathing through the mouth. However, if the entire face is to be cast, some workers use drinking straws in the nostrils while others prefer to work carefully around the nostril area. One excellent method is to cover the nostrils with PGC while the subject holds his or her breath, then with a forceful expulsion of air from the nostrils, a breathing passage will be cleared. Take care to explain this procedure carefully to the subject prior to commencing the impression so that complete confidence will be gained before the PGC is on the face.

Usually, 20 scoops of powder (177 grams) to 500 cubic centimeters of water will be sufficient for a full face. Some technicians mix the entire batch at one

FIGURE 4.5 *(A) Casting a face. The subject is prepared and the PGC is applied. (B) The PGC and the plaster mother mold are being removed. (C) An Ultracal 30 positive being cast.*

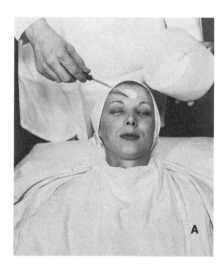
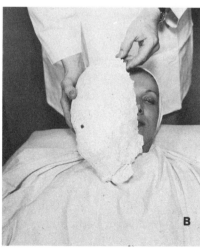

time, while others split it in half and start with one batch and then go to the second *before* the first batch sets. However, this means that at least two people must be doing the cast—one to apply and the other to mix. With the dental alginate (3-minute set time) this was necessary, but with the PGC, which has a longer working time, one person can do the impression.

Although some apply the PGC to the face with the hands, the material tends to set faster because the hands are warm while a brush or spatula is not. If you do use the hand method, it is well to have a basin of water close by to rinse the hands whenever necessary.

Don't throw excess alginate, plaster, or stone down the drain of a sink. It will stop up the trap and the pipes! It is best to work with a sink setup over a 5-gallon bucket. The liquid can be decanted off later and the residue on the bottom thrown into the trash bucket.

Mix the PGC as directed on page 000, and apply to the face with a 1-inch paint brush or a flexible spatula. The usual method is to start at the forehead area and work down the face as the PGC will run somewhat during application. Always do the nose and nostril area last. Also take care in the under-chin area that a coating of the PGC is brushed to adhere under the chin. Unless the ears are covered with the shower cap (or a huck towel), their cavities should be protected with cotton batting covered with petroleum jelly. To ensure that the mother mold will adhere to the PGC, strips of burlap (used for strengthening Ultracal molds—terry cloth may also be used) about 2 by 4 inches can be imbedded in the PGC surface before it sets. These can be placed on the forehead, cheeks, mouth and chin areas.

After the PGC is set to a rubbery mass, it must be covered with a mother mold of rigid material. Some workers prefer the fast set dental plaster made in thin mixes and brushed on in successive coats until about a half-inch thickness is obtained. A layer of cheesecloth can be placed over the plaster and another thin coat brushed in for the final application. This will provide more strength to the rather fragile dental plaster. Others use plaster bandages of the type employed by medical personnel for making broken limb casts. This is obtainable from medical supply houses and, although rather expensive, does an excellent job. Follow the directions given with the plaster bandage for application. If accelerated set is desired, warm water with a bit of salt is used for the dipping of the bandage. Short, overlapping sections can cover some of the longer ones that are placed around the head until the proper thickness is obtained. Usually ¼ inch of bandage thickness is sufficient in strength for this type of mother mold. Finally, some technicians simply accelerate the set of casting plaster with the addition of a teaspoonful of salt in a quart of water, and use this for the mother

mold. Again, take care around the nasal passages and allow breathing holes in the mother mold material.

The plaster will heat up somewhat, and when it cools off, the impression is ready to remove from the face. If the strips of burlap have been embedded in the PGC, the cast will come off the face intact with the PGC stuck to the mother mold. Having the subject make a few faces will loosen the PGC from the face and facilitate removal. A mixture of dental plaster can then be used to seal up the open nasal passages on the mother mold. Be certain to coat the inside surface of this plaster with petroleum jelly so that it will not stick to the positive to be cast. One can also fill these nostril holes with plastalene if desired.

The impression is now ready for making the positive cast (Figure 4.6). This should be done immediately as the alginate will commence to shrink as it dries out. To support the cast, one can put it in a cardboard shoe box or a plastic bowl. If the PGC begins to separate from the mother mold at the edges, metal hair clips can be used to hold them together. Another method is to use a dental product made by Johnson and Johnson called *Secure Dental Seal,* which is a paper-thin, 100 percent adhesive that can be wetted and placed between the alginate and the plaster of the mother mold to form a good temporary bond that will control a thin alginate edge and maintain the shape required. It is far better than the soft dental adhesive cream material that is used by some workers for this purpose as it does not require a heavy coating that might distort the casting.

Another adhesive material can be made by dissolving a product called Vistanex in a solvent such as toluene. This can be painted on the outer part of the alginate and the inner surface of the mother mold. It dries rapidly and will adhere the two parts on contact when they are pressed together.

FIGURE 4.6 *Various facial casts and section casts.*

A mixture of casting plaster, Ultracal 30, or stone can then be brushed into the negative PGC mold. Blowing the thin coating around with sharp breaths will remove bubbles from the surface. More liquid gypsum can then be poured into the mold. When the mixture begins to thicken, one can spatulate the mix up the sides of the mold so that the cast will be about an inch thick all around while being hollow in the center. Unless one wants a very heavy positive, it is not necessary to fill the negative cavity completely. If more than one positive is desired, don't use the burlap strips on the PGC so that the mother mold can be removed from the PGC and then it can be carefully stripped from the positive and replaced in the mother mold. Another positive cast can then be made immediately. Otherwise, one must pry the mother mold away from the PGC (often breaking it in the process), and strip the PGC away from the positive and discard it.

The positive can then be scraped free of any small casting imperfections, the nostrils cleaned out, and the edges of the cast smoothed out with a metal plaster tool. If the cast is heavier on one side than the other, a Surform tool can be used to scrape away the excess plaster or stone. Mark the back of the positive with the name of the subject, the date, and possibly a serial number for cataloging the molds. As the positive will not have thoroughly hardened yet, a sharp pencil is best to mark in this data.

Another way to take a face cast is with casting plaster. The face is prepared the same way, and a mix of casting plaster is applied directly to the face with a 1-inch bristle brush. The same precautions should be observed in applying the plaster to the nostril areas as were described for alginate.

This is a slower method because the casting plaster (salted to accelerate the set) takes a longer time to set, but no mother mold is required and if the subject is patient and does not move, an excellent impression can be taken. When the plaster is beginning to cool after its warming-up period is over, the impression can be removed from the face. A saturated solution of Ivory soap in water is then brushed into the impression as a separator. Use this soap solution copiously, brushing out the foam and bubbles until an even sleazy coating can be felt on the mold. Allow to dry for 15 minutes, then pour up a stone or Ultracal positive. When the stone has set and hardened, a few sharp blows with a chisel and mallet will crack the plaster negative from the harder positive. Do not attempt to separate the stone positive from the plaster negative until the stone has completely hardened; otherwise the positive may be damaged when cracking off the plaster.

Some technicians use plaster to take a cast of the entire head. Again the hair should be covered with a bald cap and the subject placed so that he or she is face down on a stack of towels or hard pillow. A piece of lead wire is stretched around the head just behind the ears to get an accurate outline of the head. This wire outline is then placed on a piece of strong cardboard and the head shape traced out. The outline is then cut out, and this form is slipped over the head to form a retaining wall for the plaster. The cardboard surface can be greased with petroleum jelly for ease in separation. The back of the head is then taken in plaster. When this impression has set, the subject is carefully turned around and up to the normal facial casting position. The cardboard retainer is then removed and keys can be cut into the plaster on each side and at the top of the impression with the end of a spatula. The impression should be at least 1 inch thick on the edge so that this can be done. The surface of the edge can then be coated with petroleum jelly and the cast of the face taken in casting plaster as previously described. Normally, the ear cavity is filled a bit more with cotton and petroleum jelly than with alginate for ease in separation when the cast is removed.

When the plaster impression of the face has set, it can be removed. The cast of the back of the head is then removed, and both halves are fitted together to make the positive. The inside of the impressions should be coated with the soap mixture and then, with the two halves held together with large elastic bands (made from auto tire tubes) or heavy cord, a positive can be cast.

To make the usual hollow cast, fill the mold about half full with a thin mix of stone or Ultracal 30. Carefully spread the material around the inside of the mold by rolling it in different directions to ensure an even coating. The excess can then be poured out and this flash coat allowed to semi-set before another thin mix is applied in the same manner. After three such coatings, the positive can be strengthened with small sections of burlap if desired, and more stone is poured into the mold and can be worked around inside with the hand to ensure an even coating (Figure 4.7).

When the positive has completely set, the plaster negative is carefully cracked away by tapping it with a small hammer to split the plaster. Some workers use a chisel and a wooden mallet for this. This is one of the oldest methods of making a full head cast. A newer method was devised by Dick Smith and is described and illustrated in Figure 4.10 by Tom Savini. In most cases, face casts that will be used for plastalene sculpture are coated with orange shellac or clear lacquer to seal the pores of the gypsum material and make the cast easier to clean.

SCULPTURE MATERIALS

The term *modelling clay* encompasses two types of clay-like materials. One is a water-based clay that is pur-

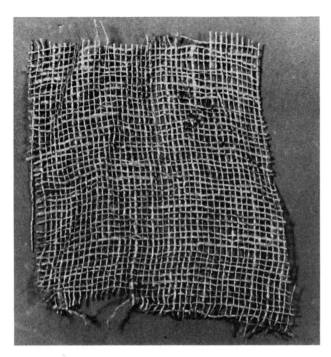

FIGURE 4.7   *The open weave burlap recommended by Dick Smith for strengthening molds and casts (see Appendix B).*

chased as a powder and mixed with water to the desired consistency for use as a modelling material. Sculptures made of this material must be kept damp so they will not dry out and crack. It finds some use in the make-up lab but is not the best sculpturing material. Make-up artists find that the oil-based *plastalene* or *plasticine* serves their purposes better. It comes in many grades from a very soft #1 to a hard #4. It can be obtained

in the normal dark green shade or in a white. Opinions vary considerably as to the most useful variety, but most technicians use the dark green in either the #2 or the #4 hardness. It comes in 2-pound blocks (see Appendix B).

The tools for use with plastalene modelling are usually small and wooden (generally much smaller than the clay sculpture tools fine artists use), and the smallest wire tools are used as well (Figure 4.8). This is mainly because the make-up lab technician starts with a face cast in gypsum material and adds the plastalene to achieve the sculpture rather than starting with a large, roughly shaped head of plastalene and carving it to shape with tools. When adding clay to a plaster or stone positive, always apply only a bit at a time until the desired shape is built up. The wooden tools with the flat ends can do this work, while the fine wire tools can be used to diminish the sculpture a bit at a time. The surface can also be scraped with a piece of coarse burlap to remove a thin layer of clay.

Texturing the surface to make it appear to have pores can be accomplished with a small knobbed-end wooden tool, with a plastic stipple sponge, or with a *grapefruit* tool made by coating the surface of various citrus fruits with a few coats of casting latex, drying this with a hand hair dryer, and then peeling off the latex after powdering it. This will take an impression of the surface of the orange or grapefruit (hence, the

FIGURE 4.8   *(A) Metal tools.* LEFT TO RIGHT: *Stiff and flexible spatulas, a plaster knife, two metal plaster carving tools. (B) Sculpture tools.* LEFT TO RIGHT: *A small spatula; two wire tools for nostrils, lines, wrinkles; three wooden carving tools for plastalene (the smallest are the most useful); a pointed ball-head wooden tool for making pores.*

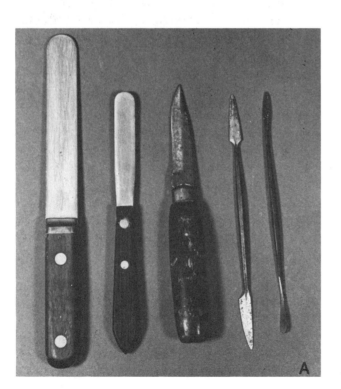

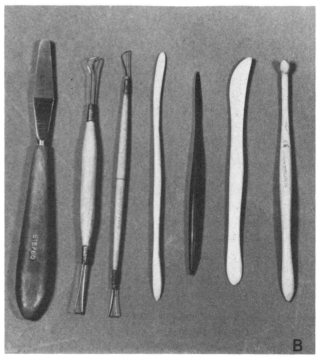

name!), which has a great similarity to the human skin.

To smooth plastalene, a brush dipped in isopropyl alcohol will serve for small areas. For a larger expanse, some petrolatum jelly or mineral oil can be rubbed sparingly on the surface with the hands or a wide brush. Take care not to use too much of the latter two materials as they will soften the surface of the sculpture. Some workers will coat a finished sculpture in plastalene with three coats of RCMA Plastic Cap Material (clear type) to provide a surface that will still take some tool and texture markings to refine the sculpture.

If one uses the sponge method, they will find that the various grades of polyurethane stipple sponges work better than the red rubber ones because the latter often leave bits of rubber imbedded in the plastalene. More often than not, a combination of the grapefruit, the sponge, and the knob tool will produce the best results for the varying skin pore textures.

Another method is to make latex stamps of skin texture areas. This can be done from the life mask cast of an older person who has good forehead wrinkles, for example. Just coat the original positive with a number of coats of casting latex (depending upon the thickness of the stamp desired), dry, and then remove it. This negative impression can be then used to press into a forehead plastalene area to obtain a reasonably good sculpture of forehead wrinkles. This method cannot be used too successfully on the soft parts of the face like the eye area, but it is suitable on the bonier parts.

Due to shrinkage of latex pieces, some size allowances can be made on appliances that cover a large area. This is one reason why many technicians make multiple appliances rather than one large face piece.

As well as wooden tools for plastalene, there are various metal tools with cutting edges for trimming plaster and stone, rasps and Surform tools for removing more material, and some labs even have machine tools with coarse wheels to rapidly cut and shape gypsum casts.

Two kinds of spatulas are used in the lab. One is the regular flexible type that is used for measuring small amounts of material for weighing, applying alginate to the face, and many other uses. The other is a stiff metal one that is obtainable from a dental supply house for mixing alginate or plaster. A strong bladed knife is needed for trimming, and a heavy screwdriver is useful for prying apart two-piece molds.

Plastic bristle 1-inch paint brushes, some with regular short handles and others with long handles (for getting into castings easier), will find much use, as will some #10 round sable hair brushes as well as some cheaper Chinese bristle brushes (for paint-in latex application) (Figure 4.9). A few wig-cleaning bristle brushes are handy for scrubbing plastalene out of plas-

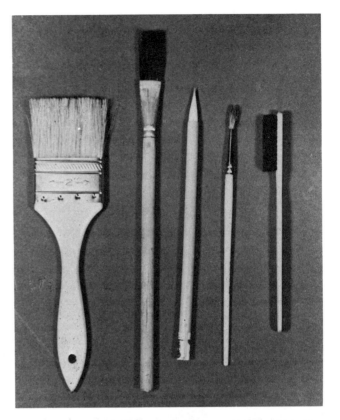

FIGURE 4.9　TOP: *Brushes.* LEFT TO RIGHT: *Soft bristle brush for cap material or other uses; long-handled bristle brush for use with plaster; Chinese bristle brush for paint-in latex work; #10R sable brush for many applications; bamboo-handled bristle brush for cleaning plastalene from castings.* BOTTOM: *Two black rubber dental bowls for mixing small batches of alginate or gypsum materials and two small polyethylene measuring cups for weighing various foam ingredients.*

ter and stone molds as are some bristle stipple brushes of small sizes.

Sculptor's calipers for measuring head size and shape are useful for making large castings and a hand or electric drill with a ¼- and a ⅜-inch bit for drilling

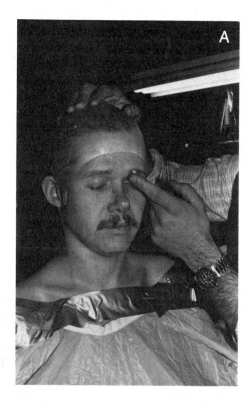

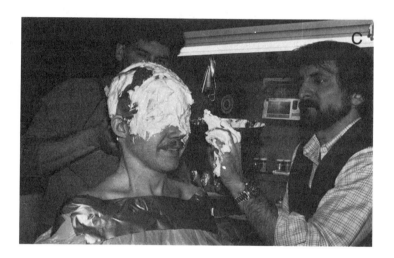

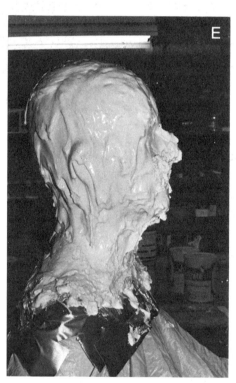

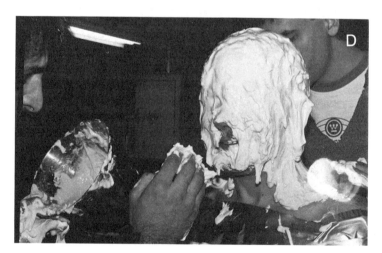

FIGURE 4.10   *Casting a full head and shoulders. (Photos and casting courtesy Tom Savini from* Grand Illusions.*) (A) The subject's head is covered with a plastic cap and adhered to cover all the hair. The brows, lashes, and facial hair are generously coated with petroleum jelly while the entire skin to be cast is also covered with a fine coat as well. (B) Tom mixes a large batch of the alginate in a kitchen mixer after weighing and measuring the proportions carefully. (C) With the aid of an assistant, he commences to apply the alginate all over the face and head, taking care around the nose section. He generally fills the ear cavity with cotton and petroleum jelly as can be seen here and, unless the ears must be part of the*

cast, fills the back of them with a plastic wax material to avoid heavy undercuts. Note that the subject has been covered with a plastic sheeting, which is held to the body with gaffer tape. (D) The mouth and nose area being worked on with care. (E) The head, neck, and shoulders covered with alginate. (F) Previously cut and rolled strips of plaster bandage are soaked in water for use. (G) The first strip goes over the head (H) and down to the neck area on both sides. (I) Plaster bandages on the neck (J) and face area, again taking care not to cover the nostril vents for breathing. The face is covered to a thickness of about four layers of bandage on the front half. (K) The front section of the head, face, and

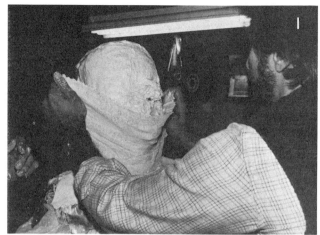

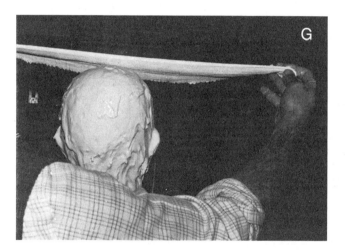

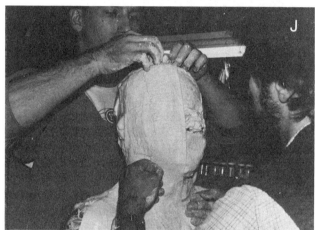

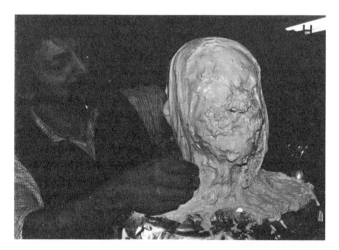

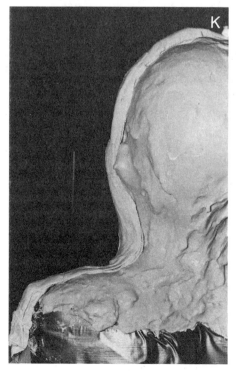

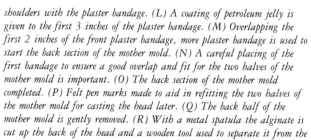

shoulders with the plaster bandage. (L) A coating of petroleum jelly is given to the first 3 inches of the plaster bandage. (M) Overlapping the first 2 inches of the front plaster bandage, more plaster bandage is used to start the back section of the mother mold. (N) A careful placing of the first bandage to ensure a good overlap and fit for the two halves of the mother mold is important. (O) The back section of the mother mold completed. (P) Felt pen marks made to aid in refitting the two halves of the mother mold for casting the head later. (Q) The back half of the mother mold is gently removed. (R) With a metal spatula the alginate is cut up the back of the head and a wooden tool used to separate it from the

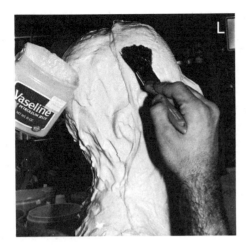

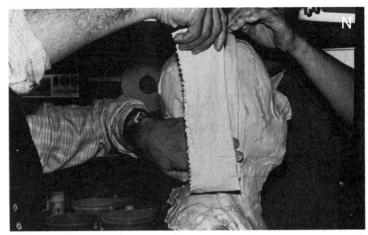

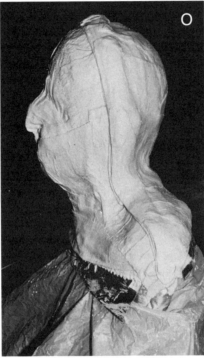

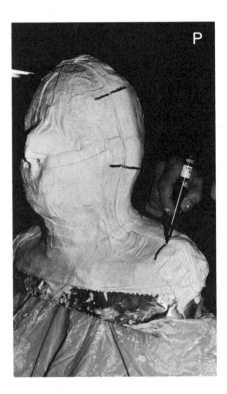

subject. (S) The head in a forward inclined position. (T) With the head forward, the alginate and front half of the mother mold are removed with care. To prevent the alginate from separating from the front half of the mother mold, he imbeds a layer of a terrycloth material into the alginate on the forehead, mouth, and chin area and down each side of the face. See page 167 for directions on adding to a set alginate surface if the alginate sets too soon before this can be done. (U) With the mold put together, the sides matching on the lines, and the alginate held to the sides of the mother mold if necessary with a false teeth gel, it can be taped, as shown, to a plastic bucket with gaffer tape and the mold held together with the same. Cord can also be used, but the tape is convenient and works well. The nostril holes can be filled with quick-set dental plaster or some plastalene forced in. A mix of Ultracal 30 is made. (V) After a splash coat is worked around the mold, the head is filled with the remaining Ultracal. Some workers prefer to make a head about one inch thick to save weight, but the usual full head is solid for strength. (W) When the Ultracal is set, the mother mold is removed and the alginate separated from the head. (X) After the usual minor clean-up around the ears and nostrils and any imperfections such as small holes or bumps are filled and removed, we have a completed perfect head cast.

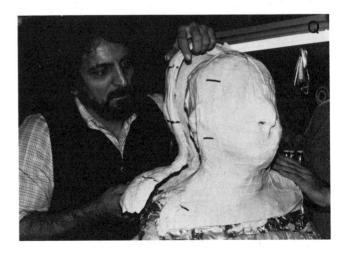

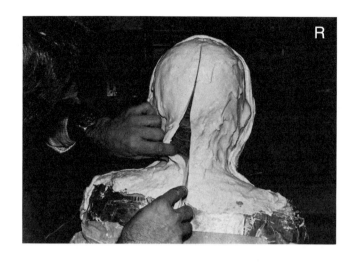

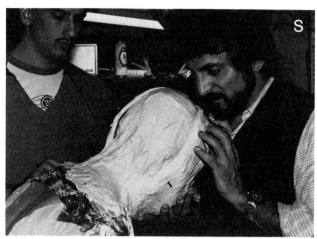

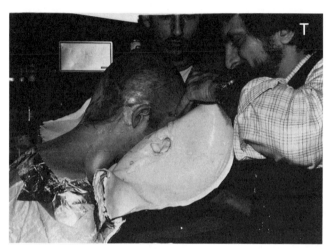

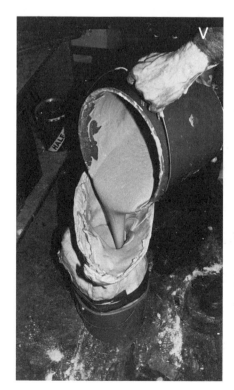

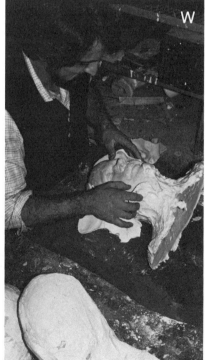

escape holes in positive casts for foamed latex or ure-thane and a ¾-inch half-round coarse reamer or rasp bit for cutting keys.

Dental sculpture tools such as dental spatulas, curved tip tools used for handling dental amalgam for filling teeth, and others will be found useful for tooth sculpture (Figures 4.11 and 4.12).

Stan Winston feels the life mask is only a guide and serves, along with many close-up photos, as a basis for sculpting in plastalene a head and face with the expression he wishes to use as a perspective for the make-up (see Figures 2.24 and 2.25 for his "Manimal" make-up). He imbeds false eyes and teeth in the sculpture to add to its lifelike qualities to aid his conceptions (Figure 4.13). He feels that many times he can capture an expression in photos that he cannot in a life mask, and the clay sculpture gives him what he seeks. P.S. One has to be a very good sculptor to do this!

MOLDS

Flat Plate Molds

The simplest of the two-piece molds is the flat plate type. With this basic casting one can make scars, cuts, bruises, moles, and other small appliances that do not require specific facial contours. When the prostheses made on the flat plate are adhered to the skin, they take on the natural curve of the area without any trouble in most cases.

To make a flat plate mold, form a rectangle whose inside measurements are about 6 by 10 inches, with four pieces of 1-by-2-inch wooden blocks (Figure 4.14). These can be held in place on a glass surface with four lumps of plastalene at the corners. The inside surface of the wood as well as the glass should be coated with petroleum jelly as a separator. Make some clay keys

FIGURE 4.12 *Various tools and clamps that are useful in the prosthetics lab.*

by rounding 1-inch balls of plastalene in the palms of the hands, then cutting them in half with a strand of thread. Place them about a half-inch from the corners of the enclosure. Make a thin coat of stone or Ultracal 30, and blow it in to remove the bubbles. (A sculptor's trick is to use sharp breaths of air blown in on a thin liquid plaster mix surface to remove all the small surface bubbles.) Then fill up the enclosure with the remaining mixture. A strip of burlap can be used as a strengthener if desired, but the basic thickness of the plate is normally sufficient for most uses.

When the stone or Ultracal 30 has set, remove the blocks and slide the cast off the glass plate. The plastalene in the keys can be pried out with a wooden

FIGURE 4.11 *1/2- to 3/4-inch rotary files for use in cutting keys in gypsum materials. They work best in a good drill press or, if need be, in a hand-held electric drill.*

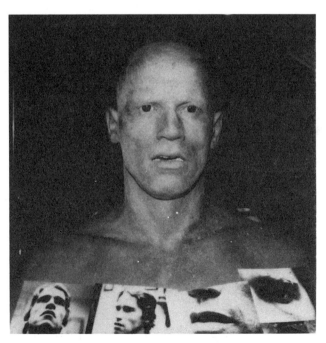

FIGURE 4.13 *Working from photographs of Arnold Schwartzenegger, Stan Winston sculpted a very accurate reproduction in plastalene as a work model for the effects he created in the film* The Terminator.

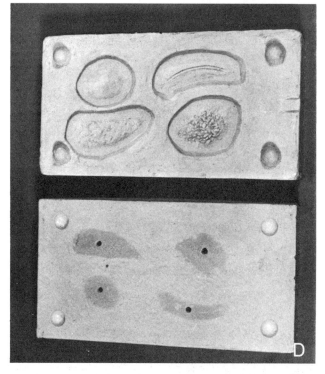

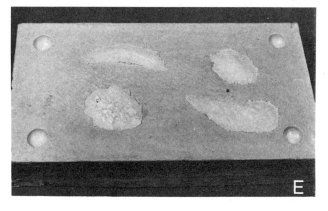

FIGURE 4.14 *Flat plate molds. (A) The sculpture of some bruises and a cut are made in plastalene. (B) After the plastalene gutters have been made, the flat plate is surrounded by wooden blocks held together with lumps of plastalene. These wooden blocks have been lacquered and coated with petroleum jelly as have the areas of the plate showing around the sculptures on the plate for ease in separation. (C) After Ultracal has been mixed and poured in, the mold set and separated, we have the two halves of the flat plate mold. (D) The plastalene is removed from the flat plate positive and 1/4-inch holes drilled into the Ultracal for vent holes. This mold was then coated with a polyurethane lacquer and employed to cast foamed polyurethane pieces. (E) The appliances (with flash removed) of foamed polyurethane.*

modelling tool. The keys can then be sanded with medium then fine sandpaper so that there are no undercuts. For use, items can be modelled on the plate with plastalene, with a ¼-inch gutter left around each of the items modelled and the remainder of the plate clayed in to a depth of about ¼-inch. Petroleum jelly can then be applied to the exposed stone areas in the gutter and keys, and surround the plate with another set of greased wooden blocks (1 by 4 inches), and secure with plastalene at the corners to form a box around the plate. Stone or Ultracal 30 can then be mixed and added in the usual way to fill the cavity. Each of the plates, when completed, should be about 1¼ inches thick.

When the stone or Ultracal 30 has set, remove the retaining wall and separate the mold. The keys may then be lightly sanded after the plastalene has been thoroughly cleaned off both sides of the mold. Acetone

can be used for this cleaning or TCTFE (trichlorotrifluoroethane) (Prosthetic Adhesive A Thinner is this
variety of solvent). The mold is now ready for use with
foamed latex or foamed urethane. The sculpted side
of this type of mold can also be employed for paint-
in plastic molding material as well. In the case of the
latter, the smooth surface side upon which the original
sculpture was done is not required as the plastic molding material uses an open-face mold.

Slush and Paint-in Molds

The basic casting latex molds are those that are taken
as a negative in casting plaster of a plastalene sculpture
on a facial cast. Noses are probably the most commonly
used prostheses in make-up work as the change of a
nasal structure can delineate a character more quickly
than any other. Many make-up artists take a full cast
of the face to get the correct proportions of the face
when modelling a new nose, chin, cheeks, eyebags,
and so on and make all their casts and molds directly
from the original positive. Others take an additional
cast only of the area (such as the nose) desired for use
in making the necessary prosthetic mold.

This individual mold can be taken in PGC or even
directly in dental plaster. The nostrils should be blocked
with cotton batting and covered with petroleum jelly,
leaving sufficient clearance to get a clear impression
of the nostril areas. During the casting operation, the
subject may breathe through the mouth as it will be
free of plaster. Paint the plaster on the face with a 1-
inch bristle paint brush, taking care not to get any in
the nostrils or the mouth. Cover about half the eye
sockets and cheeks with plaster to get sufficient edges
for the final positive. Don't forget to put petroleum
jelly on the eyebrows and lashes for ease in separation.

When the plaster is set, remove the cast and pour
up the positive with Ultracal 30 or stone using either
petroleum jelly or the soap method in a thin coat for
a separator. Another good separator for plaster to stone
is the stearic acid-kerosene one discussed on page 73.
When the stone has set, the dental plaster negative
can be easily cracked away, leaving the stone positive
ready for use.

The Nose

To make a slush or brush application mold from this
section mold of the nose (or using a full face cast),
model the desired shape in plastalene on this positive,
making certain that the blending edges are smooth so
they will be imperceptible in the finished appliance.
Take care that the nostrils are sufficiently filled on the
positive with plastalene so they will not have any un-
dercut that will prevent the removal of the negative
cast to be taken. However, sculpt the nostrils so they
will look natural and fit closely to the nose in the
finished appliance (Figure 4.15).

The nose exhibits one of the more varied skin pore

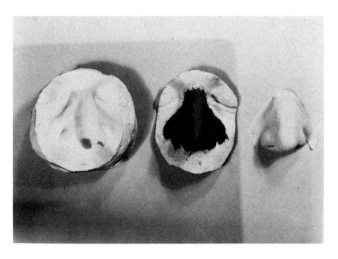

FIGURE 4.15   *Simple paint-in latex nose. A plaster negative* (LEFT)
made from a positive plastalene sculpture on a positive cast of a nose
(RIGHT). *A painted-in casting latex nose made in the negative mold.*

areas of the body. Sometimes the pores are small and
almost imperceptible on someone with fine skin, and
at other times the pores are large and the surface of
the skin quite rough. Generally, a slight overporing
is normally called for during sculpture as some of the
fine details are lost in the casting of the negative on
the surface of the appliance. Only by experience can
the technician know what is the correct depth and
extent of making pores.

For a clown nose (which is generally slush cast), no
pores are called for. Thus, the surface should be made
as slick as possible by dipping the fingers in water (or
mineral oil) and rubbing them on the surface of the
plastalene.

It should also be noted that sometimes only a nose
bridge or tip need be made so the sculpture need not
be overextensive. However, the undercuts on the nostrils must be filled as well as the outer curve of the
alae with plastalene to avoid undercuts.

When the modelling is completed, coat the remainder of the exposed positive with petroleum jelly
as a separator. The sculpture should then be surrounded with a clay wall about ¾ inch higher than
the tip of the sculptured nose and at least ¾ inch from
the sculpture all around. As the casting latex builds
up by absorption into the plaster negative, this amount
of thickness is minimal. Larger casts should be thicker
(1 to 2 inches) to allow for an absorptive surface.

Some technicians spray the surface of the sculpture
with aerosol solution or Kodak Photo Flo (1 cubic
centimeter in 200 cubic centimeters of water) to reduce
the possibility of surface bubbles in the plaster. Paint
in, then blow in, a mix of casting plaster to cover all
the sculpture and surroundings, and carefully spatulate
and pour in the remainder of the mix to fill the cavity
of the plastalene retaining wall. Some workers use a
vibrator table to hasten the removal of all bubbles while

others tap the mold on the table top to force any bubbles to the surface of the plaster.

As soon as the plaster heats up and cools, the two sides can be pried apart with the blade of a screwdriver. Any plastalene remaining in the negative should be carefully removed with a wooden modelling tool, taking care not to scratch the surface of the negative. Allow the negative cast to dry out for about an hour, then it can be cleaned of any remaining plastalene with a small bristle brush dipped in acetone or TCTFE. Rinse the negative in water before each use, and the latex appliance made in the cast will separate out easily when it is completed and dried.

If the negative is to be used for brush application, no further preparation is needed, but if a slush molded appliance is to be made, the negative requires that a plaster wall be built up in the area of the upper lip on the mold so that an even level will be achieved when the casting latex is poured into the mold.

The advantage of any slush or brush-applied latex piece is that it will fit many faces because the inner surface is not made to fit any particular face the way foamed latex appliances are. However, one cannot achieve the more skinlike quality on the outer surface of any slush or paint-in appliance that a foamed one will display (see page 96).

Whenever any additional plaster is to be added to a mold or cast, the surface should be thoroughly wetted with water before the new plaster is applied. Such additions work much better with a freshly made negative as it has a greater water content than one that has been left to dry out—even overnight.

Any repairs on the negative, like holes left by errant surface bubbles that may not have been dissipated when the cast was vibrated, can be easily made by scraping the underside of the negative with a metal tool to remove some plaster and using this to do the repair rather than making a new mix. Dental tooth filling tools are best to get into small places for these repairs.

Oriental Eyelids or the Epicanthic Eyefold

For these, a cast of the upper face from the nose to the hairline can be taken or the full face cast used (Figure 4.16). Very little poring is needed on the lids themselves. If one wishes to make a series of stock Oriental eyelids, it is well to vary the eyelid curves so they can be adjusted to fit a number of Caucasoid eyes. Again, the negative should be taken in casting plaster and made about an inch thick.

Bald Caps

Latex bald caps can be made in a negative plaster mold or painted on a positive one (Figure 4.17). To make a negative-type mold, get a small-sized balsa wood head form from a hat supply house and slice it into nine fairly equal sections by two cuts made one way, then turning the head 90° and making two cuts again. Then put the sides together and hold them in place along the neck portion of the head with heavy elastic bands. Coat the entire head with a #1 or #2 plastalene, smoothing out the surface to form a bald head sculpture. The surface can be lightly pored to give it some texture. A retaining wall of plastalene is added to the desired shape of the mold, and then it can be sprayed with the Photo Flo solution.

A good spray gadget is one made for spray painting small objects, called a PreVal Sprayer made by the Precision Valve Corporation and sold in many paint stores. It consists of a bottle for the liquid and a removable unit that has the propellant and spray tip. The latter screws onto the bottle and can be used to

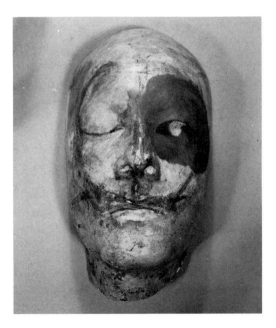
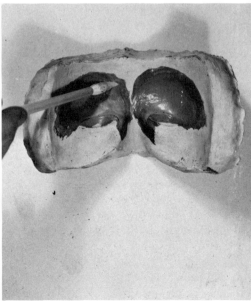

FIGURE 4.16
Epicanthic eyefold. LEFT: *A face cast with one side sculpted in plastalene of an epicanthic eyefold.* RIGHT: *The finished negative mold made from plaster being painted in with casting latex to form a large appliance that will cover the brows as well. A smaller piece may also be painted-in that will just cover the eyelid area with the same material. Such appliances can also be made of foamed urethane or latex.*

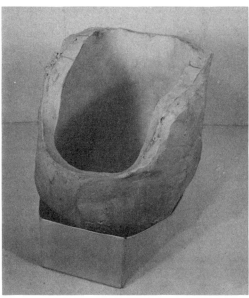

FIGURE 4.17 *Slush bald cap mold.* LEFT: *A balsa wood head (which has been previously section-cut in nine parts and held with an elastic band at the base) is covered with a coating of plastalene.* RIGHT: *A one-inch-thick plaster mold made of this form with the form removed. This mold is used for slush casting quick latex bald caps.*

spray many liquids. Buy several and keep one with the Photo Flo solution ready for use.

The retaining wall should be about 1½ inches high, and the casting plaster negative taken of the plastalene positive must be that thickness all around. When the plaster is beginning to set, cover it with cheesecloth, and brush over a bit more casting plaster to strengthen the mold. When the plaster has fully set and cooled, remove the elastic bands from the balsa wood head, and carefully draw out the center section of the cut head. This can be facilitated by passing a piece of coat hanger wire through this section before putting it together to make the mold. Once this center section is out, the others will remove easily without cracking the negative. Remove the excess clay and the mold is ready for use.

The same basic method can be used for making positive stone or Ultracal heads for plastic caps. However, do not make the casting plaster negative over ¾ inch thick, and do not use any cheesecloth reinforcement. When the plastalene has been cleaned out of the negative, coat the inside with petroleum jelly and fill the cavity with a stone or Ultracal mix. The mix should be spatulated up and around the negative so that the finished cast is about ½ to ¾ inch thick all around in a hollow shell. When the stone or Ultracal 30 has set, the plaster can be cracked away and you have a positive cast to paint or spray the cap plastic. As previously mentioned, casting latex can also be used on a positive head, but the head positive should be of plaster. Due to the separating medium (silicon grease type) used on the head molds for plastic cap material, molds so treated will not work with painted-on casting latex.

Generally, if the surface of the plastalene positive original has been pored sufficiently, the positive gypsum head will have a proper surface for painting on plastic cap material or latex as the finished cap will then be reversed for use.

To make a head mold for spraying, where the adjustment of the spray on the final coating can be made to provide a more textured coat, some technicians make the head mold as slick as possible for ease in removal, and of course, the bald cap is not reversed. John Chambers had some head molds that were chrome plated, while Bob Schiffer has made some from fibreglass, both of which are very smooth and work quite efficiently for spraying.

If one can borrow a positive head mold and wishes to make a copy, there are a number of ways that a duplicate mold can be taken. One of the basic ways is to use a flexible duplicating material such as PMC-724 or Perma Flex's Gra-Tufy CMC (see pages 71–72). Another way is to make a three-piece duplicating mold of stone or Ultracal 30. This type of mold is the same as would be made to serve as a mother mold for the flexible impression material as well (Figure 4.18).

Basically, one would divide the head mold down the center with a plastalene wall about 1½ inches high, with the division line on side one (so that when the wall is removed, the line is still on the center line of the head). A stone or Ultracal mix is then brushed and spatulated onto side one to a thickness of about 1 inch and allowed to set and cool. (Always remember that where any gypsum product meets another in casting, a separating medium is necessary.) The clay wall is then removed and keys cut into the sides of the mold (three are sufficient), and the sides are covered with a thin coat of petroleum jelly as a separator. Side two is then taken to match the thickness of side one. When this has set and cooled, two angle keys can be cut to a depth of about ¼ to ½ inch about 1 inch apart. A cap cavity is then formed out of plastalene of the top area of the head mold and this taken in the same

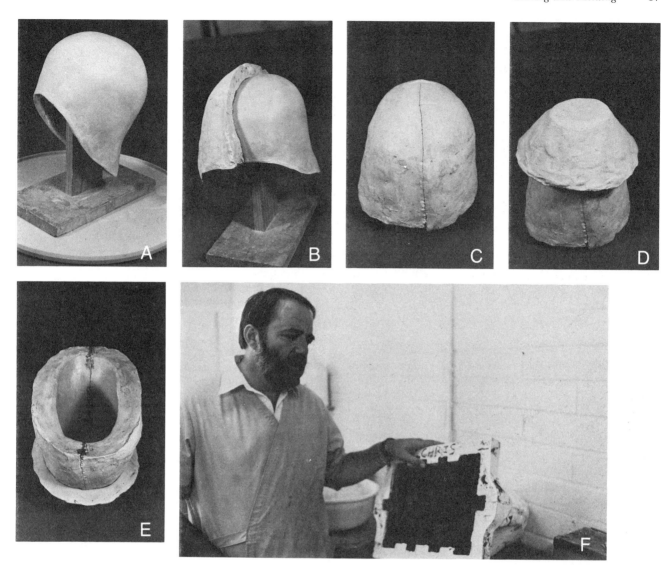

FIGURE 4.18   *(A) A positive stone or Ultracal head on a stand and turntable (for ease in spraying or painting the caps). (B) Showing one side of a section cast made to duplicate this head mold. Keys are cut (C) And the other side is made (note keys cut on top). (D) Then a cap is cast to hold them together. (E) The completed three-piece mold put together. It is a good idea to coat the inside of the mold and the rim with two coats of lacquer to seal the surface. Small chipped areas can be filled with plastalene and then the mold given a coat of petroleum jelly as a separator. Ultracal 30 can then be used to make positive heads in this mold. (F) A head mold or full head mold can also be made of polysulfide duplicating material for a seamless flexible mold (see also page 000) as shown here by Tom Burman.*

material (remember to use a separator). This third cast should have a flat top, so the plastalene wall should be higher on two sides, and the surface can be flattened with a board that has been lacquered and then covered with petroleum jelly. When this part has set and cooled, the three pieces can be separated and the original removed. The mold is then reassembled and is ready for use.

If a flexible material was used in making the mold, the procedures would be approximately the same for making the three-piece mother mold. Then in the disassembly, the flexible mold is removed from the original and replaced in the mother mold for preparing the negative for use. The negative is filled with stone or Ultracal, and a duplicate is made in the usual way. This type of duplicating mold will allow one to make a number of reproductions of the original. Check the basic shelf life of any duplicating material in the plastic varieties if you want to save the mold for future use. Of course, a stone or Ultracal 30 duplicating mold will last indefinitely with care taken in its separation from the duplicates.

Full Head Castings

Full, slip-over casting latex heads can be made with a slush cast of either one- or three-piece construction. These must be made of casting plaster and be about 2 inches thick. Such molds should be reinforced with burlap strips for strength. A mix of 20 percent Ultracal 30 with casting plaster will also add strength and not diminish the slush molding time excessively.

For use, these large molds must be securely tied together with heavy cord or rope. Take care in using clamps on plaster molds as the extra pressure exerted by the clamp may crack the mold.

Many other areas of the face and body can be cast and slush or paint-in appliances made. To get the best fit as well as the most natural appearance, however, foamed latex or urethane prostheses are far superior, especially for movement and fit.

The Two-piece Mold

The two-piece, or positive-negative, mold is required for foamed appliances or for any pressure-molded ones. In theory, the positive cast is modelled upon, with the desired shape of the appliance to be made, in plastalene. Then a negative is made of this, the clay is removed, and the mold is filled with the appliance material, placed together, cured, and separated, and the appliance is ready for use. The procedure is similar to that given for the two-part flat plate mold on page 82.

To make a mold for a foamed latex or foamed ur-
ethane small piece—say, a nose—from a full-face cast, a plastalene wall is built around the nose of the cast to a height of about ¼ to ½ inch above the tip of the nose (Figure 4.19). This cavity is then filled with PGC alginate and allowed to set. Then the clay wall is removed and the alginate separated from the face cast. This will produce a *section* negative into which is poured an Ultracal 30 or stone mix to make a positive. When set, this positive is then imbedded in another rather heavy mix of the same gypsum material. Generally, a surrounding round wall is made to hold the stone or Ultracal 30 mix out of 3-inch-wide linoleum, rubber floor mat, sheet lead, or even 6-inch plastic pipe. As the positive has still a great amount of moisture in it, it will incorporate itself into the new gypsum mix readily. Carefully place the positive in the center of the cavity, and with a dental spatula, seal the edges in so that the blend is perfect.

A good way to prepare the surface of a formica-covered table to do this procedure is to rub on a thin coat of petroleum jelly. Some workers prefer to use a glass plate or even a board with a formica top. The linoleum or other material wall can be secured with cloth adhesive tape to keep its shape.

Although with small molds there is less chance of

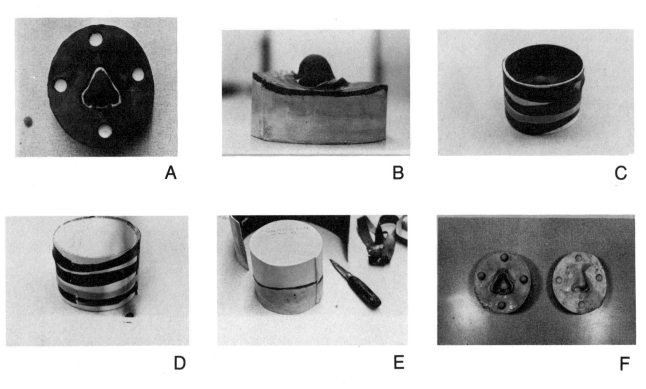

A   B   C

D   E   F

FIGURE 4.19   *Two-piece mold. (A) and (B) Two angles of an imbedded nose that has been sculpted in plastalene and the gutters made. Note that the nostrils have been employed as a run-off for the excess material when the nose is being made rather than the usual hole drilled through the positive on the tip of the nose. (C) The positive has been circled with a piece of inlaid linoleum and held together with rubber bands cut from an old auto inner tube. The inside of the linoleum has been greased with petroleum jelly. Sheet lead or rubber can also be used for this. (D) The negative portion poured with Ultracal 30. (E) The rubber bands and linoleum removed. A plaster knife is used to clean up any flash and to round the edges of the mold. The markings are made in pencil just before the Ultracal has set, giving the type of appliance, date, and if desired, a number for cataloging. (F) The finished two-part mold with the plastalene removed and the surface given two coats of clear lacquer to seal it. This mold will be used for casting foamed urethane noses.*

breakage than with larger ones, many lab technicians use fibre, fibreglass cloth, or burlap in the mold. Others prefer to use a circle of wire cloth around the positive section mold, taking care to imbed this fully within the mold.

When the stone or Ultracal starts to heat up in the set, remove the retaining wall, and while the material is not yet quite hard, scoop out three or four circular keys with the round end of a spatula or knife blade. Clean up the edges and fill any defects. The desired shape of the appliance can now be sculpted on this built-up positive form in plastalene and gutters formed for an overflow area. Clean the key areas and apply a separator on them and the overflow where the stone or Ultracal 30 can be seen. The surface can then be sprayed with the Kodak Photo Flo solution and the form enclosed in a 6-to-8-inch (depending upon the height of the sculpture) circle of linoleum or such. Heavy elastic bands or cloth adhesive tape can be used to hold the form in shape. A stone or Ultracal 30 mix is then added in the usual manner to fill the cavity, and reinforcement material is added if desired.

When the stone or Ultracal 30 is completely set and almost cool, remove the wall and separate the two sides of the mold. The plastalene is then removed and cleaned off the mold, and the keys can be lightly sanded to remove any burrs. The mold is now ready for use.

Molds made for foamed latex prostheses should not be more than 1½ inches thick to allow good heat penetration for curing the latex. Also, if the appliance is large or deep, it is a good idea to have a vent hole for overflow as well. On large noses this hole can be drilled through the positive on the nose tip with a ¼-to-⁵⁄₁₆-inch drill (Figures 4.20 and 4.21).

Two-piece molds for foamed polyurethanes are quite similar to those for foamed latex except that the urethane molds can be heavier as no baking is required.

Large molds that might be for extensive forehead pieces or for full heads can entail a positive core head and a two-piece negative. Not only are these molds made to have vent holes, but also they may be employed as filling holes for a gun filled with foamed latex that is forced into the mold. Large molds must often be clamped together as the mold is being filled, and flanges must be made to give a purchase point for these clamps. Of course, the larger the mold, the more strengthening it must have, both with a product such as Acryl 60 cement hardener and burlap or fibre added to the molds. It is also a good idea to mark one side of the molds with a heavy marking pen or to scratch a line down the sides of both of the molds to see easily how to put the molds together during use.

Some lab technicians coat the sculpted plastalene with RCMA Plastic Cap Material when making two-piece molds so that when separated after making the negative, no plastalene will stick to it, making cleaning of the negative easier. This coating should be removed from the plastalene with acetone for reuse of the clay material. There are many methods employed for making the positive-negative types of molds, and books relative to these methods may be found in the Bibliography.

Incidentally, all molds used for foamed procedures must be thoroughly dried out before use. One good way is to put them in an oven at low heat (100°–150°F) and leave them overnight.

Plastalene Transfers

Dick Smith often sculpts a facial transformation on the life mask, then removes sections of plastalene intact and transfers them to an individual section positive for making the two-piece molds. Using a clean, fresh dental stone life mask, he brushes on two coats of alginate dental separator and dries the surface with a hair dryer. He then sculpts his appliances with #2 plastalene as

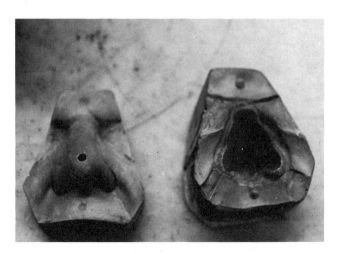

FIGURE 4.20 *A smaller foamed latex type nose mold for just a nose tip, showing the conventional escape hole bored into the tip of the positive. (Molds by Werner Keppler.)*

FIGURE 4.21 *Another Keppler mold for foamed latex for a nose tip but with channels cut for the excess rather than the hole as in the previous figure. See Chapter 5 for other two-piece molds.*

usual on the life mask, finishing the detail and the edges. He then coats the plastalene with a layer of clear plastic cap material.

The entire life mask and sculpture is then submerged in cold water for about an hour, at which time some of the plastalene sections may loosen from the life mask while others can be easily pried away. Large areas like the forehead may have to be cut in half to remove easily. These sections of plastalene are then carefully transferred to section positives. He recommends coating the section positive with petroleum jelly and then pressing on the sculpture and smoothing down the edges. The texture, edges, and minor repairs needed after the transfer can then be done as can the plastalene flashing for casting and the negatives poured up. In this manner one can get a better perspective of how the sculptured pieces will appear on the full face rather than just estimated on a section positive. RCMA makes a special heavy grade of alginate separator that is excellent for this use as well as for making acrylic teeth.

Molds for Teeth

Plastic teeth and caps that are pressure or heat cured are made in special metal flasks. However, for most make-up purposes, two-piece dental stone molds will suffice.

The first step in casting the mouth is to cast the upper or lower teeth (or both) to have a basic cast to work on. A dental supply house (see Appendix B) can furnish all the necessary materials and tools for this step as well as the materials to make the teeth. A set of impression plates, for both the upper and lower teeth, can be obtained in a number of sizes that will fit inside the mouth. They are available in plastic or metal. Also, it is a good idea to buy a set of rubber dental base molds to make neat finished castings to work with.

For a cast of the upper teeth, a mix of quick-set dental alginate can be made and placed in the tray. This is inserted in the mouth and pressed up to cast the upper teeth. This type of alginate sets quite rapidly (2 to 3 minutes) so the cast can be removed as soon as the alginate is firm. A mix of dental stone should be then brushed into the negative alginate mold (while still in the tray) and then additional stone added to fill the cast. Many dental technicians employ a vibrator to ensure that the mold is well filled and packed with the stone and to dissipate any bubbles that might be formed. The rest of the stone mix should be poured into a rubber dental base mold. When the stone is of a plastic consistency, the tray is inverted onto the stone in the base mold and the join smoothed out.

When the stone has completely set, the tray with the alginate can be removed, with the alginate attached and the casting removed from the base mold. The edges can be trimmed with metal tools to form a neat casting. The lower teeth can be cast in the same manner using the lower teeth trays and the same rubber forms. As there are a number of methods for making acrylic teeth, the special molds for these are discussed in the section on tooth plastics in Chapter 5.

Latex and Plastic Appliances

AN INCREASING NUMBER OF COMPOUNDS AND MATERIALS are being used by make-up artists to produce appliances. The criterion is always that the prosthesis looks and behaves as natural as possible for the use intended and designed. Today we have casting latex to make slush or paint-in appliances, foamed latex products, foamed urethanes, gelatins, solid molded plastics, and waxes for constructions. This chapter covers each of these materials and their basic uses.

NATURAL RUBBER MATERIALS

Of all the compounds utilized for appliances, natural rubber is by far the most popular and useful. Commencing in the late 1930s make-up artists began experimenting with various forms of these products, starting with the brush-applied method into a plaster mold and later the use of the two-piece foamed latex materials.

Beyond the making of the molds and casts, the make-up artist now had to learn a bit of chemistry to make the mixes necessary for use and to understand the variety of solvents, polymers, colorants, and so forth that were part of the vocabulary of the make-up laboratory technician. Telephone calls to manufacturers, visits to the prosthetic clinics of the Veterans Administration, discussions with chemists, and finally, comparing notes with other make-up artists interested in these new and exciting directions were all part of the education of those who wanted to learn and master these challenging techniques. Times may change but avidity for learning should never diminish.

Latex

Latex is a milky white fluid that is produced by the cells of various seed plants (such as milkweed, spurge, and poppy families) and is the source of rubber, guttapercha, chicle, and balata. Most *natural rubber* today comes from coagulating this juice and is a polymer of isoprene.

Synthetic rubberlike substances can be obtained by polymerization of some plastic materials and may also be called a *synthetic rubber,* or *synthetic latex.* The term *elastomer* means rubberlike, and there are many categories to which this term can be applied.

Natural rubber latex as employed by the make-up professional usually refers to a pure gum latex that has no fillers and is of varying density. Some are thinner for use as balloon-type rubber (for making bladders and so forth) while others are thicker (like those employed for some foam latex formulas). When rubber latex has fillers, like zinc oxide, it can be used for *casting* as it will build in thickness when left in a slush mold or can be added on with painting-in methods. Some natural rubber latices are prevulcanized—that is, pretreated so they do not require a heat cure—while others require such heat treatment to cure them.

Synthetic rubbers and latices can be polysulfides, polyurethanes, acrylics, and so on. One thus should take care in defining a material as just *liquid latex* without explaining which type or grade it might be.

The hardness of the finished product can be determined with a Shore durometer. While a reading of 40 refers to approximately the hardness of automobile tire rubber, a reading of 10 is a much softer finished product—more what a make-up artist might wish to employ as a soft duplicating material.

For make-up purposes, three types of latex molding methods are employed: the slush molding method, the paint-in (or on) manner, and the foamed latex procedures cover the general use.

Grades of Latices

Many grades of latex compounds are available from a multitude of sources and can be employed for slush, paint-in, duplicating, or foamed latex.

Natural rubber latices that have no fillers dry with a yellowish translucence and an elastic resiliency such as might be found in elastic bands or balloons. The General Latex Corporation has 1-V-10 that can be used for dipping or making thin pieces. RCMA also supplies a pure gum latex that is excellent for bladder effects: These natural rubber latices are prevulcanized and have good stability, fast drying rates, good water resistance, and excellent aging properties and flexibility.

Slush molding latices have higher solids (due to the fillers) and higher viscosities. They can be easily colored with dyes or colloidal colors and are prevulcanized. RCMA supplies a casting latex for slush molding and brush coating. RCMA also supplies a casting filler that can be stirred into the casting latex to hasten the build-up in slush casting and to provide more viscosity for brush application (see Appendix B for other suppliers). For foamed latices and their components, see the section, "Foamed Latex," later in this chapter.

Coloration

Coloration of appliances made with latices can be done *intrinsically*—that is, with color added to the initial formulation before curing—or *extrinsically*—with color added over the finished appliance. Intrinsic coloration is best done with universal colors like those supplied by RCMA or paint stores, and a drop or so of burnt sienna color is usually sufficient to color a pint of latex as a light flesh tone. Other colors such as reds, ochres, and blues can be added for coloration, but it should be kept in mind that the color of the finished material is usually quite darker than what the liquid appears before curing. Testing on a plaster plate will show the end color before adding too much.

Dyes may also be used for coloration of water-based latices, and a 10 percent solution is usually sufficient to add drop by drop to achieve the best color. Unfilled latices will deepen in coloration considerably more than the filled types of slush or paint-in latices. Some workers use 30 percent dye solutions for intrinsically coloring a foamed latex so that the higher concentration of dye in water will not affect the water balance of the mix. Colloidal colors such as universal colors, however, are considered to be more manageable and more versatile than dyes for coloring most latex products.

Extrinsic coloration of appliances requires special vehicles for the color as some affect natural rubber or synthetic rubber appliances. Cake make-up foundations, creme-stick foundations, and a number of the creme-cake foundations in general use for make-up foundations on the skin, do *not* work as a *prosthetic base*, just as the old greasepaints did not either. The main reason is that they contain mineral oil, which has a tendency either to attack the rubber or to whiten out after application. (Note: All RCMA Color Process Foundations can be used with latex appliances.) Max Factor formerly made a product called Rubber Mask Greasepaint that was essentially a castor oil vehicle base that did not attack the rubber. However, other theatrical make-up companies have copied this foundation so it is available. Also, RCMA has devised a new variety of foundation that is called Appliance Foundation that is superior to the old rubber mask greasepaint types. They also make an AF Powder that has more coverage than the regular RCMA No-Color Powder for use with these foundations (also see page 128). Powdering AF Foundations with AF Powder will produce a more matte surface on an appliance than a No-Color Powder, so sometimes a light stipple of glycerin will restore a better surface halation to an appliance.

The RCMA AF or Appliance Foundation series have replaced the RCMA PB (Prosthetic Base) materials as the newer AF series are a thicker form of foundation from which the oils do not separate as is prevalent with most of the "rubber mask greasepaint" types, nor are they sticky and hard to blend as are some of the firmer ones.

The AF series is obtainable in the basic Color Wheel primary colors of Red, Yellow and Blue, that can be combined to form any of the other in-between or secondary colors. As well, it comes in White, Black, Brown (KN-5 shade) and the earth colors of Ochre-1624, Warm Ochre-3279, Burnt Sienna-2817, and Red Oxide-6205 which are some of the main basic color ingredients that are components of the majority of skin color foundation shades. In addition, RCMA makes a number of matched shades to their regular Color Process Foundations such as KW-2 and KM-2. Other useful shades are constantly being added to the line due to the wide acceptance of the AF type of makeup for a high-coverage use.

The AF series come in various sizes and also in kit form of six colors per tray which is great convenience for carrying in the makeup kit.

The AF series can be applied with brushes or sponges and provides a super-coverage of both skin and appliances made of foam latex or plastic as well as for slush or paint-in molded rubber.

The mixing of earth colors with the bright colors and the dilution with white will produce almost any shade of foundation. As most make-up artists who employ appliances in their work prefer to mix their own shades for the particular intended use, this provides an excellent basic method. The colors are easily spatulated together on a glass or plastic plate to the required shade. It is a good idea to mix more than is required so that one does not run out of special color during the job at hand. The extra can be stored in a container for future use. It is also well to keep track of the mix by marking down the amounts of the basic materials used, such as so many spatula tips or spoonsful of one shade to another in case additional material must be mixed.

The AF Kits are numbered as #1, #2, etc. #1 has 1624 (Ochre), 2817 (Burnt Sienna), 3279 (Warm Ochre), 6205 (Red Oxide), KW-2 and KM-2. Kit #2 has Red, Yellow, Blue, Black, White and Brown-KN-5. Other kits with regular matched Color Process shades are also being made. Special kits are available to order for specific use.

Although the viscosity of the AF series is high, its blendability and coverage is superior for any type of appliance.

A new concept of extrinsic coloration is being done with acrylic emulsion colors. Dick Smith devised a mixture of RCMA Prosthetic Adhesive B and acrylic paints that coats a foamed latex appliance with an excellent surface material. His basic formula is an equal mix of PA-B and Liquidtex tube colors. This he stipples on the appliance with the urethane stipple sponges after giving the appliance a stipple coat of PA-B and powdering. To lessen the halation, he might stipple on a coat of Liquidtex Matte Medium.

For temporary coloration (as it has a tendency to crack off with age), Craig Reardon painted the ET heads with universal colors mixed with regular rubber cement (Figure 5.1). Also, some firms make a paint for latex castings with xylol as the solvent. The latter seems to incorporate the color quite well into the latex but does not give as fleshlike a look as the Dick Smith mixture (he calls that PAX).

RCMA also makes a special line of flexible acrylic foamed latex or foamed urethane paint colors for make-up use, which are similar to the PAX material which can be painted or stippled on to the appliances. There are matting agents that can be added to produce a less shiny coating as well. A new series with FDA certified colors has also been developed by RCMA, called Appliance Paint (AP) series, and is available in colors matching the Appliance Foundation (AF) series.

pH Value

Natural rubber latices are suspensions in ammoniacal water, and the correct pH value for most systems is between 10 to 11. pH test papers can be obtained from chemical supply houses. The excess ammonia loss of natural rubber latices can be corrected with a 2 percent solution of ammonium hydroxide in water, testing as one adds the solution to obtain the proper pH.

Fillers

Latices used for slush or paint-in casting can be adjusted for various degrees of stiffness or hardness of finished product by the addition of a filler. This filler can be prepared by adding 25 grams of zinc oxide to 100 cubic centimeters of distilled water, or it can be purchased from RCMA as Casting Filler. Depending upon the degree of opacity and stiffness required, anywhere from 1 to 10 percent of filler can be added by stirring into any prevulcanized latex for slush use.

Softeners

To make softer latex pieces, any latex compound can have a plasticizer added to it which consists of 400 grams of stearic acid, 500 grams of distilled water, 100 grams of oleic acid, 12 grams of potassium hydroxide, and 12 grams of ammonium hydroxide (28 percent). This mixture can be added 5 cubic centimeters (to 100 cubic centimeters of latex compound) at a time, testing a finished piece in between, to achieve the degree of softness required. Such products also affect the drying time of the latex as well as the durability of it.

Thickeners

Most natural and synthetic latices can be thickened to a soft, buttery consistency in a few minutes by stirring in Acrysol GS. This product is the sodium salt of an acrylic polymer and is supplied at 12 to 13 percent solids in water solution. For most applications, the use of 0.10 to 2 percent Acrysol GS (solids on latex solids) is adequate. Natural rubber has approximately 60 percent solids, and thus, 5 to 10 cubic centimeters of Acrysol GS added to 100 cubic centimeters of latex will thicken it considerably. This mix can then be spatulated into a mold to add bulk to a particular section for paint-in or slush molding. Note that thickeners retard the drying time of any latex compound.

As the Acrysol GS is a very heavy, viscous liquid, a diluted solution in water will work better for additions to latices. Therefore, if the Acrysol GS is diluted 50-50 in water, it will have half the strength of the stock solution and should be used accordingly. Tincture of green soap can also be employed as a latex compound thickener for some applications.

Latex Appliances

Slush or Slip Casting

Casting latex is poured into a slush-type mold and allowed to set for a period of 10 to 30 minutes, de-

FIGURE 5.1 *Craig Reardon with one of the ET heads that he painted.*

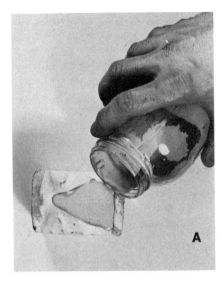
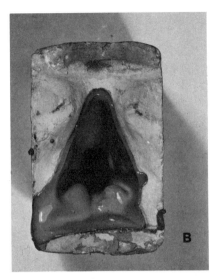

FIGURE 5.2   *Slush casting. (A) A nose mold is filled with casting latex and allowed to set until the buildup is about 1/16 to 1/8 inch. (B) The latex is poured out of the mold and the surface of the latex dried with a hand-held hair dryer. Unless oven cured in a low heat for about 1 hour, the mold should be left to air cure for about 8 hours after the latex has been thoroughly dried. (C) The nose is then removed and trimmed for use. Clown noses are usually made by this method as their edges do not need to* be thin for blending into the skin. As with all slush- or paint-in-type molds, to reuse them after they are dry (especially after oven curing), they should be rinsed in clean water before use. This restores some of the moisture in the mold and prevents the latex from adhering strongly to the plaster when the appliance is removed. Otherwise, no separating medium is required for latex-to-gypsum castings.

pending upon the thickness of the desired appliance (Figure 5.2). The excess latex is then poured back in the container and the mold turned upside down to drain. It can be force dried with a hand-held hair dryer, set under a large hair dryer, or placed in a low-heat oven. Drying time varies with the thickness of the prosthesis, but separation from the mold is relatively simple due to shrinkage of the latex. It should be noted that the appliance will have rather heavy edges and is unsuitable for blending into the face during application.

A slush cast nose is generally made for clowns as they will last longer than the delicate paint-in or foamed pieces. Full heads often found in joke and costume shops are made in this manner as well as full or partial appliances made for extras in a production where special make-ups are required but do not have to have any facial movement.

Paint-in or Brush Application Molding

This method consists of painting casting latex into the mold in successive overlapping coats with the thinnest being closest to the edge of the prosthesis. While a slush molded piece has a heavy ungraduated edge, the brush application method will allow the blending edge to be carefully controlled. This is quite necessary because a casting latex edge cannot be dissolved into the skin area as can many of the plastic types. Another advantage of a painted-in piece is it can be built up more heavily where it is necessary. For example, the alae and the bridge of the nose will require extra coats to produce an appliance that will hold the proper shape.

Sometimes workers add small pieces of paper towelling in to strengthen a piece. The towelling should always be torn into shape rather than cleanly cut to produce more graduated edges. It is then placed where desired with a brush and additional casting latex coated over the paper to make it a part of the prosthesis.

Medium-sized Chinese bristle brushes are used for this work by many technicians due to their size, configuration, and cost. Always work up a good lather of soapsuds on a cake of Ivory Soap with the brush and wipe it lightly before putting it into the casting latex. This procedure prevents the latex from solidifying or building up on the bristles of the brush and facilitates its cleaning in cold running water after use. It is a good practice to pour some casting latex in a 16-ounce wide mouth jar for painting use. The brush should always be left *in* the latex when not in use between coats so that it will not dry out. Leaving the latex-covered brush on a counter top for just a few minutes can ruin it for further use. Sometimes a coated brush can be salvaged by soaking it in RCMA Studio Brush Cleaner overnight.

Some appliances require special attention and painting—for example, Oriental eyelids where the lid area must be painted heavily enough to hold the proper shape while the upper portion that is attached to the skin must blend off in a thin coat. It is a good idea to have a series of eyelid molds (see Figure 4.16) and to paint up a sample of each for try-ons when a number of them are required. Then the eyelids can be individually fitted and the area to be painted in casting latex noted (as eyes tend to be different, some lids may be attached higher or lower on the frontal bone for the best effect).

Another case is the making of latex bald caps for extras or large casts. This method consists of pouring some casting latex into the mold cavity and turning the mold back and forth, with the latex being carried higher and higher each time and forming an edge. This procedure should be carried out carefully so that the leading edge around the forehead line of the hair receives only one or two such coatings of casting latex. Don't let the latex sit in the mold without this turning agitation because it will build in rings that might be apparent when the piece is dried out for use. Experience will show how long this procedure must be kept up to obtain a bald-effect cap that is both fine at the edges and heavy enough in the crown to hold its shape.

Pour off the excess out of the back portion of the mold, and drain fully before drying the surface with a hand-held hair dryer. Half an hour of drying is required generally, and then the mold can be set aside for another hour or so to cure fully. The cap can then be peeled off the mold, and to insure that it will retain its shape, it should be placed over a head form for about another hour so the surface can fully dry out. It is then ready for use (see mold shape in Figure 4.17).

Inflatable Bladder Effects

Many special effects transformations or illusions employ the use of some form of inflatable bladder whose effect is to ripple the surface of the skin to indicate violent changes taking place systemically (Figure 5.3). In essence, these bladders are inflatable plastic or latex balloons that can be controlled in size and flexibility by the introduction of air into them through fine plastic tubing. Such bladders may be concealed under surface appliances made of foamed latex, urethane, or plastic molding material so when they are inflated and/ or deflated, it appears that the surface of the skin is expanding as air is introduced into the bladder or contracting as the air is let out. As such, a rippling effect can be created like that on William Hurt's arm in Dick Smith's make-up in the film *Altered States* (Warners, 1980) and Rick Baker's *Werewolf*.

To make a simple bladder, pure gum latex can be used. Make a plaster flat plate (a good size would be 6 by 12 inches and about an inch thick for a permanent stock plate) with a smooth surface. Sketch an outline with a #2 lead pencil of the two sides of the bladder, and paint on three even coats of RCMA Pure Gum Latex, right to the edges of the outline, drying each coat thoroughly between with a hand-held hair dryer. This will normally give a sufficient thickness for the walls of the bladder, but larger-sized bladders can be made with additional coats for more strength.

Cut out a piece of heavy waxed paper, allowing about ½-inch clearance to the edge of the outline. On larger bladders, allow at least 3/4-inch (for an adhering

edge). This waxed paper will delineate the inside dimension of the bladder, which of course can be made in many shapes.

Dust this waxed paper cutout with RCMA No-Color Powder on both sides, and lay it down on the latex-painted shape on one side. Take care not to powder the surface of the latex. Carefully peel up the other side of the bladder and fold it over to fit exactly the outline of the other side. Press the edges together firmly so that the latex will adhere to itself to form the two sides of the bladder. Strip off the other side of the bladder from the plaster, and trim the latex nozzle end to within about 1/8 inch from the waxed paper end.

To remove the waxed paper, push in a small rounded wooden modeling tool to force an entrance and then remove it. Insert in its place a drinking straw whose end has been dipped into No-Color Powder. Blow in the powder into the bladder cavity on each side. Then the waxed paper insert can be teased out with a pair of dental college pliers or tweezers. The bladder with a nozzle end is now complete. Clear plastic tubing can be obtained from a medical or chemical supply house and inserted into the nozzle of the bladder. This can be sealed in with Johnson & Johnson 1/2-inch Dermicel Clear Tape and then coated over with pure gum latex. The bladder is then ready to be attached and used.

Although the illustrated bladder has no excess edge

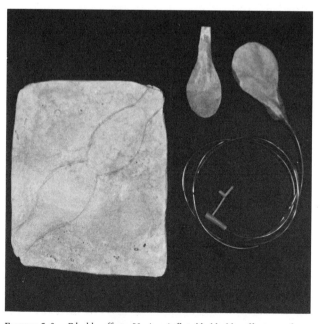

FIGURE 5.3 *Bladder effects. Various inflatable bladder effects are often seen in transformations. These can be made of PMC-724 (see page 49) or in pure gum latex. This is a plaster flat plate with an outline inscribed in pencil. A finished bladder is shown after having been attached to the tubing with Dermicel tape and a coat of pure gum latex as a sealer over it. In the center is the cutout wax paper used to keep the sides of the bladder from each other when it is folded over.*

for attachment to the skin, the 1/2- to 3/4-inch excess previously described during manufacture can be used for the adhesion area. RCMA Prosthetic Adhesive A is best for these bladders as it has excellent retention (see page 52 for other bladder uses).

Foamed Latex

The present-day ultimate in prosthetic appliance use for make-up purposes is the employment of foamed latex. It is unsurpassed for the best possible effects as well as adhesion to the skin. Since MGM's classic, *The Wizard of Oz* (1939), when Jack Dawn, then head of the make-up department, employed foamed appliances for the unforgettable characters of the Cowardly Lion, the Tin Man, and the Scarecrow as well as many others in the film, foamed latex has been the mainstay of tri-dimensional character work in motion pictures. In the early days of television in New York in the 1940s and 1950s, studios relied mainly on painted-in casting latex appliances for their low cost and rapidity of making them that was needed due to the lack of preparation time allowed to make-up artists for television shows. Today, foamed latex has become the standard for most appliances for professional make-up work.

Like many laboratory procedures that have been developed strictly in the make-up field, the parameters of the chemistry and mixing of foamed latex have been found to extend beyond the seeming restrictions of the expensive scientific or special equipment to ordinary, easily obtained ones (Figure 5.4). At first, special hand-made beaters, bowls, and laboratory ovens were considered to be required, but many labs today use kitchen-type Sunbeam Mixmasters with regular beaters and bowls, along with either standard electric kitchen ovens or the newer air convection table-top type. Only when full heads and bodies must be made are larger ovens required and restaurant-type Hobart mixers employed.

However, still some conditions do not vary much, and general room temperature and humidity do affect foaming procedures. The optimum is 68 to 72° F and a midrange of humidity. It is not difficult to maintain such with air conditioning and heating today. Higher temperatures will cause faster gelling and setting, while lower temperatures will extend the time. Successful foaming operations are impractical below 60° F.

Small quantities of ingredients can be weighed in plastic cups and the standard bowls of the Mixmaster used. Some artists mark the foaming volume on these bowls (five volumes is approximately correct for most appliances). All measurements given are for wet un-foamed ingredients, and a basic mix can often do quite a few small pieces. As it is rather impractical to mix very small amounts, most workers fill the molds that they are presently working on and, with the remaining material, fill some stock molds for extra pieces. Otherwise, much foamed product is wasted.

Wholesalers of foamed latex ingredients normally sell 5 gallons as a basic lot, but 1-quart sizes of both the three-part latex and the four-part Burman formula are available through RCMA. Some other suppliers will furnish 1-gallon lots. It should be noted that a lot consists of the measured amount of the basic latex material plus all the necessary chemicals for the foaming operation, although they are also available separately from most sources. European users will find a very soft and excellent foam available through Christopher Tucker in England.

The Three-part Foamed Latex

1. Mix Parts A, B, and C thoroughly to be sure there is no material separated and caked on the bottom of the containers.
2. Combine 170 grams (6 ounces, or 3/4 cup) of Part A and 22 grams (1 tablespoon) of Part B in a mixing bowl.
3. Mix with electric mixer to three to six times the original volume, depending on the firmness desired.

FIGURE 5.4 *Mixing foamed latex. (Lab work by Werner Keppler.) (A) Paper cups used to measure ingredients by weight. (B) Beating foam in a kitchen mixer with regular beaters. (C) The latex mix beat to correct volume and refined.*

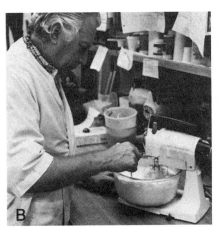

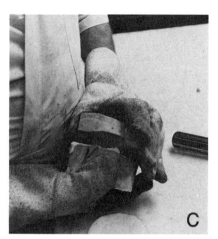

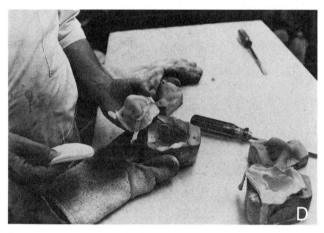

FIGURE 5.5   *A nose mold for foamed latex. (A) Filling the negative with a spoonful of the foam. (B) The positive set on and hand pressure applied. (C) After baking, the mold is separated. Gloves are used to hold*

the still hot mold. (D) The appliance removed. Flash or run-off can be seen. (E) Comparison with a file photo upon which the nose was based for duplication.

4. Add 6 grams (1/2 teaspoon) of Part C, and mix until uniformly mixed (about 1 minute).
5. Pour or inject into your mold and allow to stand undisturbed until gelled. Place in oven and cure (bake) at 200° F for 4 to 5 hours. If the material gels (sets up) too fast, reduce the amount of Part C used gradually until you get the amount of working time you need. Normally it is not desirable to exceed 10 minutes after the addition of Part C.

However, one of the most knowledgeable lab technicians in California, Werner Keppler, who formerly headed the Universal Studio laboratory and is now at TBS in Burbank, has modified and simplified the foaming procedures, making small to large appliances with a minimum of difficulty. He prefers to use the three-part material and makes minor adjustments for each run if need be (Figures 5.5 and 5.6).

Using the regular Mixmaster bowls, Keppler's overall mixing time is 10 minutes, and his measurements are made in plastic cups. One cup of Part A (the latex) in the small bowl is about the minimum, and this will do half a dozen noses, while four cups in the large bowl will suffice for a full head.

His molds are prepared by coating a fully dried out, cool mold with two coats of thinned-out clear lacquer. After this has dried, he coats them with a thin brushing of castor oil and then uses Mold Release prior to use. He also prefers the Kerr Toolstone (about 2 inches thick) with fibre (hemp casting fibre) reinforcement for making his molds.

To prepare for a run, Keppler lays out his molds side by side coated with Mold Release. The foamed ingredients are measured on a scale and poured into the mixing bowl along with a few drops of burnt sienna universal color to make slightly flesh-tinted appliances. If he decides that he wants softer than usual foam, he adds two drops of glycerin per cup of Part A. He then hand mixes the ingredients a bit and places them under the mixer, starting at a slow speed and gradually turning the speed wheel up to the desired one. Timing begins when mixing by machine starts.

With the small bowl, he mixes at a speed of 7 the measured ingredients Part A (latex) and Part B (curing

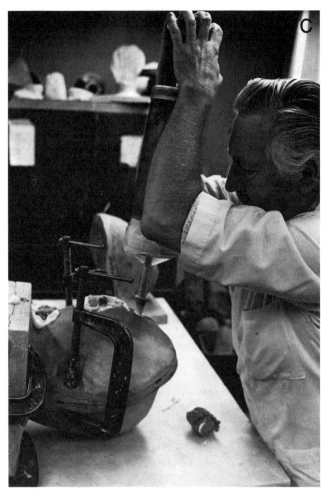

FIGURE 5.6   *A full head mold for foamed latex. (A) Coating the negative with separator. (B) For a large mold with many surfaces, a special gun is filled with the foamed latex mix and injected into a hole drilled into the mold surface for this purpose. This particular mold is a three-piece affair with a front, back, and core all held securely together for casting with large screw clamps. (C) As the mold fills, two exit holes for the excess material are seen. As the foam bubbles through the one closest to the injection hole, it is stopped up with plastalene. The second hole has just been plugged with the clay material before removing the injection gun. (D) The injected molds are placed in the large oven for baking at the proper temperature and timing. (E) The cured appliance is removed from the oven and the front half of the mold opened and powdered. (F) The*

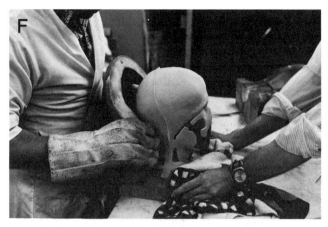

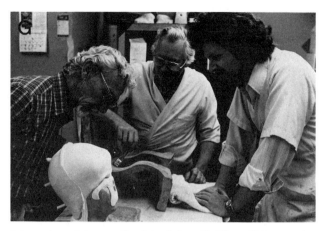

back half of the mold is removed as the latex head remains on the core section of the mold. Note that as the piece is a head and forehead appliance only, the core face portion has been cut away to remove any undercuts. Note also the excess foamed latex that has flowed into the prepared channels away from the front blending edge of the appliance. (G) Leo Lotito, make-up department head of TBS Studios (LEFT), views the completed appliance with Terry Smith (RIGHT), the make-up designer for the production (The Last Star Fighter, Lorimar Productions, 1984). Note also the two approximately half-inch projections that are the injection

point and one of the excess flow holes of the mold. These will be removed, and the hair portion of the appliance will cover them. For a large piece like this, Werner often paints the inside of the mold with a coating of the latex used for the foaming procedure to give a skin to the surface of the appliance. Werner (CENTER) is seen recoating the molds with castor oil prior to allowing them to cool off slowly before another use. Large molds are covered with towels or blankets to slow cooling process. These molds were made of Kerr Toolstone.

agents) and with the large bowl, the speed is 12, for 4 1/2 minutes. He then tests the mix by dipping a kitchen knife into the mass. If the mix does not fall off the blade readily, he estimates that it is ready. He then turns the mixer to speed 1 to refine the foam for 3 1/2 to 4 minutes. He then adds the Part C (gelling agent) and beats for the remaining time (about 1 minute), stirring down to the bottom of the bowl with his knife blade to insure that the gelling agent is thoroughly mixed in. He also hand reverses the motion of the spinning bowl to aid in removing all the excess or large bubbles that might have formed. If the piece is a large one, he often adds the same amount of water to the gelling agent to slow down the gell time.

He then pours into his molds immediately and holds them shut until the excess material gells to the touch. Large molds are filled with an injection gun and are clamped shut during this procedure as they are filled.

Keppler bakes the molds in a 200° F oven for 2½ hours for a small piece and full heads or large molds for 5 1/2 to 6 hours. On completion of bake time, the molds are removed from the oven with welders' gloves and taken apart. Small molds are opened and the piece is left out to air dry, while larger appliances are left on the positive side of the mold after being taken apart and replaced in the oven for about 1/2 hour so that their more extensive surfaces can fully dry out.

He then coats the molds, while hot, with some castor oil with a paint brush and sets them aside to cool off. Large molds are covered with towels to slowly dissipate the heat. The molds must cool off completely before another use.

He fills small holes in a finished foam appliance with a mixture of pure gum latex into which Cabosil

M-5 has been stirred to thicken it. Sometimes, when the head is a large one, he will coat the negative mold surface with a brush coat of Part A before pouring in the foam mixture, especially if the modelling is intricate and detailed on the finished piece. This "skins" the mold and becomes a part of the appliance during the baking.

Some additional notes on the three-part foamed latex are from Dick Smith, who uses it only occasionally since he seems to prefer the four-part latex mix. He does not recommend the use of the castor oil separator but does lacquer-coat his molds and uses a stearic-acid-type mold release. When beating the foam he sets his mixer on the highest speed for about 2 minutes so that the volume of the mix will be increased to about four volumes. Three volumes will make a firm foam, four volumes a soft foam, and five volumes a very soft piece. He then turns the machine down to a speed of about 3 and refines the foam for 3 minutes. This way the volume remains about the same, but the foam cell structure becomes finer.

He measures out the gelling agent with a spoon that has been waxed (the gelling agent won't stick to a waxed surface) or a small receptacle such as a cut-off paper cup that has been coated with a paste wax. A level teaspoon of gelling agent is about 8 grams, which he normally uses. If the foam mixture doesn't gell within 15 minutes after the mix is stopped, it will start to break down and collapse the foam. A good average time is between 5 and 10 minutes for gellation, when the room temperature is in the mid-seventies.

He also mixes his color in the gelling agent, using casein artist tube colors slightly thinned with water. A light flesh tone is provided with a teaspoon of color with 1/4 teaspoon of water for a standard mix (using burnt sienna as the colorant).

Like Keppler, Smith uses a spoon to scoop out the foam from the mixing bowl and pours it carefully into the mold, taking care not to entrap any bubbles. If the negative has deep texture or pits, the foam mix should be poked into these with a pointed wooden modelling tool. Special care should be taken with nose tips.

Smith cautions that too much foam should not be placed in a small mold as it will make it too difficult to press completely closed. He recommends a preheated oven of 210° F. With a mold about 4 inches high, 3 hours' baking time should be sufficient. When the foam is believed to be cured, the mold should be removed from the oven and gently pried open. The foam should be poked in an inconspicuous spot (such as an overflow area). If it stays indented, it is not baked enough. Leave the piece on the positive half of the mold, and return it to the oven for another half-hour. Test it again before removing completely. He also recommends that all molds be wrapped or covered in old bath towels to prevent rapid cooling or cracking.

Foam can be made softer to the touch by adding 3 grams of Nopco 1444-B from Diamond Shamrock Chemical Company to the 22 grams of Part B and then adding it to Part A. If you want to beat to volume 5, also add 10 grams of water to the ingredients before beating.

As one can readily see, foamed latex mixtures can be varied by different technicians to achieve what they consider to be the most efficient or simplest method of use. Certainly there is little contradiction in the methods, and they show the versatility of the material as well as slightly different approaches to achieving the same end result.

Most lab technicians that employ dental or tool stone molds will coat them when hot with castor oil, but this method should not be employed for Ultracal molds as it often leaves the edges of the appliances gummy. Use only the Mold Separator with the latter after the mold has cooled off and before the next use.

The Four-part Foamed Latex

Some basic differences in the three-part and the four-part foamed latex procedures are noted here.

Sponge rubber will cure properly only in a *thoroughly dry* mold. When one mixes gypsum products a large amount of water is used. Some of this water goes into the molecular change when the gypsum sets up, but the rest has to be removed from the mold before it is suitable for molding sponge rubber. Separate the two halves of the mold, and bake at 200° F for 4 to 6 hours if a small mold and from 10 to 12 hours if larger.

Once the mold is dry, it should not be heated above 200° F as the water of crystallization will leave and the mold material will break down. Mold separator should be applied in a *thin* coat to both halves of the dry mold only where the modelling occurred. Do not allow this material to get into the keys. When the mold is thoroughly cold and the separator has dried, the sponge can be poured in.

Room temperature and humidity have a great bearing on the operations and results. With an optimum room temperature of 68 to 72° F, it may be necessary to vary the amount of gelling agent from between 9 and 16 grams to have the foam jell in about 10 minutes.

Using the deluxe model of the Mixmaster with the small bowl, the beater speeds and times should be carefully noted for each batch. (Note that some other kitchen mixer models usually beat too fast at their slowest speeds and so are unsuitable.) As the latex is stabilized with ammonia, the recommended speeds will assure that sufficient remains in the mix so that it will gell with 14 grams of gelling agent. If it is beaten faster or to too high a volume or the temperature of the latex or air is too warm, the mix will gell too fast—even during the mixing process. Conversely, if the latex or air is too cold, 15 minutes of beating time will not remove enough ammonia and the foam will not gell in 30 or more minutes. If, during the final refining process of slow beating, the speed of the beaters is too fast, a nice fine foam cannot result and the mix will set up too fast. Also, with some other beaters that do not fit the contours of the bowl correctly, poor mixing of ingredients will result.

To insure a very slow low speed, one can connect a light dimmer fixture (or studio light dimmer) in series with the Mixmaster. The controls of the Mixmaster are then set at 12 (the highest speed) and all the speeds set up with the dimmer. One must carefully calibrate the dimmer switch with markings to indicate the speeds of 1, 5, and 6 for correct operations. This way, the Mixmaster runs much cooler and quieter, and infinite speed control is possible.

Although the latex is simply stirred carefully to remove any lumps, the three other components—curing agent, foaming agent, and gelling agent—should be thoroughly shaken up just before weighing them; otherwise the heavier ingredients will settle to the bottom while the lighter ones will be poured off first. Thus, the first batch mixed and the last will have the same mix if they are properly shaken. Otherwise the formula will vary considerably—and so will the foaming operation. The four-part latex is considerably thicker than the three-part one, so turning the containers every 2 weeks on the shelf is quite important to avoid settling and extend shelf life.

To prepare the foam mix, pour 12 grams of curing agent into the mixing bowl and add 30 grams of foaming agent and 150 grams of the latex, and mix thoroughly with a rubber spatula. Adjust the beaters so they fit to the sides of the bowl and then:

Begin the mixing and foaming cycle.
1 minute at speed #2 (mixing)
7 minutes at speed #8 (whipping)
4 minutes at speed #4 (refining)
2 minutes at speed #2 (ultra-refining)

Then add 14 grams of gelling agent (shake bottle first!) taking 30 seconds to do so and staying at speed #2. Finally, continue mixing at speed #2 for 1 more minute, turning the bowl back against the beating action to assure a complete mix. This gives a total beating time of 15½ minutes. (Timings are for 70°F.)

The mix can then be poured into the prepared molds. Roll the molds around to cover the necessary surfaces, then slowly set on the other half of the mold and add weights to close it tightly. The remaining foam can be poured on a glass or formica sheet where it should set to a solid mass in 10 to 30 minutes. When you can press it down with a finger and a permanent indentation is formed, you may put the molds in the preheated oven and *bake 5 1/2 hours at 200° F.* When the time has elapsed, the now vulcanized piece can be removed from the molds and the molds put back into the oven to cool slowly. Don't forget to turn the oven off! To prolong the shelf life of the latex, it should be kept as close to 70° F as possible.

Four-part foamed latex formulas, such as GM Foam or Burman Foam, do not recommend the castor oil treatment for the molds. Rather, after the new mold is thoroughly dried out in an oven of about 150° F for four hours (more for larger molds) and allowed to cool, it should be liberally coated on the inside surface with a stearic acid type of *Mold Release* and allowed to set. When dry, the surface should then be carefully whisked dry with a bristle-type brush. Before each use, the surface of the mold should be coated with a thin application of the GM or Burman Mold Release. In general, the mold surface preparation is similar for most four-part systems, as the repeated castor oil application often makes the edges of the finished appliances gummy.

Another suggestion is to add the color directly to the latex, tinting a gallon at a time, and then storing the latex in 1/2-gallon brown glass wide-mouth bottles until ready for use.

Most workers agree that overcuring in an oven of no more than 200° F will neither ruin the appliance nor the mold, but careful watch should still be paid to *all* timings for foamed products. Large-sized batches might require double the beating time—for example, batches that cannot be handled in the large Mixmaster bowl and that require the large restaurant kitchen-type Hobart mixers.

Regarding the injection by gun of large molds, breathing holes or exit holes placed along the line of the injection flow are necessary, and as the foam begins to escape from each successively, they can be plugged with a blob of plastalene until the mold is filled and the material has gelled. These blobs of clay can be removed before the mold is placed in the hot oven.

Carl Fullerton, who often works with Dick Smith, considers the four-part foam to be superior and experiments constantly with it to get better results. In a move to save the molds from calcining due to excessive heat, as well as the shock of going to and from a hot oven, he does not preheat his oven, but turns it on just before putting his filled molds into the oven. In this way, the cold mold goes into a relatively cold oven. He turns the oven up to 200° F, or just under sometimes, and bakes for only 1 to 1 1/2 hours. He then turns off the oven and leaves the mold to cool for about 3 hours. At that time both the oven and the mold should be cooled off. He then takes the mold out and separates it. His theory is that the shorter baking time not only saves the mold but also makes a stronger appliance. Again, personal experimentation will allow the lab technician to devise individual methods and techniques based on the experiences of others as well as researching new ideas.

Some of the main differences between the two systems, the three- and four-part formulas, is the lacquer sealing of the molds for the three-part foam that is not recommended for the four-part method; the amount of beating time—for example, only 10 minutes for the three-part formula and 15½ minutes for the four-part one; the speed recommendations for each; the baking timings; and, of course, the basic chemistry of each formulation. As well, the three-part materials carry a somewhat greater latitude for storage as well as use temperature than the other. Nevertheless, in all cases, the final product is the ultimate criterion, and whichever one the make-up artist decides upon to use, he or she might also be smart to test the other system to have a means of comparison on a particular project. Also, although simplification of any manufacturing process leads to faster and less complicated procedures, the final outcome should not suffer unless the compromise will accomplish the same result.

In this vein, the newer flexible polyurethane foams might be considered. Certainly, with more experimentation and possibly even more improved products, these materials will gain more favor and use by make-up artist technicians as their two-part formula does not require any beating with a machine or baking in an oven as well as the piece being completed in less than an hour from the start of the entire operation.

Repairing and Cleaning Foamed Latex Appliances
When an appliance first comes out of a mold, it may have small defects (especially in a large section or a

full headpiece). These can be repaired by mixing some pure gum latex with Cabosil M-5 (see page 116), or the inside can sometimes be strengthened by brush coating in a thin piece of netting or nylon stocking.

Rips or tears made when the mask or large piece is removed from the performer can sometimes be repaired by using Prosthetic Adhesive A on each side of the tear, drying a few minutes, and then contacting the sides for adhesion to take place. Then both surfaces, inner and outer, can be stippled lightly with some pure gum latex to disguise the line.

Normally, any foamed latex appliance can be cleaned of most adhesives and make-up coloration by immersing it in acetone and squeezing the solvent through the foam. Two baths will normally take out all the color and adhesion, but the piece will shrink. Shrinkage can be somewhat controlled by a method recommended by Dick Smith in which he adds 1 part of light mineral oil to 6 parts of Ivory Liquid or Joy detergent in a bowl large enough to immerse the piece. The liquid should be squeezed through the foam until it is saturated—about 2 minutes. Then rinse out the detergent from the appliance with about 10 to 20 rinses of cold water. The foam should have expanded about 10 percent. If the detergent mix is decreased to about 4 parts with one of mineral oil, this results in about a 20 percent enlargement. The appliance can then be placed in a warm oven to dry. He also states that this procedure is not exact and to make tests before trying it on a valuable appliance. Generally, such methods may be employed when a fresh prosthesis is not available but are not normal practice.

Basic Procedures for Handling Latex Appliances

As both natural and synthetic latices will stick to each other and the edges may curl and be difficult to straighten out, it is standard procedure to powder any appliance before removing it from any mold. This also can be said for plastic caps, plastic molding materials, and the like. RCMA No-Color Powder or unperfumed talc can be used because they will not impart any color to the appliance. Also, when the prosthesis is removed from the mold, it is a good practice to powder the outside or face of it as well as the back.

PLASTIC MATERIALS

Plastics are widely used by make-up lab technicians for a variety of uses and appliances. For such they can be divided into foamed urethanes, solid urethanes, cap materials, molding materials, tooth plastics, special construction plastics, and gelatin materials.

Foamed Urethanes

A number of these products see increasing employment in the lab. The semiflexible types can be used for filling or supporting certain molds or constructions, while

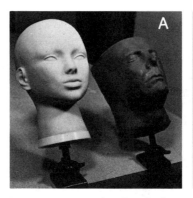

FIGURE 5.7   *Foamed urethane heads. (A) A commercial plastisol full head form* (LEFT) *from a beauty supply firm (RMCA can furnish these) that is suitable for some applications. It fits on a standard adjustable wig block stand that can be clamped to a table top.* (RIGHT:) *The latex filled-with-foam heads made by Werner Keppler for beard laying (see Chapter 3). (B) A self-skinning type of urethane foam head made by Gary Boham with a plastic PVC pipe insert that will also fit on the wig block stand.*

the flexible types can replace some foamed latex applications.

Semiflexible Types

What industrial chemists think is a *flexible* type of urethane may not be quite flexible enough for the make-up artist. *Rigid* urethanes, in the strict sense, are those with little or no flexible qualities, but the semiflexible types do have *flex* to them but might not be as resilient to the touch as what a make-up artist might class the foamed or sponge rubber appliances. There are, however, some new skinlike urethanes with which we will deal later.

One product we might put in the semiflexible class is made by the Hastings Plastics Company and is excellent as a filler product when a slush molded item must be made that will hold its shape. Werner Keppler has made some heads using this technique that are suitable for laying on premade beards (Figure 5.7). Using a face cast in casting plaster, he cut out all the undercuts around the nose and removed part of the

FIGURE 5.8   (opposite page) *Making a foamed urethane face block. (Photos and lab work courtesy Gary Boham.) (A)* (TOP) *The pipe sections are shown.* (MIDDLE) *The elbow covered with fiber glass material.* (BOTTOM) *The finished support with the extended elbow finished to fit a wig block stand. (B) A plywood board with the gasket channels cut and the holes drilled for the support rod and for pouring. (C) The plaster mold sealed to the board with plastalene. (D) RTV 700 flexible mold is made. The keys shown at the sides were made of cut foamed urethane and sealed into the flexible mold with the material. (E) The base of the plaster mother mold must be flat so that it will set straight upon inversion to make the heads. Rigidity is maintained with the particle board box. (F) Placement of the support rod. (G) IASCO two-part self-skinning flexible urethane foam and the flesh colorant material. (H) The mixed foam material is poured into the closed mold. Note the positioning of the clamped pipe support and the stage weights. (I) The foam having set, the mold is opened. (J) The flexible duplicating mold is stripped from the foam head still attached to the board. (K) The foam head pulled away from the board. The finished head can be seen in Figure 5.7(B).*

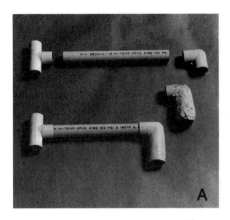

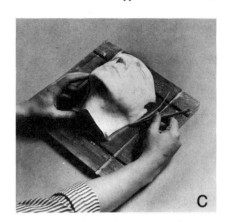

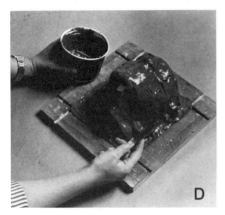

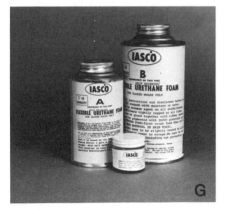

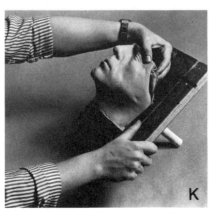

forehead area, only keeping intact the area of the face where the beard normally grows. The ears were also cut down, leaving only an indication so that sideburns can be laid in the correct area. He then made a negative mold of this face in casting plaster about 2 inches thick. Separating the two, he had a negative of the face. Into this he poured a lightly fillered casting latex and let it build up to about 1/8 inch in thickness. He then poured out the latex and *almost* dried the slush piece (so that it would not shrink too much). At this point, he made a mix of the Hathane polyurethane 1640C-54 and filled the cavity. As it foamed up, he laid a silicon-greased board and weight over the top of the mold so that the foam would not spread but be confined. It is necessary to determine exactly how much foam mixture to add as it does expand. Also, the mold must be so made that it has a flat top so that the board can be put on top of it. When the foam has set, the head can be removed and a hole drilled up through the bottom and fitted with a plastic tube so that the form can be set on a head form support. This particular polyurethane comes in a range of densities from 4 pounds per cubic foot to 16 pounds per cubic foot. Many companies make numerous varieties of this type of foaming product (see Appendix B).

Gary Boham makes his beard block as well as full heads for ventilation hair with a flexible self-skinning urethane foam that has a 5-pound density and sets rapidly (Figure 5.8). The support rod is made of 3/4-inch PVC tubing. A T-connector is cemented to one end of the pipe and imbedded in the foam during manufacture of the head. A special elbow joint is made by using a regular PVC joint covered with fibreglass resin. The tapered portion of a wig clamp is covered with masking tape to serve as a release agent and then inserted into the open end of the 90° 3/4-inch elbow joint. A thin layer of fiberglass resin is applied and then wrapped with fiberglass cloth or tape. The continuous-strand type gives slightly more strength than the cloth. After curing, the wig stand can be removed by twisting and pulling and the completed fiberglass connector sanded as necessary.

The head form can be any ear-to-ear cast of a male head of average size that is either cut to shape and flattened on the top and bottom portions to form a block of the desired size. Although the one illustrated in Figure 5.7B does not include the forehead, it is a good idea to do so if the block is to be used to make any eyebrows. Another way is to make a section mold of a face cast using alginate for duplication (if one does not wish to ruin a good original face casting).

A wooden base is made as illustrated in Figure 5.8B with plywood or 3/4-inch particle board that is at least 3 inches longer and wider than the plaster mold. Center the mold on the board and trace its outline. Using a router or table saw, cut gasket channels all around the four sides of the mold, 1 inch away from the widest portions. These channels should be about 1/4 inch wide and 1/4 inch deep. One inch below the center of where the mold will fit on the board, drill a hole about 1/4 inch larger than the outside dimension of the plastic pipe to serve as a support rod for the head form. Then 1 inch up from this hole, drill a 1 1/2-inch hole for pouring in the foam and to allow an exit hole for the excess during the foaming procedure. Seal both sides of the board with two coats of a polyurethane lacquer. Then center the head on the board, and seal down with plastalene.

To make a flexible duplicating mold, a number of products can be used, but the one recommended here is GE's RTV 700 with Beta 2 curing agent (see Appendix B for suppliers). The surface of the original plaster mold should be sealed with lacquer before use in most cases. This is a high elongation and tear strength material with a variety of curing agents available for room temperature use. No heating is required. An amount of 10 parts of base to 1 part of curing agent is recommended, and mixing is done by hand using a spatula or paint stirrer. Avoid rapid stirring so as not to induce bubbles into the mass, and mix for about a minute; then apply to the mold with a spatula. Any bubbles should be broken by passing the spatula over the surface. The pour time is about 1/2 hour and the work time about an hour more. Allow to stand at room temperature until the mass has completely set, but with this curing agent, a minimum of 3 hours is required. Take care that the molding material extends just beyond the gasket channel. A minimum thickness of about 1/4 inch is desirable so add additional layers as required. The edges may be reinforced with gauze to prevent any tearing when removed from the mold. Make certain to shake the curing agent well before mixing it into the base. The finished mold has a Shore A Durometer reading of 30 and an elongation of about 400 percent. Shrinkage for this use is minimal. A three-piece mother mold of plaster is recommended, and it can be confined in a box made of particle board as shown in Figure 5.8E. The flexible mold is stripped from the plaster head, the mother mold is inverted, and the flexible mold is set in. Keys can be made to ensure proper and correct fitting. The wooden portions of the mother mold, the base board, and all tools can be coated with paste wax for a separating medium, as well as the surface of the flexible duplicating mold. Trewax is a good product for this.

The support rod is placed inside the negative flexible mold and passed through the board, which is carefully fitted into the gasket portion of the mold. The correct height of the plastic pipe can be maintained with a spring clamp as shown (Figure 5.8H), lifting it up about an inch from the surface of the flexible mold to be embedded there. Stage weights (wrapped in plastic wrap as a separator) can be employed to hold down the spring clamp and board during the foaming procedure or a clamp arrangement can be devised.

The foam material used was IASCO's two part self-skinning flexible urethane foam using 240 grams of Part B to 80 grams of Part A. This can be tinted with fleshtone plastisol pigment if desired, mixing it into the Part B before adding the Part A. Mixing time is about 20 seconds before the foam will start to rise when the material should be poured into the large hole of the cast. Expansion and exotherm action start immediately, so steady the support pipe and apply some body weight to the mold to aid in weighting it.

The foam will set in about 1 minute, and the mold can be opened in 5 minutes. The flexible mold can be removed and the head stripped from the base board. The excess can be trimmed with a sharp knife or shears. The block can be cleaned with acetone to remove any excess wax, and the special elbow joint can be glued with PVC cement to the end of the pipe support. The length of this pipe support can be varied to suit, but 6 to 8 inches is normally long enough.

With experimentation, full heads, prosthetic arms or legs, and other items can be made with this same self-skinning foam. Imbedding wire forms in it is also possible to govern the position of appendages. A burnt sienna shade of colorant will be found to be useful for most Caucasoid appliances, while Negroid or Oriental skins can be simulated by the addition of a burnt umber or ochre shades, respectively. This foam has excellent solvent resistance for normal usage and is rather easy to use overall.

Flexible Polyurethane Foam

A unique material is made by BJB Enterprises called TC-274 A/B, which is a two-component flexible foam system specifically developed for low density molding, and like most of these polyurethane foams, it is just a matter of mixing A with B, noting how much time is allowed to mix, then how long it takes to foam, and finally, how long the cure time is to complete the project. This particular material has a density range about 3.5 to 4 pounds per cubic foot, but it is very soft. It has a cream time of 90 seconds at 75° F and a cure time of 15 to 20 minutes at room temperature, depending upon part size and cross section. It offers low oral, skin, and eye toxicity; low vapor pressure; and good storage stability. Shelf life is six months at room temperature, but may last considerably longer.

For molding, a regular two-piece mold similar to that employed for sponge rubber is used, although one can make it a trifle heavier to last longer (Figure 5.9). The mold should be prepared by coating it with a polyurethane lacquer to seal the gypsum material. It should then be warmed slightly and coated with BJB Mold Release #86 or RCMA MR-8 (which is a wax

in solvent) two or three times, drying in between coats. A single nose will take about 8 grams of Part B and 2 grams of Part A mixed and then poured into the negative. The positive is then pressed on and the mold clamped for about 20 minutes. Test the overflow foam

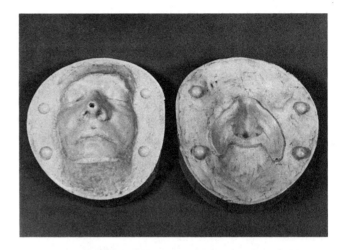

FIGURE 5.9 *Flexible urethane appliance.* TOP: *A two-part mold for making flexible urethane appliances. Note that it is constructed in a heavier form than the normal foamed latex molds for a similar-sized appliance.* MIDDLE: *The male portion of the mold.* BOTTOM *A finished piece showing the fine edges possible with this versatile material.*

with the finger, and keep clamped until the foam is not tacky any longer. The molds can then be separated and the piece removed for immediate use.

Considerable research has been done on this product by Werner Keppler and David Quashnick of California, and some very fine foamed work has been done with it. The Part B can be intrinsically colored with universal colors or RCMA Color Tint Light (1 drop per 10-gram mixture) before mixing. It will be noticed that the manufacturer recommends a 4-to-1 (B to A) mix, while experimentation may prove that a 5-to-1 mix will produce a softer product more suitable for make-up use.

Werner Keppler makes gang nose molds for the TC-274 mix with five different noses (Figure 5.10). It takes a 30-gram B and 6-gram A mixture just to fill the cavities and give sufficient overflow. These appliances can be attached and made up like any other. The TC-274 A/B polyurethane foam material is available from RCMA as is the MR-86 and MR-8 Mold Release.

Solid Polyurethane Elastomers

It is sometimes convenient to make a core mold or an item in a more solid compound that has some elastomeric qualities. BJB makes a multipurpose elastomer

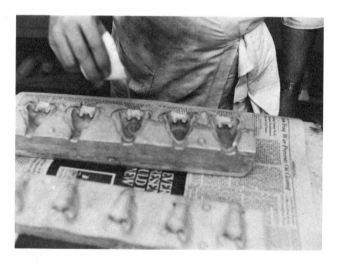

numbered TC-430 A/B that is suitable for a variety of applications (available from RCMA in small quantities). This material has a high tear strength, ability to accept coloration, and being odorless, a high acceptance in the medical prosthetic industry. It can be used to make both positive casts and negative molds, and most thermoset liquid plastics and gypsums can be readily cast in molds of TC-430 A/B.

TC-430 A/B is available in two versions: TC-430 A/B for casting and TC-430 A/B-10 as a brushable grade. The standard versions of these are white, but they also come in clear (which yellows with aging).

Equal weights of the two parts are mixed together and have a work life of 30 minutes at 75° F in a 100-gram mass. Cure time is 24 hours at room temperature and 48 hours for full properties. Heat cure of 200° F only accelerates demold time, which is 4 hours at room temperature and 2 hours at 200° F. Again, good ventilation is recommended during its use and avoid skin contact with the liquid materials.

To increase the hardness, use 60 percent Part A and 40 percent Part B. To make the end product softer, use 40 percent Part A and 60 percent Part B. This will make a difference of ± 10 durometer hardness.

When TC-430 A/B is used to reproduce molds from gypsum or other porous materials, a silicon release #1711 is recommended. Shrinkage is very low and the material has good tensile strength and elongation, plus with a 50/50 ratio mix, the durometer A hardness is 50 to 55. A note about this durometer A reading: This is a means of comparing the relative hardness of a mass with a scale of 0 to 100. Soft, very flexible materials will be 6 to 10, while a stiffer product (such as auto tire) would be 40 to 50 (also see page 93 for further information).

FIGURE 5.10   *A gang mold for noses.* TOP LEFT: *Werner Keppler pours flexible urethane into a gang mold.* BOTTOM LEFT: *The mold is clamped shut. Note the excess coming out of the overflow holes, which were made in the nostril area of the noses.* ABOVE: *The separated mold, showing the noses in a row still in the negative portion of the mold.*

Some general basic notes on urethanes of all varieties will help those who handle these materials. Storage in an area between 70° and 90° F is best. During colder weather the resin should be inspected to assure that there is no crystallization. If the resin appears cloudy or the hardener becomes gummy, the component should be heated to 120° to 160° F and stirred until the material returns to its proper smooth liquid consistency.

Use only metal or plastic mixing containers and spatulas as paper cups and wood stir sticks have been known to contaminate the ingredients as they are porous and can absorb moisture in storage.

Weigh all parts accurately and always mix thoroughly. Polyethylene mixing containers are good because the cured urethane will not adhere to them.

Molds should always be quite dry and made nonporous. A slightly warmed mold is preferred. The sealing process must be done with a material that will withstand the exotherm generated when the urethane cures and must not melt at the peak temperature.

There will be some shrinkage as in all rubber or urethane materials, but this depends greatly upon the thickness (cross section) and configuration of the casting.

Always use any urethane with adequate ventilation, and avoid skin contact with the uncured ingredients. Protective barrier creams are recommended for the hands, and brushes and equipment may be cleaned with MEK if the solid urethanes are being mixed and have not hardened. General cleaning can be done with soap and water or a 1-to-1 mixture of toluene and isopropyl alcohol.

RCMA can furnish 8-ounce quantities of both foamed and solid urethane materials for laboratory work.

Cap Material

Bald front wigs and fully bald head appliances have been made with a number of materials and in a variety of ways, but the only really good bald cap material is made from a vinyl resin of the Union Carbide Corporation called VYNS. There are a number of formulas in use employing MEK or acetone (or a mixture of the two) as a solvent plus a plasticizer to control the degree of desired softness. A basic formulation is 25 grams of VYNS to 75 grams of MEK and adding 10 to 25 grams of plasticizer.

There are many plasticizers on the market, among them, dibutylphathalate (DBP) and dioctylphathalate (DOP). The Monsanto Company also makes a series of plasticizers called *Santicizers,* and their #160 is used where DBP is called for and #711 for DOP. The DOP will retain the soft quality of a cap material and be less affected by ultraviolet than DBP.

After dissolving all the solid in the liquids, cap material can be tinted by using some of the RCMA PB Foundation shaken in. To make a bald cap one

requires a positive mold made from plaster, stone, metal, or even fiberglass. One of the production methods to make thin caps is to spray the cap material with a Pasche L head airbrush with a medium (#3) nozzle. John Chambers sprays about five heads at a time, one after the other, with about six coats of spray. In this way, the first head sprayed will have just about set when the second coating is applied after spraying head number 5 in the sequence. Careful guiding of the spray, plus a rather rough final coating spray is best as the caps, when removed from the molds, will not be reversed. As such, head forms for spraying are made quite smooth for ease in removal of the plastic cap from the form.

A more tedious method, but one that allows full control over the thinness of the blending edge wherever one wants it and a heavier weight of material on the hairline or the pate, is done by painting the plastic cap material on a head form that has a slight pore effect on the surface. When completed, this cap will be reversed to show this pored surface.

The best way to make caps is to have a ventilated spray hood for either the spraying or the painting due to the fumes of the solvents. Otherwise, this operation should be carried out in the open air on a calm day or with a fan blowing the fumes out a window. The cap plastic can be brushed on with a 2 1/2-inch oxhair or sable hair brush in a flowing manner rather than brushed back and forth the way one would paint. The brush should always be well wet with material as it will evaporate very rapidly. Most metal molds do not require any separating medium, but others should be lightly rubbed with a silicon mold release and wiped almost dry for ease in separation. Head molds can be lightly marked in pencil in the general shape of the hairline so that a reference point is available when graduating the coats to make a fine blending edge on the cap.

For a full, regular thickness cap, brush on 5 coats over the entire head form. Then brush on 25 coats just up to the hairline marking, graduating the coats to form a thin edge. Finish off with a few more coats over the entire head. Coats should take about 10 minutes to dry between each one, so again, doing a number of heads one after the other will save overall time.

Always remove any stray hairs immediately if they fall out of the brush while painting the cap on the mold. A small sable brush is best for this operation. The same precautions about dust and dirt in the air should be observed about painting caps as with any fine varnish or lacquer. Never sweep the room or in other ways disturb any settled dust while caps are being sprayed or painted as dirt specks will ruin the caps.

Allow the cap to remain on the mold overnight to air cure. Caps can also be cured and much shrinkage prevented by placing the finished cap on the mold in an oven at 150° F for 5 minutes.

To remove the cap from the mold, cut a line with a sharp knife or razor blade around the base of the head mold through the plastic material, and carefully strip the cap from the mold. To prevent edge turnover or the cap sticking to itself, a good powdering before removing the cap from the mold and on the other side after removal is best (No-Color powder is good for this). Some very shiny (chrome-plated metal) molds need only the edge to be started and then the cap can be easily rolled off.

Another way of making a partial bald cap is to use a try-on cap on the performer and carefully mark out the hairline that must be covered and where the hairpiece is to be added on top of the bald cap area. As the cap will be made quite heavy, it is often not necessary to make a blending edge in the back of the neck area as it will not be adhered there. The top or pate area can be made quite heavy with 45 to 60 coats, depending upon the desired weight. Also, when the cap is made for one particular performer, the edge can be painted with a finely graduated painting that becomes heavier and thicker more quickly than on a stock cap.

Cap material can also be used to make thin sections that will be used to cover eyebrows. Generally these can be made by painting cap material on a flat plate and building edges and sufficient weight for covering the hairs. Some brows will require heavier buildups than others to cover the coarse hairs.

Clear cap material is also employed by some sculptors to cover their plastalene modelling. Additional sculpture can still be done over the coating, or fine lines can be refined (see page 77). RCMA supplies two grades of cap material: one tinted for cap use and the other clear for sculpture. It is fast drying and can be thinned with acetone if it thickens during use. For a slower set, thin with MEK.

Molding Plastics

Molding plastics can be divided into two categories: those that are simply painted into a negative mold in layers to form a piece and those that are pressure molded in a two-piece mold.

Paint-in Plastic Molding Material

RCMA furnishes a Molding Material in Light (KW shade), Deep (KM shade), and Dark (KN shade) that can be painted into a negative mold in successive coats to build an appliance. This Molding Material also is available in a thicker, quicker drying form in a tube under the name of Scar or Blister Making Material by RCMA. Essentially, they are methacrylates in a solvent with plasticizer and are excellent for temporary appliances. Due to the manner in which they are made and the basic qualities of the material, appliances should be produced only a day or so before use. Otherwise there is a tendency (of all such molded plastics) to lose

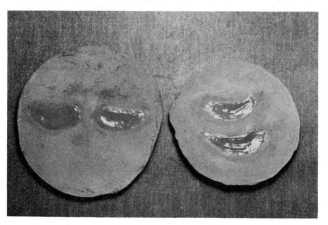

FIGURE 5.11   *Plastic molding material.* TOP: (LEFT) *A set of eyebags sculpted in plastalene on a plaster flat plate.* (MIDDLE AND RIGHT) *Finished plastic molding material appliances.* BOTTOM: *The appliances painted into mold before powdering and removal.*

some of the sculptured surface during long storage periods. However, appliances made with this material are soft and flexible and are easily adhered to the skin with Prosthetic Adhesive A. (Formulas for similar materials can be found on page 111.)

Negative molds should be coated with RCMA Silicon Mold Release or silicon grease before use, taking care not to brush too much into the fine sculpturing. This type of material is especially good to make eyebags when time and budget do not allow foamed ones to be made. The liquid Molding Material should be put in a small wide mouth jar with an easily cleaned stopper or cap and thinned out a bit with acetone. Make certain that you stir the stock bottle to disperse all the coloration that might have settled to the bottom during storage.

Eyebags can be sculpted on a flat plate and a negative mold of stone or Ultracal 30 made (Figure 5.11). After the silicon separator has been applied, give the bags (don't overpaint for a blending edge) 10 coats of the thinned-out Molding Material, allowing them to air dry (don't use the hair dryer as it will bubble the material) between coats. Slightly heavier coats can then be applied as the cavity of the sculpted eyebags begins to fill up. Dry between coats. Finally, lay in a heavy

Latex and Plastic Appliances 111

coat of material so that the level of the eyebag is built up higher than the mold surface, and set aside to dry overnight. As the solvent evaporates completely, the level of the built-up portion will shrink down to slightly below the surface level of the mold so the appliance can be attached flat to the skin. To remove, powder the surface and tease an edge up with a sharp tool and then peel out the appliance. It is then ready for immediate use.

This material can also be used to make interesting forehead pieces for gunshot wounds, veins that pulsate, and such. For example, for a gunshot wound, take a negative cast of the forehead area in salt-accelerated casting plaster (Figure 5.12). The surface can be sealed with the RCMA Silicon Mold Release agent and the coatings built up by brushing the Molding Material into the form to cover the entire forehead area, making a good blending edge just above the eyebrows and at the point where the nose meets the forehead, as well as all around the hairline edge. The thickness of the appliance can be increased near the center of the hairline where either the performer's own hair or a small hairpiece will cover this edge.

After painting on about 15 coats of thinned Molding Material, a small-diameter polyethylene plastic tube can be imbedded with its end about in the middle of the forehead. This tubing should be about 4 feet long so that the other end will be off camera with a blood syringe attached. Hold the tube in position and carefully paint in a few coats of material to imbed it into the surface of the appliance. Adhesive tape can be used to position and hold the tubing where you want it to stay. Then add more coatings of the Molding Material

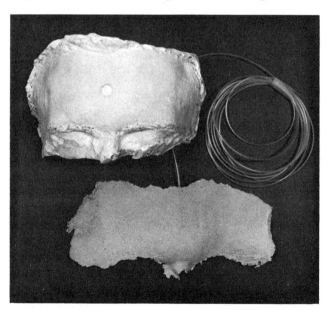

FIGURE 5.12 TOP: *A plaster cast of a forehead with a bullet hole cut into the center to show where the tubing must end.* BOTTOM: *After painting into a negative mold, an appliance with a tube imbedded into the material. The hole is cut with a sharpened metal tube and the plug saved for later insertion.*

over that to fully seal and cover the tubing, graduating the coatings away from the tubing so that it won't be seen as a bulge when the appliance is attached to the face. Thicker coats can be applied until the desired amount is reached.

Let the appliance dry on the mold overnight, and strip it off, taking care that the tube remains firmly imbedded in the appliance. Always select a color of Molding Material that will be closest to the skin coloration of the performer so that little foundation will be required for coverage. Next, with a sharp, round punch, about the size of the bullet hole, cut out a circle *just* below the end of the imbedded tube. The hole in the tube can then be cleared with a sharp instrument. A needle about the tube size can be imbedded in a wooden dowel point first. The protruding head portion makes a good tool for this. Save the cutout portion of the plastic as this will be used as a plug. Attached to a length of clear filament, this plug can be pulled out as part of the bullet-hit sequence before the blood flows through the tubing.

Dick Smith has imbedded removable strips cut in the shape of veins in this material and, in use, filled the spaces with a fluctuating air stream to simulate the pulsation of forehead veins. Small bruises, cuts, scars, moles, burn tissue, and many other marks can be made similarly with this type of Plastic Molding Material. One of the main advantages of the Molding Material is that its blending edges are soluble in acetone. Thus, it can be washed in to be imperceptible.

Press Molding Material

This is a polyvinyl butyral plastic that is employed to make appliances with a method devised by Gustaf Norin a number of years ago. Although it is employed relatively seldom, the procedure is an interesting one that produces an appliance whose edges are soluble in isopropyl alcohol (Figure 5.13).

The original formulation consists of 4 1/2 *fluid* ounces (by measure) of Vinylite XYSG (a white powder, polyvinyl butyral) dissolved in 32 fluid ounces of isopropyl alcohol. Then add a plasticizer mixture of 25 cubic centimeters (cc) castor oil, 25 cc DBP, and 50 cc isopropyl alcohol. If a harder appliance is desired, use 10 cc castor oil, 10 cc DBP, and 25 cc alcohol. Mix well and keep tightly capped until use.

To prepare the plastic for molding, pour some of the compound into clean, cold water, and with clean, well-scrubbed hands knead the then coagulated mass until it stiffens into a ball (Figure 5.14). This squeezing will press out all the solvent alcohol into the water and should take about 3 minutes (for a piece large enough to form a nose). Remove the plastic from the water and it will now be a semitranslucent white mass. Stretch a clean, lintless dish towel, often called a *huck towel,* over the knee, and carefully roll the plastic back and forth for about 15 minutes to dry out all the water from it. It is important that, when ready to color and place in the mold, no water content remains in the plastic as this will cause shrinkage.

When the mass is dry to the touch, dip the roll of material into some dry calcium carbonate to give it some opacity, and knead this well into the material. A slight coloration can be imparted by rubbing the material lightly on a cake of a pale shade of dry cheek-color and kneading the color into the material. To hasten the drying out period, a stream of warm air from a hand-held hair dryer may be used, taking care that the material does not stick to the fingers due to the heat. It is well to keep dipping the fingers into No-Color Powder to prevent sticking during this part of the operation. Do any coloration gradually, a bit at a time, and do not color deeply as the plastic has a propensity to deepen in shade as it cures and, again, a pale shade is easier to cover with make-up than a dark one.

The material is now ready to place in the mold, which is a pressure type made of dental stone (see page 201 for pressure-type molds). Grease the female side with petroleum jelly, and *lightly* wipe the male side with the same separating medium. Place the material on the negative female side, spreading it out into the general shape of the desired prosthesis, and put the two sides of the mold carefully together. Place about 200 pounds of pressure on the mold for about 15 minutes. Large sections may require up to 400 pounds of pressure to get a fine blending edge and correct construction of the material. Twenty-five-pound iron stage weights are very good for applying this pressure. Build them up by crossing two over two at right angles

FIGURE 5.14   *Press molding.* TOP LEFT: *Plastic poured into water and coagulated.* TOP RIGHT: *Opacity and color kneaded into plastic.* BOTTOM LEFT: *Stage weights used for pressure on mold.* BOTTOM RIGHT: *Finished appliance on the male side of the mold after pressing and trimming edges.*

until the correct weight is achieved. Sitting on the built-up weight platform will increase the pressure if necessary.

After the required pressing time, remove the weights and open the mold carefully. The negative side, which was greased, should release quite easily and leave the completed prosthesis on the positive male side. If the appliance is well made with no bubbles or defects, let it stand overnight on the open mold. However, if the appliance has defects such as thick edges or lack of completeness, add a bit more molding material where necessary and repress the material for about 10 minutes. Separate and check once more. If perfect, leave the mold open overnight, but if still defective, repair in the same manner. Sometimes rearranging or replacing the material is necessary to get a perfect pressing.

The prosthesis can be removed from the mold the next day by lightly brushing under the edge of the appliance with a small flat brush covered in No-Color Powder or very fine talc. Then the overflow excess plastic material that forms in the gutters during the pressing can be cut away from the appliance, leaving just enough of the thin blending edge to adhere the appliance to the skin. This blending edge can be thinned out to a very fine edge against the positive mold with a flat sable brush that has been dipped in isopropyl alcohol. It is best to keep the appliance on the male mold or another positive cast of the same until ready

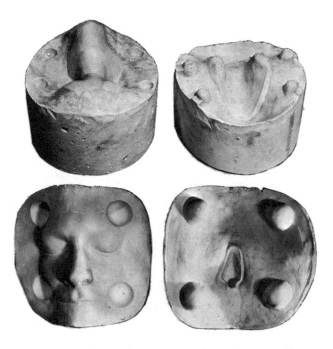

FIGURE 5.13   *Comparative casts.* TOP: *A foamed latex nose mold.* BOTTOM: *A pressure casting or foamed urethane sized mold.*

for use. It is also a good idea to make up plaster duplicates of the male side of the mold for this purpose so as to leave the actual mold free to do another pressing if necessary.

To adhere this type of appliance to the skin, cover the area where the prosthesis is to be placed with a coating of the liquid plastic molding compound and dry thoroughly. Powder this area with No-Color Powder, and center the appliance in place. With a small brush carefully touch under the appliance with isopropyl alcohol. This will immediately dissolve the appliance into the adhesive coat of molding compound, attaching the prosthesis firmly to the skin. Carefully wash the edges of the appliance into the skin with the alcohol, and powder the appliance and the edges with No-Color Powder or very fine talc. Do not use the so-called translucent or neutral powders for this type of appliance as these powders do have color and fillers that will affect the coloration of the piece. Extrinsic coloration can be done with a high-pigment creme-type foundation like RCMA Color Process Foundations or similar types.

Tooth Plastics

Dental acrylic resins of methyl or ethyl methacrylates are supplied as a *monomer,* a colorless liquid, and a *polymer,* a fine powder that comes in a number of shades. For additional coloration, there are liquid stains that can be painted over any finished denture material.

When the monomer and the polymer are mixed together, the polymer is partially dissolved so that the mixture becomes a doughlike plastic mass. The monomer in the mixture is then polymerized to form the solid acrylic resin. Two types of acrylic resins are used by dental technicians and dentists. In one, the polymerization is activated by heating the mixture, and in the other, polymerization is activated chemically. The latter type is self-curing and is generally the variety employed by make-up lab technicians for teeth. One of the best textbooks on oral anatomy and techniques, titled *Dental Technician, Prosthetic* (1965), is published for training prosthetic dental technicians in the U.S. Navy and is available through the U.S. Government Printing Office (NAVPERS 10685-C).

The Lang Company makes a number of materials for dental use that can be adapted by make-up lab technicians:

Jet Tooth Shade Acrylic   A very fast-setting, self-curing powder and liquid combination available in shades 59, 60, 61, 62, 65, 66, 67, 68, 69, 77, 81, 87, and Light and Dark Incisal.

Jet Denture Repair Acrylic   Strong and fast setting, this self-curing acrylic is colorfast in Pink, Fibred Pink, Translux, and Clear and is used for simulating gum tissue.

Colored Jet Acrylic   Self-curing resins that set hard in less than 10 minutes. Available in colored powders with clear liquid monomer or with clear powder and colored liquids. Tans, greens, reds, blues, yellows, violet, and black are available in sets.

Flexacryl-Soft Rebase Acrylic   An ethyl methacrylate formulation that is plasticized to remain resilient in a cushionlike consistency for a number of months. This material is nonirritating and dimensionally stable.

Warm weather and humidity will affect these self-curing polymers during mixing. Working time can be extended with chilled mixing containers for large batches.

In most cases, the polymer powder is wetted with the monomer to make the casting. Many workers coat the negative cast with a brushing of monomer and then add a bit of powder to start, then drop powder and liquid a bit at a time to form the mass. As long as it appears glossy, it can be worked and brushed into a form.

To make teeth, one can employ a number of techniques. Each one is a bit different and more designed for make-up use than regular dental application. The simplest way to make flat-form teeth for imbedding in gum material is to fill preformed plastic crown forms with tooth shade acrylic and allow them to set. Odd-shaped or special teeth can be made by spatulating additional material on these formed teeth. One can also obtain various preformed teeth from supply houses that serve dentists to identify tooth shades and shapes. Sometimes dentists have a set of discontinued artificial teeth that they will give you if you ask for them.

One method is described by Lee Baygan in his book on prostheses for make-up, *The Techniques of Three-Dimensional Make-up* (Watson Guptill, 1982), where he sculpts the desired teeth in plastalene on the positive dental stone cast. Using petroleum jelly as a separator on the gypsum portion of the cast, he takes a negative of the sculpted teeth in alginate in the dental tray. When the alginate is set, he removes it and, since the next step may take some time, immerses the alginate negative in water to prevent any shrinkage due to air drying. The plastalene is removed from the positive (or negative if any becomes imbedded), and the positive is given a coating of petroleum jelly. The negative is then removed from the water and the surface quickly dried (don't use heat). Self-curing tooth shade acrylic polymer powder is added to the tooth cavities. The liquid monomer is added with an eyedropper, and the mass is mixed with a small narrow tool. Adding a bit of each at a time will fill the teeth and allow some extra for flash over the gums (which he has allowed for in the plastalene modeling). The positive is then placed carefully over the negative and the two pressed together and held for a minute or two until set. Put aside and let the acrylic fully harden for about 30 minutes.

The two sides can then be separated and the teeth pried from the positive cast. The casting of the teeth is then trimmed with a Mototool and polished so that no rough edges are felt. The teeth may be colored (or discolored) with acrylics and then given a coat of 5-minute epoxy. This can be yellowed for some effects. The epoxy will gloss the teeth to a natural shine. Baygan then recommends that a bit of flesh pink be added to an epoxy mix and painted on the gum section of the acrylic to simulate the gums.

Tom Savini's *Grande Illusions* (1983) on special make-up effects shows a method of making a set of vampire teeth by building up a wax covering over the teeth in the stone cast and then imbedding some artificial teeth into this wax in front of the teeth on the cast. He also makes some long incisors by mixing the polymer-monomer into a heavy paste and, wearing surgical gloves, rolls the material to get the shape of the desired tooth. Filing and grinding produce the finished teeth. Using a medicine dropper, monomer is used to wet the area above the teeth, and some pink gum shade polymer powder is sprinkled on. The process is repeated until the proper amount is built up to surround the teeth in front. The wax is removed after the acrylic is set (about 10 minutes), and the back of the teeth are treated in the same manner to form around them. Small dental tools can be used to sculpt around the gums and teeth.

When the material is set, it can be removed from the positive form, and you will have a dental plate that fits directly over the subject's own teeth. They can be finished with acrylic lacquer if need be to restore the shine. Dental powder or cream can be used to hold the teeth in for use in the mouth.

If someone has teeth with a space between, a set of snap-on tooth caps can be made by making a cast of the front teeth and then imbedding them in a heavy stone-reinforced mold or a dentist's flask (Figures 5.15 and 5.16). Make a mix of the proper tooth shade, and after coating the positive side with an alginate release agent, put on a layer of the mix and place a sheet of cellophane separator on top of the plastic. Close the mold and put it in a dental press for a minute or two. Remove the mold from the press, separate the two halves, lift the cellophane separator sheet, and using light pressure, with a sharp scalpel trim off the excess flash material from the appliance, then repress the appliance in the mold press for a minute or so. Repeat this until no excess is extruded from the prosthesis. Replace the cellophane sheet with a new one each time a repress is made. When the appliance is complete and perfect, leave the mold halves separated until the material sets. Then ease the appliance off the positive cast and clean and polish it with burrs, abrasive paper discs, rubber cups, and felt wheels (with a paste of chalk or

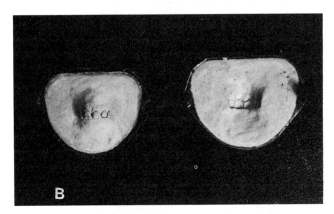

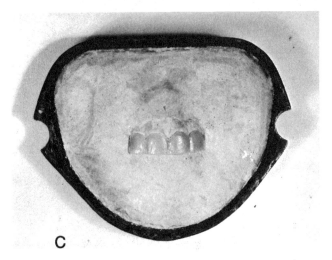

FIGURE 5.15   *Tooth caps. (A) Flasked male mold of actual teeth. (B) Male and female mold before pressing. (C) The finished caps on the male mold.*

tin oxide and water) in that order. These very thin caps should then clip on to the real teeth and look perfectly natural. By the way, they are not made for eating and are rather fragile, so keep them in a small plastic box when not in use.

Variations of these methods include sculpting the teeth in an inlay wax material rather than in plastalene or using a Flexacryl-Soft Rebase Acrylic for making the pink gum material for teeth, which may be easier on the wearer. Colored acrylics can be used to make teeth of any shade for certain effects, while the Flexacryl-Soft material can be used alone to make an appliance that would cover all the teeth for a toothless gum effect.

It is not a good idea to apply any of the polymer-monomer mixture directly into the mouth to form teeth as it may firmly attach itself to the subject's teeth. Work only from a tooth cast, and always trim the finished plate so that the performer's speech will not be impaired—unless that is the desired effect. If too much acrylic is formed on the inside portion of a tooth prosthesis, it may produce lispy speech patterns.

Special Construction Plastics

Certain special effects require construction plastics such as epoxies, fiberglass, polyester resins, and other such industrial materials often employed by auto repair shops (see page 44). Most of these are rigid materials although some technicians are also using the flexible urethanes and polysulfide products as well. None of these is for application to the skin, and they represent mostly substances that are being adapted to make the dummies, figures, puppets, and simulations of humans or animals that are usually mechanically operated that serve to replace a living thing to achieve situations that might either be physically impossible or that might prove to be dangerous to a living person or animal.

Sometimes these materials are used as part of an overall make-up effect and the finished piece attached to the body. See Tom Burman's special make-up on page 121. In general, the special construction plastics and other materials serve as a stimulation to new make-up effects, and in the future, more industrial products designed for other uses will find their way into the laboratories of the creative lab technician/make-up artist.

Again, great care should be taken with researching not only the finished qualities and restrictions that might affect the human skin on all these products but also whether or not any dangers exist in the use of the raw materials to laboratory personnel. None of these materials is classified for cosmetic use so great care should be taken whenever their use is contemplated. Also see the section "Duplicating Materials" earlier in this chapter.

One use of two-part epoxy is for glossing over latex or plastics to make false eyes. One method is to paint ping-pong balls with artist's enamels in the shape and color of eyes and then giving them a coating of the epoxy. This material comes in a handy two-barrelled ejector type of dispenser that can be purchased in hardware stores. This fast-drying epoxy can also be used to put a gloss on teeth in latex masks.

Polyester resin used by auto repair shops with fibre-glass cloth comes with a can of resin and a tube of curing agent plus some open fibre or mesh cloth to soak into the compounded resin. Also available from the same source are the filled polyester resins that are used as auto body fillers. Both types set hard and can be worked with files and sandpaper to make various constructions.

Gelatin Materials

In addition to synthetic processed materials, one can also include animal gelatin for the manufacture of special constructions (see page 34). A basic formula recommended by Tom Burman is as follows:

20 grams of gelatin powder,
12 cc of distilled water,
100 cc of glycerin.

Set this mixture aside to saturate for 45 minutes. First, heat to 140° F in a water bath to melt the mass, then pour into a plastic bag (Ziplok type) and flatten out to cool. For use, this gelatin compound can be made opaque with talc and titanium dioxide, and water-soluble vegetable colors can be used for various shades. Dry colors could also be ground into the dry mixture of talc and titanium dioxide, while kaolin can be used as a filler if required. Tom Burman uses this formula gelatin with a red coloration for blood effects for certain projects. Nonmetallic powders were incorporated into

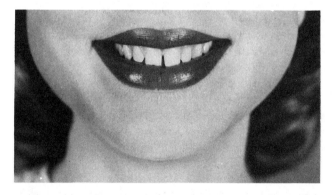

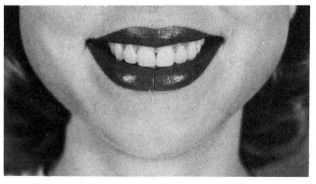

FIGURE 5.16 *Tooth caps.* TOP: *The natural teeth without caps.* BOTTOM: *Appearance after adding temporary caps. Bonding can produce the same effect on a more permanent basis.*

the gelatin mix by Stan Winston for his robot make-ups.

Softer constructions can be made with 15 grams of gelatin and 25 grams for harder ones in the given formulation. Another formula calls for 50 cc of Sorbitol and 50 cc of glycerin with 1 gram of salicylic acid as a preservative or a few drops of oil of wintergreen.

The molds used are similar to any type of pressure mold that is well greased with petroleum jelly as a separating medium. In use, the gelatin material is melted, fillered, and colored and then poured into the negative, or female, mold. The positive is then placed on and weights or clamps applied to hold the molds together. When the material is cold, the molds are separated and the appliance powdered and removed.

ADHERING APPLIANCES

Books on make-up seldom stress the importance of selecting the proper adhesive to keep the appliances firmly attached to the skin or one material to another so that the overall effect is never destroyed by an appliance, hairpiece, or other special material coming loose. Oftentimes, re-attachment takes more time and clean up than the time that should have been taken to attach the item properly in the first place. No matter how well the molds were made and the appliances formed, if they are not properly adhered, the entire effect is lost.

There are many varied adhesives used for make-up work, some very versatile and others very specific in use. The directions for use must be accurately followed. Certainly new adhesives will be found in the future, and make-up personnel should research and experiment with any new ideas they come across. However, take care with any adhesive that it can be *removed* from the skin before using it for any make-up purposes or application of hair goods. Some of the fast-drying super-glues used for pottery, metal, and other materials (such as Cyanoacrylate types) should *never* be used on the skin because they are very difficult to remove. Therefore, a good adhesive should be easy to apply, set rapidly, be dilutable for use, and be removable with a solvent that is not harmful to the skin. In addition, the adhesive should be a proper one for sticking one surface to another without adversely affecting either one. Finally, never use any adhesive on the skin without testing it first—preferably on yourself—and if any adhesive causes any skin irritation on a performer, discontinue its use and seek another for the job.

Matting and Thixotropic Agents

Many materials, among them adhesives and sealers, can be made to set with less shine or be made thicker for certain applications by the addition of special clays or earths or with microsilicas that are made in many grades and particle sizes. The Cabot Corporation makes a number of grades of Cab-o-sil, which is a fumed silicon dioxide used to increase solution viscosity. They also will reduce sheen but do not produce a truly flat or matte effect as will some of the larger-particle silicon dioxide types. Cab-o-sil, like all the others of this type, is a very fine white powder that is quite light in weight. M-5 is the lightest weight grade (2.3 pounds per cubic foot) that the make-up technician might employ, and it can be dispersed in a solution under low rates of shear. The MS-7 (4.5 pounds per cubic foot) is almost twice as heavy and is best dispersed with high shear equipment. Both will thicken many liquids (such as latices or resin gum solutions) by forming a network of particles. A nonionic surfactant such as Triton X-100 (Rohm and Haas Co.) can be added (0.5 percent) to further thicken some solutions. The nominal particle size of Cab-o-sil is 0.014 microns, and it can be used in combination with larger-particle silicon dioxides to promote suspension and reduce hard settling. A variety of this material is the processed silica like Tullanox, which makes the product superhydrophobic.

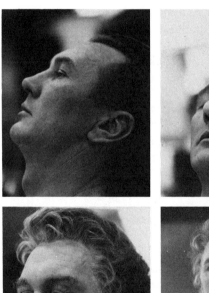

FIGURE 5.17 *Application of small appliances.* TOP LEFT: *Kenneth Smith before make-up for the NBC production of* War and Peace *in which he played General Kutuzov.* TOP RIGHT: *A foamed latex nose is attached with Matte Plasticized Adhesive as is a slush molded blind eye appliance.* BOTTOM LEFT: *A scar is added on the cheek with scar material along with a wig and sideburns, and the eyebrows are grayed with some hair added as well.* BOTTOM RIGHT: *The completed make-up as designed by Dick Smith and applied for the production by the author.*

The larger-particle Syloids (Grace Chemical) or De-gussa's TS-100 have more matting effect. Syloid 244 (4 pounds per cubic foot) has an average particle size of 3.3 microns diameter but can settle out of solution—even after dispersal by high shear—unless suspenders are added to the mix. TS-100 varies in particle size from 2 to 10 microns with an average value of 4 microns in diameter. Its particular quality is that it can be added to a solution under low shear and will increase in thickening effect at about the same rate that the flattening resultant increases. For example, 1 ounce of a basic resin adhesive can be matted with 1 gram of TS-100 to produce an adhesive that can be finger tacked to remove the shine, while 2 grams of TS-100 will produce a gell that dries matte without tacking.

Clays such as kaolin and the Attapulgus varieties of AT-40 or Pharmosorb produce a flattening if added to resin adhesives, but although they do settle out readily, they are easily shaken back into solution. However, an excess of the latter has a tendency to whiten or gray upon full drying after application. It takes almost 3 teaspoonsful of Pharmosorb in 1 ounce of resin adhesive to give an adequate matting effect but, unlike some of the silicas, does little to add to the adhesive quality of a resin gum solution. Also see pages 14 and 15 for further explanations of the use of matting materials in RCMA adhesives and sealers.

General Applications

Most appliances, slush or paint-in latex, foamed latex or foamed urethanes can be attached with Matte Plasticized Adhesive. This type of adhesive is a Matte Adhesive with special plasticizers added to provide an adherent that sets with more tack and does not crystallize like ordinary spirit gums.

With small prostheses, apply a coat of the adhesive to the edge of the appliance, and allow some of the solvent to evaporate (Figure 5.17). Then carefully place the appliance on the desired area and press into place. Take care that adhesive is painted on the blending edge but not over it. If some of the adhesive is left on the surrounding skin, carefully remove it with a Q-Tip lightly dipped in alcohol. Never paint over the edge of an appliance with adhesive after it has been adhered to seal the edge as this excess adhesive will darken with the application of any foundation. Instead, to seal the edge, use a material that will seal but not discolor. Some make-up artists use RCMA Matte Plastic Sealer, while others prefer a latex-type eyelash adhesive. Either one of these products can be lightly stippled on with a small section of stipple sponge held in a pair of curved dental college pliers. Before using an edge sealer, check that the appliance is fully attached right to the edge. If there are any loose spots, lift the appliance with the college pliers, carefully brush

a touch of adhesive under the edge, and press down the appliance to the skin with a damp huck towel.

Some make-up artists prefer to attach the pieces with eyelash adhesive and to stipple over the entire surface of foam appliances with the same adhesive to seal the surface. Others use Prosthetic Adhesive A or B. These are contact-type adhesives and so both surfaces, the skin, and the appliance must be coated. As neither one of these adhesives fully dries to the touch, it should be lightly powdered with No-Color Powder on the surface of the adhesive coatings before centering the piece on the skin, then pressed in to complete the adhesion.

On a large piece, many artists adhere only the center portion of the appliance by coating just the skin area, leaving about half an inch of blending edge adhesive free. A brush with a small amount of adhesive is then passed under the edges, and the piece is pressed in to the face or body part with a damp towel. Take care that the blending edges of the appliance do not roll over to form a visible demarcation to the surrounding skin area. Such folds can be eased out with a brush dipped in alcohol and re-adhered if Matte Plasticized Adhesive is used.

Coloration may be done with any RCMA Color Process Foundation that has been slightly thinned with Foundation Thinner, or any shade of RCMA AF Foundation may be used. Some of the latter are heavier and stickier than others, but all are designed to give a heavy cover to both the skin and the appliances. Both the polyurethane sponge and brushes can be used for application and then the surface powdered with either PB Powder for a matte effect or No-Color Powder for one with more halation. The latter does not absorb the oils in the PB Foundations as well as the PB Powder, however. If the surface appears too dry, appliances can be overstippled with a bit of glycerin or RCMA Tears and Perspiration to restore some surface shine without affecting the foundation. Some make-up artists make a mixture of glycerin and a bit of isopropyl alcohol for a thinner mix for the stippling.

Foamed urethane appliances can be attached in the same manner, but if the outer skin of the foam is porous, it can be coated with RCMA Matte Plastic Sealer before applying the foundation. Either Color Process Foundation, AF, or PB Foundations will work over this type of appliance; liquid or water-based cake foundation does not. RCMA also makes a very flexible acrylic-base foundation called Acrylid, specially compounded for use with foamed latex or flexible urethane foam appliances in a number of basic colors (AP series).

Latex and Plastic Bald Caps

Latex bald caps are employed solely for mob scenes or extra work but are still effective except for close shots. Films on American Indians in the eighteenth and early

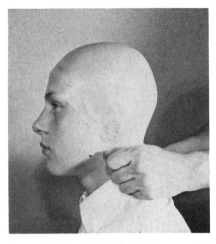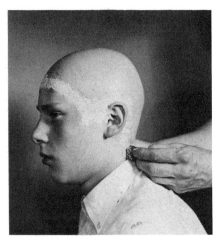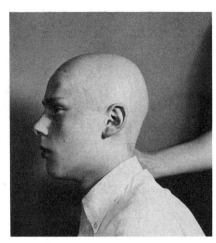

FIGURE 5.18 *Applying a bald cap.* LEFT: *A plastic bald cap is marked at the hairline with a brown pencil and is stretched to estimate the fit on the head.* MIDDLE: *After cutting and adhering, the edge is being stippled with eyelash adhesive or edge stipple to further disguise the blend and seal the edge of the cap.* RIGHT: *The completed attachment of the cap.*

nineteenth centuries when the scalp lock was worn can use latex caps, and the front blend edge is often disguised by a streak of warpaint. These caps can be generally applied with RCMA Matte Plasticized Adhesive or Prosthetic Adhesive A. Plastic bald caps are much thinner and more fragile than the latex variety but can be applied to have an imperceptible edge. The same adhesives as recommended for latex caps can be used.

Applying a Latex Cap

Slip the cap over the performer's head, and mark line with a brown make-up pencil about a half-inch from the edge of the front of the hairline, close around the ears, and allow about 1 inch below the hairline in the back. Remove the cap and cut along the line, then replace it on the head.

The front edge can be adhered by passing a #10 round sable brush dipped in Matte Plasticized Adhesive under the blending edge and pressing out the excess with a damp huck towel. The cap can be adhered around the ears and back in the same way, then the edges stippled with eyelash adhesive and dried with a hand-held hair dryer.

The cap can be made up with AF or PB Foundations or with RCMA Color Process Foundation on a sponge dampened with Foundation Thinner. If the head is to appear with a scalp lock, the rest of the hairline should be stippled with a dark gray beard stipple to simulate stubble growth. For some bald effects where the cap does not fit well in the back of the head, costume design can sometimes cover this defect.

Applying a Plastic Bald Cap

As plastic bald caps are generally thinner and more translucent than the latex variety, it is easier to trace

the hairline for cutting the excess cap material (Figure 5.18). When the cap has been refitted to the head, start attaching the forehead area first by passing the adhesive brush under the edge with some Matte Plasticized Adhesive. Avoid using too much adhesive so as not to dissolve the edge of the cap. Press the front down with a slightly dampened huck towel to make

FIGURE 5.19 *A partial bald cap used to cover the hairline of Sarah Churchill as young Queen Elizabeth I for a Hallmark Theatre production. This cap was not attached at the back and a wig was used for the hairstyle that covered the back of the neck as did the costume (hairstyling by Jack (M) LeGoms).*

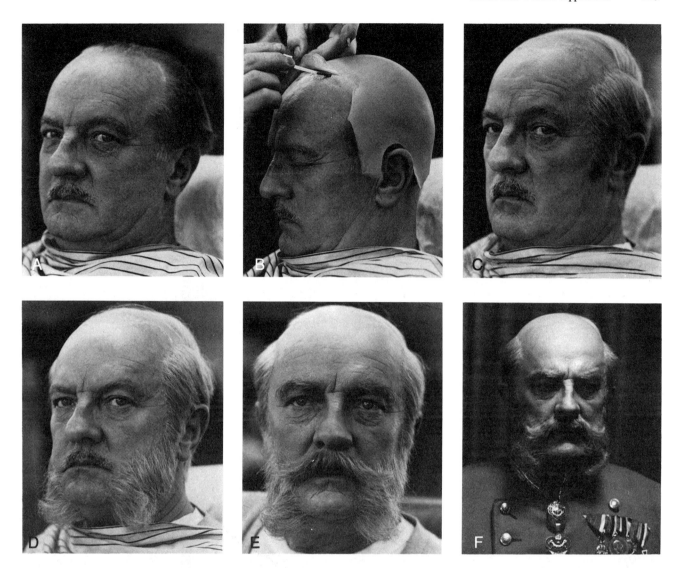

FIGURE 5.20 *Partial bald cap. (A) Basil Sydney before make-up. (B) A heavy (50 coats painted) bald cap has been made to fit the actor's hairline exactly and is being attached with Matte Plasticized Adhesive. (C) The wig and sideburns are added with RCMA Special Adhesive #1. (D) Added mutton chops lengthened sideburns. (E) After the addition of the moustache, the face was covered with a light coating of foundation and then blended carefully. As the Special Adhesive #1 was used on the lace and attached to the bald cap, the foundation was blended right over it. Shadows, highlights, and age lines were then added. (F) The completed make-up for Emperor Franz Josef of Austria. (Make-up by the author for an NBC production with make-up design by Dick Smith.)*

the edge smooth. Then stretch the sides downward by the sideburn tab, smoothing out the front and side so that no wrinkles appear, and pass the adhesive-dipped brush under the edges and press them in place with the towel. It is easier to attach a cap with two make-up artists working together since then one can stretch one side while the other side is being stretched and attached so that both sides will have approximately the same tension. However, one person can still do it. The cap area at the back of the ears can be adhered to the head and along the hair line in the back.

The back of the head is the most difficult to attach if the hair is not cut close. If the costume will cover the back of the head, don't adhere it so the wearing of the cap will be more comfortable for the performer.

If the rear of the cap is to be attached, then the back of the neck where the adhesion must take place should be cleanly shaven; otherwise the hair will prevent positive adherence. If the cap must be applied to a woman or man with long hair, carefully pin the hair as flat to the head as possible, taking care that no bobby pins point outward to puncture the cap. It is also a good idea to place the crown of a previously used cap over the top of the head prior to application of the outer cap to protect the cap further from bobby pins and to smooth out the rough surface created by the pinning down of the hair. This extra inner cap need not be adhered as the pressure of the outer cap will hold it in place.

Sometimes when just the front of the head need be

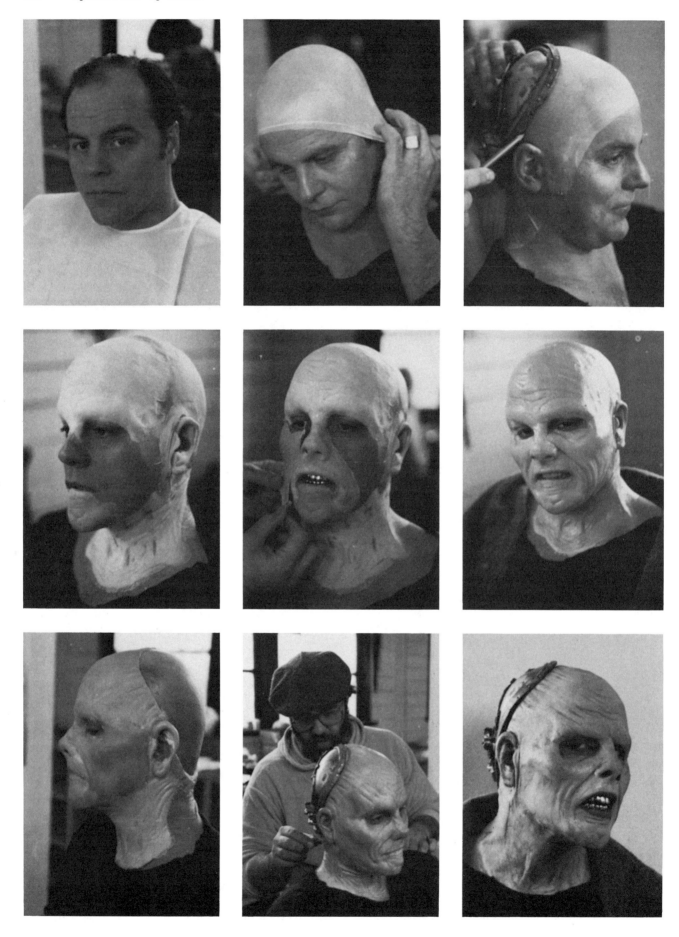

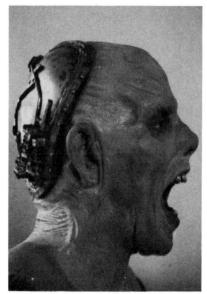

FIGURE 5.21 *Character creation for Michael Ironside in* Spacehunter. *(Make-up and photos by Tom Burman.)*

bald, there is a Velcro type of hair bandage that can be wrapped around the forehead area and then slid up to flatten out and push back the hair (Figure 5.19). Prosthetic Adhesive A can also be used to attach a bald cap by cutting the cap completely to shape and size and then coating the inner surface of the blending-attaching inside edge with a half-inch strip of Prosthetic Adhesive A. This will dry quickly and it should then be powdered with No-Color Powder. Then place and center the cap on the head, and roll back the leading edge on the forehead line and carefully coat the skin with Prosthetic Adhesive A, dry it, and lightly powder it. This adhesive does not really dry to the touch as it is a contact type, so the light powdering simply takes out some of the tack. Then carefully roll the edge back on to the forehead, and when perfectly centered, roll the sides back one at a time and repeat the process. When this is done start pressing the blending edge of the cap firmly into the skin with a dry towel or a polyurethane sponge. This will complete the contact, and the cap will be securely attached. Unlike the Matte Plasticized Adhesive, once the bond is made, the cap cannot be repositioned by lifting an edge and regluing.

Do around the ears and back of the head in the same manner. The blending edges can then be washed into the skin with a brush lightly dipped in acetone. Take care in this operation that you do not get much acetone on the cap as it will eat right through the thin edges and ruin the blend. The edge can then be additionally disguised by stippling the blend area with RCMA Matte Plastic Sealer, or eyelash adhesive may be used. The stipple should be thoroughly dried with a hand-held hair dryer before applying any foundation. Color Process Foundations, or AF Foundations may be used,

or the cap may be stippled with the Prosthetic Adhesive B and tube paint mixture described on page 94 or RCMAAP series.

Heavy Partial Bald Caps

The heavier, painted-on bald cap described on page 119 can be attached with Matte Plasticized Adhesive by placing the cap on the head in the required position (Figure 5.20). The edge is then turned up, first on the forehead, and a coat of adhesive is applied to the skin, allowed to set for a few minutes, and then pressed down on the skin. The same process is repeated on the sides. The cap can then be blended into the skin with acetone and pressed with a small-bladed dental spatula to smooth the edge. Stipple on Matte Plastic Sealer or eyelash adhesive as previously described. The Prosthetic Adhesive A method can also be used.

Lace hair goods can be attached to the cap with RCMA Special Adhesive #1. This has a heavy matting material in a solution similar to cap material and must be well shaken before use. The hairpieces are held in the proper position, and the adhesive is applied *over* the lace. This adhesive dries very quickly and totally matte, incorporating the lace into the cap so that it is imperceptible. Other adhesives may dissolve the cap material or produce an excessive shine in the lace area. This Special Adhesive #1 is only for use on the cap, so Matte Adhesive can be employed where the lace meets the skin.

For coloration, some make-up artists stipple the entire cap area with Matte Plastic Sealer that has been colored with foundation to the desired shade. Any RCMA Color Process Foundation can be used for this and the color worked into the sealer with a dental spatula on a glass plate.

The incorporation of a number of appliance elements is used in the make-up shown in Figure 5.21 by Tom Burman on Michael Ironside for the film, *Spacehunter,* where he plays a character being kept alive by a mechanical support system controlled by his brain—hence, the special steel cranial plate with its attached circuitry. First, the performer's head was covered with a plastic bald cap with an extra long neck length attached with RCMA Prosthetic Adhesive A. Next, foam latex appliances on the forehead, chin, nose, nasolabial folds, ears, neck, and cheeks were adhered with RCMA Prosthetic Adhesive B. The edges of the latex appliances were blended together with a mixture of eyelash-adhesive-type latex and the PA-B. The foundation and other coloration are prosthetic bases of Tom's manufacture, with shadows and highlights to complete the effect. The cranial plate was made of vacuum-formed sheet butyrate and painted with a silver lacquer. The rivets and other circuitry were made of clear dental acrylic cast in alginate and tinted with a gold-colored lacquer. The whole plate was then assembled and adhered to the head with Prosthetic Adhesive B (so as not to dissolve the cap material base).

The special teeth were made by taking an impression of the actor's teeth, sculpting the desired look in dental wax, and taking a cast with a polysulfide mold. The bases of the teeth were made in Flexacryl-Soft acrylic, and a veneer was made of wax. This was then turned over to dental lab technician, Armando Ramos, who cast the teeth in chrome and polished them. Due to their close fit, the teeth were simply held in place by suction. The final photos show the extreme versatility allowed by the soft foam appliances as well as the actor's feeling for the role.

PROFESSIONAL MAKE-UP PRODUCTS

EQUIVALENCY CHARTS

The one basic factor that separates *professional* make-up foundations, shadings, counter-shadings, cheekcolors, and lipcolors from their *commercial,* or even *theatrical,* counterparts is accurate consistency of shades and colors. With commercial and theatrical make-ups, exact day-to-day color matching does not have the importance that mediums of the screen demand, as the former are only seen in person for *that* day, while the latter require day-to-day constants in tonality. Skin testing is a necessity to maintain exact color matches for all professional make-up materials. However, shades of make-up with either the exact names or for similar uses do vary somewhat from manufacturer to manufacturer, depending upon their assessment of values for specific purposes. Actual screen tests are the final method of determination, so that equivalency charts are approximations of the color or shade value as they are expected to appear on screen under normal lighting conditions rather than the same number or name of the shade.

It is not practical to simplify the multitude of foundations made by various manufacturers of professional products in a basic comparison chart so we shall only show some former Max Factor numbers that were quite familiar in the field to the current approximate RCMA equivalents. We shall then list the recommendations of the other two leading professional cosmetics for screen/theater use, and a listing of a theatrical make-up firm as well.

RCMA	MAX FACTOR
KW-1	CTV-2W
KW-2	CTV-3W
KW-3	Olive or CTV-4W
KW-4	Deep Olive or CTV-5W
KW-5	725 A
KW-6	725 B
KW-7	725 BC
KW-8	725 CN
KM-1	CTV-6W
KM-2	CTV-7W
KM-3	CTV-8W
KM-5	725 EN
KM-36	665-G
KM-37	665-I
KN-3	665-O
KN-4	665-P
KM-8	665-L
F-2	Fair
K-1	K-1
K-2	K-2 or 665-J
K-3	665-K
KN-5	Eddie Leonard (Pancake shade)
KN-6	Negro 1
KN-7	Negro 2 or 665-R
KT-3	Light Egyptian
KT-34	Dark Egyptian
KT-4	Tahitian
RJ-2	KF-7 (Pancake shade)
KW4M3	Golden Tan
KW-38	Natural Tan

The futility of matching printing inks with how foundations appear either in the container or how differently on the skin precludes professional manufacturers from attempting to make commercial *color charts* as exact comparatives but only for advertising purposes in brochures and such.

CUSTOM COLOR COSMETICS BY WILLIAM TUTTLE

An Academy Award, 20 years as head of the make-up department at MGM, and over 400 feature film credits have distinguished William Tuttle in the field of make-up artistry. His line of cosmetics, albeit limited to basic straight make-up materials, has been designed for professional use. His personal preferences in average situations are as follows (Light to Dark):

WOMEN

NORMAL	TAN EFFECT
Medium Beige	Suntone
Deep Olive	Natural Tan
Medium-Dark Beige	Tawny Tan
	Tan-del-Ann

MEN

NORMAL	TAN EFFECT
Dark Beige	Desert Tan
Natural Tan	Xtra Dark Tan
Tan	K-1
	Jan Tan

NEGROES
(MEN AND WOMEN)
All colors from Toasted Honey through Ebony

These recommendations are interchangeable for film or tape, although for live television or talk shows one shade deeper than the norm is employed due to the overall set lighting that is flatter than for normal production lighting.

COLOR FOUNDATIONS

Ivory	Warm Tan
Truly Beige	Tan-del-Ann
Fair & Warmer	Tawny Tan
Light Peach	Fern Tan
Pink 'n' Pretty	Bronze Tone
Peach	Jan Tan
Rose Medium	TNT
Light Beige	Light-Medium
Light-Medium Beige	Peach
Medium Beige	Deb-Tan
Medium Dark Beige	Suntone
Bronze	Medium
Tan	Beige Tan II
Xtra Dark Tan	Shibui
Hot Chocolate	Deep Olive
Sumatra	Chinese I
N-1	Chinese II
Natural Tan	Western Indian
Dark Beige	Tawn-Shee
Toasted Honey	BT6
Cafe Olé	BT7
Rahma	11019 (Dark Tawny
Bronze	Tan)
Natural Tan	K-1
Chocolate Cream	Hi-Yeller
Tan Tone	Tan
CTV-8W	Ebony
BT5	Desert Tan

CORRECTIVE CONTOURING
Special Hi-Lite (For erasing circles under eyes)
Hi-Lite (For contouring)
Shadow I (For contouring)
Shadow II (Darker than Shadow I)
Blusher
Tan Rouge (Used with dark foundations)
Sunburn Stipple (For an outdoor look)
Red-out (For erasing darkened areas)
CTV Rouge
Mauve Blusher
Persimmon Piquant
007

EYE ESSENTIALS

20-30-40 Eye Shadow
CoCo Bare
O-Dee
Frosted Eye Shadow Duos
  Chamois/Burnt Spice
  Pearl Blue/Caribbean Blue

PROFESSIONAL PENCILS

Black	Light Brown
Charcoal Grey	Auburn
Midnight Brown	Taupe
Dark Brown	Beige
Medium Brown	

LIP ESSENTIALS

Mango Mist
Lip Glosses
  Ming Coral
  Bacchante Brown
  Castiliana Red

SKIN CARE ESSENTIALS

Cleansing Lotion (Dry and Normal Skin)
Freshener (Dry Skin)
Freshener (Normal Skin)
Oily Skin Cleanser
Oily Skin Astringent
Moisturizer (Dry and Normal Skin)
Skin Conditioner (Very Dry Skin)
Facial Scrub (All Skin Types)
Sun Screen Moisturizing Lotion

Also, Extra Fine Translucent Powder and Prosthetic Make-up can be had on special order to match any listed color.

CREME CHEEK ROUGE

DRY CHEEK ROUGE

Red	Red
Dusty Rose	Raspberry
Raspberry	Coral
Dark Tech	Dark Tech
Coral	
Blush Coral	

CHEEK BLUSHERS	CREME HIGHLIGHT
Dusty Pink	Extra Lite
Nectar Peach	Medium
Golden Amber	Deep

CREME BROWN SHADOW	FACE POWDER
#40 Character (Purple-Brown)	Translucent Coco Tan (For dark skins)
42 Medium (Brown)	Special White (Clowns)
43 Dark (Warm Dark Brown)	
44 Extra Dark (Rich Dark Brown)	

LIPSTICK

#1 Lip Gloss	9 Plum
3 Coral	10 Bordeaux
5 Garnet	12 Natural Brown
6 Plum Pink	14 True Red
7 Natural	15 Siren Red
8 Cranberry	

PRESSED EYESHADOW

Toast	Navy Blue
Silver	Rust
Lavender-Mist	Gold Leaf
Plum	Iridescent Taupe
Burgundy	Dark Brown

CAKE EYELINER

Black	Blue
Brown-Black	Iridescent Turquoise
Brown	Green
Plum	Iridescent Green
Silver	Iridescent White

PEARL SHEEN LINERS

White	Bronze
Green	Copper
Turquoise	Mango
Royal Blue	Dusty Rose
Sapphire	Cabernet
Shimmering Lilac	Rose
Ultra Violet	Brown
Amethyst	Walnut
Gold	Charcoal

BEN NYE MAKE-UP

Ben Nye was the director of make-up for 20th Century Fox for many years, and his make-up line is a reflection of his high standards of artistic quality. Now operated in Los Angeles by his son, Dana, this firm has an extensive list of products for use in screen make-up as well as being the leading supplier to college drama and visual arts departments around the country.

For the screen, Dana Nye recommends N-3, Deep Olive, N-6, and T-1 for Caucasoid women and M-1, M-2, M-3, Y-3, and M-5 for men. The most popular Negroid shades are 27, 28, and Dark Coco. In the N series, N-1 is the fairest for light complexions.

CREME-CAKE FOUNDATIONS

White

Black
Ultra Fair
Old Age
Bronzetone
Dark Coco

Tan Series: Natural Tan colors

T-1 Golden Tan	T-2 Bronze Tan

Twenty Series for Asians, Latins, and Negroids

22 Golden Beige	White
23 Fawn	Forest Green
24 Honey	Green
25 Amber Lite	Yellow
26 Amber	Orange
27 Coco Tan	Sunburn Stipple
28 Cinnamon	
29 Blush Sable	
30 Ebony	

L Series: Lighter value shades

L-1 Juvenile Female
L-2 Light Beige
L-3 Rose Beige
L-4 Medium Beige
L-5 Tan-Rose

Y Series: Olive skin tones

Y-3 Medium Olive
Y-5 Deep Olive Tan

American Indian Series

I-1 Golden Copper
I-3 Bronze
I-5 Dark Bronze

Mexican Series: Olive brown tones

MX-1 Olive Brown
MX-3 Ruddy Brown

Natural Series

1, 2, 3, 4, 5, 6
Deep Olive

M Series: Medium warm brown tones

M-1 Juvenile Male
M-2 Light Suntone
M-3 Medium Tan
M-4 Deep Suntone
M-5 Desert Tan

CREME LINING COLORS

Dark Sunburn	Gray
Fire Red	Beard Stipple
Blood Red	Black
Maroon	White
Misty Violet	Forest Green
Purple	Green
Blue	Yellow
Sky Blue	Orange
Blue-Gray	Sunburn Stipple

COLOR LINING PENCILS

Red	Iridescent Violet
Maroon	Iridescent Blue
Rust	Iridescent Green
Violet	Gold
Blue	Silver
Green	White

EYEBROW PENCILS

Light Brown	Dark Brown
Auburn	Charcoal Gray
Medium Brown	Midnite Brown
Black	

Mellow Yellow (To mute redness)
Five O'Sharp (Beard cover in Olive and Ruddy)
Clown White
Nose and Scar Wax
Mascara (creme) (In Black and Brown)
Silver Hair Gray
Custom Flat Brushes (Synthetic Bristle) #2, 3, 5, 7, 10, and 12
Sable Brushes (Round) #1 and 2
Dry Rouge, Lipstick (Retractable), and Powder Brushes
Latex Foam Sponges, Nylon Stipple Sponges, and Velour Powder Puffs
Crepe Hair in White, Blond, Light Brown, Auburn, Medium Brown, Dark Brown, Light Gray, Medium Gray, Dark Gray, and Black
Liquid Latex (Casting)
Spirit Gum
Stage Blood
Make-up Remover
Brush Cleaner

Ben Nye also furnishes student make-up kits for individuals in the following:

White Female	Olive Male
White Male	Black Medium
Olive Female	Brown
	Black Dark Brown

Each kit contains three foundations plus an assortment of cream rouges, highlights, shadows and lining colors, silver hair gray, natural lipcolor, nose and scar wax, make-up remover, translucent face powder, two custom flat brushes, two pencils, dry rouge and brush, stipple sponge, powder puff, latex sponge, and spirit gum. This is the best-buy kit for student make-up in its field and far better than others offered by some competing theatrical manufacturers.

STEIN'S MAKE-UP

Since 1883, the M. Stein Cosmetic Company has been making theatrical make-up for both amateurs and professionals. Many items have been on their lists for years, and they still will supply both the old stick greasepaint, soft tube greasepaint, colored face powders, liquid make-up, stick liners, and other classic items.

GREASEPAINT
(Cardboard Tube)

1 Pink	14 Gypsy
2 Pale Juvenile	15 Othello-Moor
3 Juvenile	16 Chinese
4 Juv. Flesh Auguste	14 Amer. Indian
5 Dpr. Flesh Clown	18 Carmine (red)
5L. Ivory Yellow	19 Negro
6 Robust-Juvenile	20 East Indian
7 Light Sunburn	21 Vermilion
8 Dark Sunburn	22 White
9 Cream Sallow	23 Yellow
10 Middle Age	24 Brown
11 Sallow Old Man	25 Black
12 Robust Old Man	26 Japanese
13 Olive	27 Cinema Yellow
13L. Red Brown	28 Cinema Orange

LIQUID MAKE-UP
(Plastic Bottles, Water Soluble)

2 Pink Natural	15 White
3 Flesh	16 Negro Brown
5½ Orange	17 Black
6 Tan	17½ Green
6½ Blue	18 Carmine (Red)
7 Olive	18½ Vermilion
7F Dark Sunburn	19 Light Negro
8 Light Sunburn	20 Dark Negro
8½ American Indian	21 Peach Bloom
9 Indian Brown	22 Rachel
9½ East Indian	23 Brunette
41A Special Indian	24 Sun Tan
10 Hindu Brown	27 Lt. Egyptian
11 Mulatto Brown	28 Dk. Egyptian
12 Mikado Yellow	29 Light Creole
12½ Bright Yellow	30 Dark Creole
13 Purple Sallow	31 Hawaiian
14 Gypsy Olive	32 Frankenstein Gray

Bright Colors

6½ Bright Blue	17½ Green
17 Black	15 White
12½ Bright Yellow	18 Red

LIQUID MAKE-UP METALLIC

25 Gold	26 Silver

CAKE MAKE-UP PAINTING PALETTE

Five colors; in water soluble White, Black, Blue, Yellow, and Red.

CAKE MAKE-UP

Natural Blush	44 Middle Age
Natural A	45 Robust Juvenile
Natural B	46 Green
Cream Blush	47 Blue
Cream A	48 Red
Cream B	49 Lavender
Tan Blush	50 Sallow Old Age
Tan Blush No. 2	51 Negro Brown
Tan Blush No. 3	52 Dk. Negro
Tan A	53 Sunburn
Tan B	54 Pink
2 Russet	55 Olive
7 Sun Tan	56 Spanish Mulatto (New)
9 Red Brown	
21 Peach Bloom	7N
22 Rachel	725 A
23 Lady Fair	725 B
24 Brunette	T.V. 1
25 Rose Brick	T.V. 2
26 Toffee	T.V. 3
27 Burnt Toffee	T.V. 4
28 Clove	T.V. 5
29 Mesa Brown	T.V. 6
30 Toast	T.V. 7
31 Cinnamon	T.V. 8
32 Othello	T.V. 9
33 Black Minstrel	T.V. 10
34 Gray Frankenstein	T.V. 11
	T.V. 12 (TV Black)
35 Light Creole	C-1 Light
36 Dark Creole	C-2 Very Fair
37 Hawaiian	C-3 Fair
38 Light Egyptian	C-4 Medium Fair
39 Dark Egyptian	C-5 Lt. Brunette
39½ Japanese	C-6 Brunette
40 Chinese	C-7 Dk. Brunette
40½ Mikado Yellow	C-8 Golden Tan
41 Indian	C-9 Copper
41A Special Indian	C-10 Bronze Tone
42 East Indian	C-11 Walnut
43 White Clown	C-12 Ebony

SOFT GREASEPAINT
(Collapsible Tube)

1 Yellowish Pink	11 Mulatto Brown
1½ Light Pink	12 Mikado Yellow
2 Pink-Natural	13 Purple Sallow
3 Flesh	14 Gypsy Olive
3½ Deeper	15 White
4 Cream	16 Negro Brown
5 Ivory Yellow	17 Black
5½ Orange	18 Carmine (Red)
6 Tan	19 Light Negro
7 Olive	20 Dark Negro

7F Dark Sunburn	21 Peach Bloom
8 Light Sunburn	22 Rachel
9 Indian Brown	23 Brunette
10 Hindu Brown	24 Sun Tan

SOFT SHADOW LINERS

1 Lt. Flesh	17 Black
2 Medium Flesh	19 Bright Green
3 Lt. Gray	19¼ Lt. Green
4 Medium Gray	19½ Dk. Green
5 Dark Gray	20 Blue-Green
6 Lt. Brown	21 Purple
7 Dark Brown	23 Lavender
8 Lt. Blue	24 Pearl White
9 Med. Bright Blue	25 Gold
10 Dark Blue	26 Silver
11 Special Blue	27 Silver Blue
15 White	28 Rose Sallow

VELVET STICK
Matching
Cake Make-up in Colors

SPECIAL SOFT LINERS
(Do not use in eye area)

12 Crimson	16 Bright Yellow
13 Dk. Crimson	18 Carmine Red
14 Vermilion	22 Red Brown

LINING COLORS STICK

1 Golden Yellow	15 White
2 Flesh*	16 Yellow*
3 Light Gray	17 Black
4 Medium Gray	18 Carmine* (Red)
5 Dark Gray	19 Green*
6 Light Brown	20 Blue-Green
7 Dark Brown	21 Purple*
8 Light Blue	22 Light Green (New)
9 Medium Brown	23 Brunette
10 Dark Blue*	24 Tan
11 Sky Blue	25 Red Brown*
12 Crimson*	26 Lavender*
13 Dark Crimson*	
14 Vermilion*	

*Do not use in area of eyes.

METALLIC LINING STICK

Gold	Silver

CREAM (MOIST) ROUGE

1 Twilight	10 Youth Flame
2 Light Red	11 T1 Dk. Pink
3 Medium Red	12 T2 Rusty
4 Dark Red	13 Orchid
5 Youth Blush	14 Light Rose
6 Real Red	15 Rose
7 Royal Red	16 Brunette
8 Pink Tone	17 Carmine
9 Brown (Male)	

DRY ROUGE

5 Youth Blush (T1)	18 Evening Glow
12 Dawn (T2)	20 Tropical
14 Twilight	22 Youth Flame
16 Raspberry	

BLUSH-ON STICK

1 Pink Pearl	4 Bronze
2 Summer Gold	5 Peach Pearl
3 Dawn	

LIPSTICK

1 Twilight	13 Green (New)
2 Evening Glow	14 Blue (New)
3 Raspberry	15 Purple (New)
4 Dark Red	Video Pink 1 Lt.
5 Youth Blush	Video Pink 2 Med.
6 Real Red	Video Pink 3 Dark
7 Royal Red	Video Blush 1
8 Pink Tone	Video Blush 2
9 Brown (Male)	Video Light Red
10 Lip Gloss	Video Medium Red
11 Youth Flame	Video Dark Red
12 Witches Black	

LIPGLOSS

1 Cherry Red (Regular)	3 No Color
2 Frosted	

EYESHADOW STICK
(Swivel Case)

1 Natural	7 Taupe
2 Tan (Video)	8 Lilac
3 Blue (Video)	9 Silver
4 Pale Blue	10 Gold
5 Irr. Blue	11 Green
6 Turquoise (Video)	12 Pearl

CAKE EYESHADOW
(With Applicator, Wet or Dry)

1 Aqua	5 Blue
2 Turquoise	6 Jade
3 Lavender	7 Brown
4 Green	8 White

CAKE EYELINER
(With Brush)

1 Black	6 Lt. Blue
2 Brown-Black	7 White
3 Brown	8 Hi-Lite
4 Smoke	9 Green
5 Med. Blue	

FLUID EYELINER

1 Black	6 Green
2 Brown-Black	7 White
3 Brown	8 Hi-Lite
4 Smokey Gray	9 Navy
5 Ultra-Blue	10 Plum

PRESSED PEARLITES
(Pressed Shadows in High Shimmering Colors for Lids, Face, and Body)

1 Copper	6 Temptation
2 Silver	(Blue-White)
3 Grape	7 Blue
4 Raspberry (Red-Blue)	8 Dark Gold
5 Champagne	9 Pale Gold
	10 Bronze

PEARLITES POWDER
(Loose Powder Shadows in High Shimmering Colors for Lids, Face, and Body)

1 Plum	6 Temptation
2 Silver	(Blue-White)
3 Amethyst (Purple)	7 Sapphire (Blue)
4 Raspberry	8 Autumn Leaves (Gold)
5 Turquoise	9 Sea Green
	10 Bronze
	11 Pale Gold

NAIL ENAMEL

Black	Green
Purple	Yellow
	Blue

NAIL ENAMEL GLITTER

Red	Silver
Blue	Purple
Gold	Multicolor

BODY GLITTER (CREAM)
(Only the Glitter Shows)
(Do Not Use in Eye Area)

1 Gold	4 Green
2 Silver	5 Blue
3 Multicolor	6 Red

LUMINOUS MAKE-UP

Phosphorescent Glows in The Dark	Fluorescent Glows in U.V. Light

MAKE-UP CREAM
(Collapsible tube, water soluble, 1.25 oz.)

Minstral Black	Green
Light Creole	White Clown
Glow Face	Blue
Dark Creole	

LIP LINING PENCIL
(7 inch)

Tawny (Maroon)	Red

EYEBROW PENCIL
(7 inch)

Black	Auburn
Blue	Silver Gray
Brown	

MASCARA (CAKE)

Black	Brown
Blue-Green	White

FACE POWDERS
(Plastic Jar)

1A Neutral (Colorless)	13 Othello Dk. Brown
1 White Clown	14 Chinese
2 Light Pink	14½ Japanese
4 Flesh	15½ East Indian
5 Brunette	24 Light Brown
5½ Dark Brunette	24½ Red Brown
7½ Suntan	25 Black
8 Tan	26 Gray
9 Sallow Old Age	Frankenstein
11 Healthy Old Age	27 Blue
12 Olive	28 Green

RUBBER MASK GREASEPAINT

C-1 Light Skin	C-7 Medium Skin
C-4 Fair Skin	C-11 Dark Skin

COLOR CROWN TEMPORARY HAIR SPRAY
Fluorescent Colors

Ripe Red	Shining Silver
Yummy Yellow	Glowing Green
Blazing Blue	Gorgeous Grape
Jet Black	Wild White
Passion Pink	Obvious Orchid
Outrageous Orange	Glimmering Gold

Glitter Colors

Blue	Burgundy Red
Green	Gold
Silver	Multi-Color

CREPE HAIR WOOL

1 White	7 Light Gray
2 Light Brown	8 Medium Gray
3 Medium Brown	9 Dark Gray
4 Dark Brown	10 Blonde
5 Auburn	10½ Dark Blonde
6 Black	11 Red

In addition, Stein's also furnishes toupee tape, collodion (flexible and nonflexible), nose putty, black tooth wax, Derma (mortician's) wax (three shades), latex, spirit gum, clown white (regular and water soluble), blemi-sticks (three shades), stage blood, hair wax sticks (three shades), temporary liquid hair color touch-up, eyebrow and lipliner pencils (several shades), sponges, puffs, paper stomps, brushes, cold cream, liquid make-up remover, spirit gum remover, and a variety of student kits and masquerade, clown, and face-painting kits.

RCMA COLOR PROCESS MAKE-UP
The Research Council of Make-up Artists (RCMA) was formed as a membership organization in autumn 1955 by Vincent J-R Kehoe with a group of leading New York make-up artists. In 1962, it was incorporated as a membership corporation, and in 1965 it changed to a sales corporation under the laws of the State of New York. Since its inception in the sales field, it has serviced only the professional industry with products designed especially for their use. Research and Supply offices were set up in Lowell, Massachusetts, in 1966, and the company was moved in 1985 to Somis, California, to better serve the industry while new laboratories were built for advanced research in plastic and latex appliances, modern adhesives, and special products for make-up artists. Although RCMA Professional Make-up cannot be purchased in any drug or department stores, it is available through authorized distributors in major production areas as well as sales outlets in many parts of the United States.

Color Process Foundations
These are some shades matched to some other manufacturer's discontinued numbers that are still being requested by certain make-up personnel:

Ivory	K-1	K-3 (665-K)
Tantone	K-2	RJ-2 (KF-7, Pan-Cake match)

There are also some four-part containers with special colors:

Bruise Kit Violet, Black, Raspberry, Bruise Yellow
Burn Kit Red, Raspberry, Black
Clown Kit Red, Yellow, Blue, Black
Old Age Spots Kit Four shades to simulate old age discolorations and spots.

Lipcolors

These lipcolors contain no staining dyes
and no perfumes.

NUMBER	APPROXIMATE COLOR
CP-1	Coral Pink
CP-3	Browned Pink
CP-4	Bright Pink
CP-5	Orange Red
CP-6	Blue Red
CP-7	Blue Pink
CP-8	Light Pink
CP-9	Orange
CP-10	Grape
CP-11	Brown Red
CP-12	Special Red
CP-13	Mix CP-1 and 3
CP-14	Rose
CP-15	Dark Red-Brown
CP-1	Pearl
CP-3	Pearl
CP-4	Pearl
CP-5	Pearl
CP-6	Pearl
CP-7	Pearl
CP-8	Pearl
CP-9	Pearl
CP-10	Pearl
CP-11	Pearl
CP-12	Pearl
CP-13	Pearl
CP-15	Pearl
CP-6	Copper
CP-12	Silver
CP-1	Gold
CP-4	Gold
CP-6	Gold
CP-7	Gold
CP-11	Gold
CP-12	Gold
CP-14	Gold

Gena Special Red
Gena Special Red-Gold
Gena Special Red-Silver
Gena Special Red-Copper
DP Special
Pink Frosting
Special Pink #1
Special Pink #2
Special Pink #3
Pink Cocoa
Pink Gloss
Gena Pink
Gena Coral
Gena Pearl
Tomato Soup
Fantasy Red
Candy Apple
Pure Pearl
Bronze
Copper
Silver
Gold Sparkle

LS-1	Fuchsia
LS-2	Garnet
LS-3	Cranberry
LS-4	Orange Brown
LS-5	Peach Pearl
LS-6	Rotten Apple
LS-7	Natural Rose
LS-8	Light Pink Pearl
LS-9	Orange Pearl
LS-10	Salmon Pearl
LS-11	Dusty Rose
LS-12	Dusty Coral
LS-13	Peached Brown
LS-14	Browned Peach
LS-15	Rust
LS-16	Plum
LS-17	Purple Brown
LS-18	Bright Red
LS-19	Dark Blue-Pink
LS-20	Special Rust
LS-4	Pearl
LS-7	Pearl
LS-13	Gold
LS-16	Gold
LS-2	Silver
LS-3	Silver
LS-6	Silver
LS-18	Silver
LS-639	Special Coral
LS-739	Light Special Coral

Lipgloss

CP-1   CP-10   CP-12
CP-4   CP-11   LS-12
Gena Special Red
No-Color
Clear
RCMA Lip Balm (Semigloss)

Within these shades and colors, one can
find lip make-up for every period and fashion
time. New shades are added from time to
time according to fashion trends.

Eyecolors

#1 WATER APPLIED

Black	Silver Green
Midnite Brown	Olive
Gray Brown (Dark)	Aqua
Royal Brown	Turquoise
Light Brown	Silver Turquoise
Charcoal	Silver Lilac
Light Gray	Silver
Midnite Blue	Gold
Light Blue	Cream
Silver Blue	White
Green	Yellow
Light Green	Plum

#2 DRY APPLIED

Royal Brown	Turquoise
Light Brown	Silver Turquoise
Royal Blue	Silver Lilac
Silver Blue	Silver
Wedgewood	Cream
Silver Green	White
Gold Green	Yellow

DRY BLUSHES

Plum	Brown Pearl
Red	Gold Brandy
Mocha	Blush Pink
Pink Pearl	Flame
Peach Pearl	Candy Pink
Bronze Pearl	Garnet

Rust Pearl	Claret
Raspberry Pearl	Lilac

#3 PEARLIZED AND GOLD SHADES

Pearl Black	Gold Huckleberry
Pearl Charcoal	Gold Brown
Pearl Smoke	Gold Burgundy
Pearl Brown	Gold Emerald
Pearl Royal Brown	Pearl Wine
Pearl Light Brown	Pearl Mocha
Pearl Cinnamon	Pearl Plum
Pearl Rust	Pearl Pink
Pearl Cafe	Pearl Rose
Pearl Yellow	Pearl Apricot
Pearl Cream	Pearl Salmon
Pearl Olive	Pearl Violet
Pearl Green	Pearl Lilac
Pearl Turquoise	Pearl Blue
Pearl Teal	Pearl Light Blue
Pearl Pure White	Pearl Slate Blue

These also come in kits of 12 colors of EC
#1 or EC #3 and kits of 6 in EC #2 or Dry
Blush, made to order for make-up artists in
their choice of colors in a flat plastic box.

Special Materials

RCMA has the most extensive and varied
selection of special materials, and although
mentioned throughout the text, this is a complete list of the items that are available in a
number of sizes. Where designated, PMA is
the abbreviation for a special line of Professional Make-up Artist materials.

PMA Plastic Wax Material

Light
Women (KW-3 shade)
Men (KT-3 shade)
Negro (KN-5 shade)
Violet No-Color

Also, there is *Dental Wax* in Red Gum shade
and Black.

Latex

Pure Gum
Casting Latex
Casting Filler
Foamed Latex (four-part formula)
Foamed Latex (three-part formula)

Mold Release

PMA Silicon Mold Release
MR-8 Urethane Mold Release
PJ-1 Mold Release
FL-1 Mold Release (four-part foamed latex)

Old Age Stipple

KW-2 (Light)	KM-2 (Deep)
KW-4 (Medium)	KN-5 (Dark Brown)

Adhesives

Prosthetic Adhesive A (Solvent based)
Prosthetic Adhesive B (Water based)
Special Adhesive #1
Special Adhesive #2
Eyelash Adhesive
PMA Matte Lace Adhesive
Matte Adhesive
Matte Adhesive #16
Matte Plasticized Adhesive

Sealers

Matte Plastic Sealer

PMA Matte Molding Sealer

Molding Materials

PMA Press Molding Material

PMA Molding Material (Light, Deep, and Dark shades)

Thinners

Prosthetic Adhesive A Thinner

Foundation Thinner

AF Foundation Thinner

Scar Materials

Scar Material

Scar or Blister Making Material

Plastic Cap Material

This comes in clear and pale tinted shades.

PMA Blood Series

Type A (Water soluble)

Type B (Plastic base)

Type C (Cream variety in tube)

Type D (Dried blood effect)

RCMA also makes *Beard Setting Spray, Artificial Tears and Perspiration, AF Klenzer, Alginate Separator,* and two-part *Flexible Urethane Foam* and *Solid Urethane* materials.

Appliance Foundation Series

RCMA originally made a PB (Prosthetic Base) series which was similar to the old Rubber Mask Greasepaint of Max Factor and others. However, this has been replaced with an advanced type of material which has higher coverage, no oil separation, and is extremely opaque while spreading very easily with a brush or sponge. (See page 94 for full discussion of this series.)

The *Appliance Paint* (AP) series includes paint-on shades matched to the RCMA Color Process series for latices or urethanes in certified colors. There is also a clear *Acrylid* for coating latices or urethanes. RCMA also furnishes Universal Colors in 1-ounce squeeze bottles that dispense just one drop at a time to tint any type of casting or slush latex or latices and urethanes during foaming operations.

Make-Up Cases

RCMA furnishes three styles of make-up cases (also see Appendix B). The accordion style is lightweight, compact, and easy to transport but holds a considerable amount of make-up materials. Also there are two solid walnut drawer styles that can carry more make-up than the accordion style.

RCMA also sells a variety of raw materials for molding and casting, dental acrylics, chemicals, and so forth under Make-up Lab Specialties Company. They also will furnish empties of all their containers for make-up artists who wish to mix special colors or add to their kits.

There are a number of other firms that supply theatrical make-up with similar products to some of those mentioned herein. However, those included are generally representative of the major items employed by professional make-up artists or the procedures and make-ups employed in this book.

SUPPLIERS AND PROFESSIONAL ADDRESSES

It is not possible to list every supplier of materials that is or can be employed for professional make-up. As well, new sources are always being found as technology advances and old sources either discontinue items or businesses. However, listed here are a number of representative manufacturers and suppliers that will be useful as a current source of materials.

CHEMICALS
General
City Chemical Corp., 132 West 22nd St., New York, NY 10001

Kem Chemical Co., 545 S. Fulton Ave., Mt. Vernon, NY 10550

Ruger Chemical Co., Box 806, Hillside, NY 07205

Special
Carbopols Goodrich Co., 3135 Euclid Ave., Cleveland, OH 44115

Methocels Dow Chemical Co., Midland, MI 48192

Plasticizers Monsanto Chemical Co., St Louis, MO 63166

Surfactants BASF Wyandotte Corp., Wyandotte, MI 48192

Rohm and Haas Co., Philadelphia, PA 19105

Separators (Silicons) Dow Corning Corp., Midland, MI 48640

DENTAL SUPPLIES
The *Yellow Pages* of the telephone book will provide local sources for both medical and dental supplies. However, dental and prosthetic grades of alginates can be found at the following:

Mid-America Dental, 160 Center Dr., Gilberts, IL 60136

Teledyne Getz Co., 1550 Greenleaf Ave., Elk Grove Village, IL 60007

HAIR AND HAIR SUPPLIES
Frends Beauty Supply, 5270 Laurel Canyon Blvd., N. Hollywood, CA 91607 Wool crepe and yak hair and hairdressing supplies.

Seigfried Geike (Ziggy), 14318 Victory Blvd., Van Nuys, CA 91401 Real and prepared hair goods of all kinds.

Ideal Wig Co., 38 Pearl St., New York, NY 10004 Rental and sales of theatrical-grade wigs.

Polly Products Co., 1 Plummers Corner, Whitinsville, MA 01588 Styrofoam heads.

Ira Senz Co., 13 East 47th St., New York, NY 10017 Wigs, hairpieces, beards, and other lace pieces.

Stein Cosmetics Co., 430 Broome St., New York, NY 10013 Wool crepe hair of excellent quality.

Josephine Turner, 12642 Kling St., N. Hollywood, CA 91607 Real hair lace-front wigs and falls.

LIGHTING MATERIAL
(Special Sunlight-Rated Bulbs)
Luxor Lighting Products, 350 Fifth Ave., New York, NY 10001

PROFESSIONAL AND THEATRICAL MAKE-UP SUPPLIES
Alcone Co., 575 8th Ave., New York, NY 10018

Ben Nye Inc., 11571 Santa Monica Blvd., Los Angeles, CA 90025

Cinema Secrets, Inc., 4400 Riverside Drive, Burbank, CA 91505

Custom Color Cosmetics, Box 56, Pacific Palisades, CA 90272

Frends Beauty Supply, 5270 Laurel Canyon Blvd., N. Hollywood, CA 91607

Joyce Daniel Make-up, 97 Jamestown Pk., Nashville, TN 37205

Kryolan Corp., 747 Polk St., San Francisco, CA 94109

MIS Retail Corp., 736 7th Ave., New York, NY 10019

Naimie's Beauty Supply, 12801 Victory Blvd., North Hollywood, CA 91606

RCMA (Research Council of Make-up Artists, Inc.), P.O. Box 850, Somis, CA 93066

Stein Cosmetics Co., 430 Broome St., New York, NY 10013

In United Kingdom: Screen Face Dist. Ltd., c/o Mitastyle, 24 Powis Terrace, Westbourne Park Rd., London, W11 1 JJ

In Canada: Mavis Theatrical Supplies, 46 Princess St. East, Waterloo, Ontario, N2J 2H7

In Australia: Josy Knowland, 46 Young St., Annandale, NSW 2038

In Far East: Modern Film & TV Equipment Co., 23 Chatham Rd. S. Ocean View Ct., Tsimshatsui, Kowloon, Hong Kong

MAKE-UP EFFECTS STUDIOS
(Prostheses, Special Make-up Effects)
Rick Baker Studio, 12547 Sherman Way, N. Hollywood, CA 91607

TBS, 4000 Warner Blvd., Burbank, CA 91505

The Burman Studios, 4706 West Magnolia Blvd., Burbank, CA 91505

Terry Smith Studio, 330 South Myers St., Burbank, CA 91506

Werner Keppler Studio, 23740 Albers St., Woodland Hills, CA 91364

Dick Smith Company, 209 Murray Ave., Larchmont, NY 10538

Stan Winston Studio, 19201 Parthenia, Northridge, CA 91324

MEDICAL SUPPLIES
(Plaster Bandages, Tubing, Scissors)
Lomedco, 55 Church St., Lowell, MA 01852

Also see local telephone book for other suppliers.

PLASTICS
(Casting Plastics, RTV, Silicones, Acrylics, Urethanes)
Adhesive Products Corp., 1660 Boone Ave., Bronx, NY 10460 Foamart, Adrub RTV, Kwikmold, Casting resins, adhesives, and so on.

BJB Enterprises Inc., Box 2136, Huntington Beach, CA 92647 Various solid and foamed urethanes.

Devcon Corp., Endicott St., Danvers, MA 01923 Devcon WR, metallic varieties, Flexane 60, and others.

Dow Corning Engineering Products Division, Midland, MI 48640 Silicone elastomers, RTV rubbers.

General Electric Co. Silicone Products Division, Midland, MI 48640 Silicone adhesives and sealants, RTV silicone rubber.

Hastings Corp., 1704 Colorado Ave., Santa Monica, CA 90404 Various urethanes.

Industrial Arts Supply Co., 5724 West 6th St., Minneapolis, MN 55416 IASCO products: Plastics, molding supplies, and so on.

Perma-Flex Mold Co., 1919 East Livingston Ave., Columbus, OH 43209   Blak Tufy and Stretchy, Gra-Tufy, UNH, Regular CMC, P-60s.

Smooth-On Corp., 1000 Valley Rd., Gillette, NY 07933   PMC-724, Sonite Release Agents.

RUBBER
(Latex Products Including Slush, Foamed, and Pure Gum)

A-R Products Inc., 8024 Westman St., Whittier, CA 90607

Burman Foam Latex (Sandra Burman), 20930 Almazan Road, Woodland Hills, CA 91364

General Latex Co., 11266 Jersey Blvd., Cucamonga, CA 91730

General Latex Co., High Street, Billerica, MA 01853

G.M. Foam Co., 14956 Delano St., Van Nuys, CA 91411

R & D Latex Co., 5901 Telegraph Hill Rd., Commerce, CA 90040

R.T. Vanderbilt Co. (latex chemicals), 30 Winfield St., Norwalk, CT 06855

SILICAS AND CLAYS

Attapulgus Clays, Englehard Minerals, Menlo Park, NJ 08817   AT-40, Pharmasorb.

Cabot Corp., Tuscola, IL 61953   Cab-O-Sil grades.

Degussa, Rt. 46, Teterboro, NJ 07608

Wyoming Bentonite, National Lead Co., 111 Broadway, New York, NY 10006

SCULPTORS' SUPPLIES

Chavant, Inc., 42 West St., Redbank, NJ 07701   Plastalene, many varieties.

Dick Ells, 908 Venice Blvd., Los Angeles, CA 90015   General supplier of all types of materials.

Knickerbocker Plaster Co., 588 Myrtle Ave., Brooklyn, NY 11205   Plaster and Ultracal.

Sculpture Associates, 40 East 19th St., New York, NY 10003

Sculpture House, 38 East 30th St., New York, NY 10016

Waldo Bros., 202 Southampton St., Boston, MA 02118   Plaster and Ultracal.

Westwood Ceramic Supply Co., 14400 Lomitas Ave., City of Industry, CA 91744

SPECIAL ITEMS
Artificial Eyes

Jonas Brothers, Inc., 1037 Broadway, Denver, CO 80223

Schoepfer, Inc., 138 West 31st St., New York, NY 10001

Tech Optics, 2903 Ocean Park Blvd., Santa Monica, CA 90405

Van Dyke Co., Woonsocket, SD 57385

Mechanical Materials

Edmund Scientific, 101 East Gloucester Pike, Barrington, NJ 08007

Hobby Lobby International, Rt. 3, Franklin Pike Circle, Brentwood, TN 37027

Jerryco, Inc., 601 Linden Place, Evanston, IL 60202

The Joint Works, P.O. Box 9280, Marina Del Rey, CA 90295

Small Parts, Inc., 6901 NE Third Ave., Miami, FL 33138

Techni-Tool, 5 Apollo Road, Plymouth Meeting, PA 19462

UNIONS AND ORGANIZATIONS

IATSE, Make-up Artists and Hairstylists
Local 706, 11518 Chandler Blvd., North Hollywood, CA 91601
Local 798, 31 West 21st. St., New York, NY 10010
NABET, Make-up Sections
Local 15, 1776 Broadway, New York, NY 10019
Local 531, 1800 North Argyle, Hollywood, CA 90028

SCHOOLS AND SEMINARS IN MAKE-UP

Years ago, when the major film studios in California were thriving and live television was centered in the New York networks, most had a form of apprentice program to bring eligible people into the unions. However, this entrance to the field is now very limited, and attending a make-up school or studying with individual make-up artists is more prevalent today. College-level make-up classes are mostly for student performers who wish to learn the basics for self-use and for degree credit. There are no degrees in professional make-up artistry. Hairdressing/beauty schools do not teach studio make-up artistry but prepare students to take a state license in hairdressing and/or skin care to work in a beauty salon—not a film or television studio. Studying with an established union member provides a better insight into the professional field, but choose one who has teaching ability and has never failed a union exam!

Small class groups are best (eight to ten) rather than unwieldy large ones, and adequate facilities for all phases of the sessions are necessary. As well, take care before enrolling that one is guaranteed hands-on demonstrations and practical work rather than a steady stream of prepared videotapes of normal make-up procedures. Tapes should always supplement, but not supplant, teaching methods. Of course, videotapes of important special character make-up effects from films are valuable for illustration of specific make-ups as an adjunctive tool.

Finally, students should not expect miracles and should devote a great amount of time practicing all make-up principles before asking to take a union examination. Know your profession first and thoroughly prepare for it.

Vincent J-R Kehoe holds two-week intensive professional level seminars in basic and advanced make-up, and information on these is available through RCMA, PO Box 850, Somis, CA 93066. Marvin Westmore Academy of Cosmetic Arts, 12552 Cumpston Ave., North Hollywood, CA 90010, specializes in training for cosmetico-medical procedures.

PROFESSIONAL MAKE-UP KITS

MAKE-UP CASES

Two basic styles of cases are generally utilized for make-up kits by professionals. While many East Coast artists prefer the accordion-style case, the West Coast people generally carry the wooden, drawered variety.

RCMA stocks both of these cases in the most popular and versatile sizes. The accordion-style case is black fibre with chromed fixtures and is reinforced with steel frames (Figures C.1 and C.2). It is large enough to hold a full professional assortment of make-up materials. The wooden case with drawers is often hampered in capacity in the style with many small drawers (and often contains more wood than space!). However, RCMA stocks two kinds of these in solid walnut that have only three wide, full-depth drawers plus a generous hinged-top space on top. One has an overall size of 16 inches long, 12¼ inches high, and 8½ inches deep. It has chromed fixtures and a comfortable handle for carrying. This type of case has a lock (the accordion-style fibre case does not) in addition to three strong clasps. Its capacity is larger than that of the accordion case, but its carrying weight is more due to its solid construction.

The second wooden case is a combination design of the old on-set kit and the regular wooden one in use for many years (Figures C.3 and C.4). However, this new concept case made exclusively for RCMA combines all the good features of both and eliminates the main problems of weight and loss of space. Essentially, by removing much of the metal hardware, which is unnecessary, the case weighs empty only 8 pounds and fully loaded, with tissues attached, only 21 pounds, an easy weight for anyone to carry.

A spring clip on the side holds a box of tissues for easy use, and all the drawers are metal lined for ease in cleaning. The top section does lock, and all the drawers are on spring catches so they will not fall out when opened. One can open the drawers without opening the top or cover of the case. This case is not only elegant but also practical for professional make-up artists and is especially designed to fit the newest professional containers without waste of space.

Two types of make-up kits of materials and tools are listed here. The first is a basic RCMA kit recommended by Vincent J-R Kehoe for his Professional Make-up Seminars. It contains all the primary materials and tools and allows room for individual selection of additional items for expansion. The items will fit in either of the case styles, with the multiple color ones such as foundations, lipcolors, pencils, shadings and countershadings, cheekcolors, beardcover, lipgloss, and eyecolors, as well as brushes and tools, all boxed as units for ease in both storage and use.

THE BASIC KIT

CP Foundations: KW-13, KW-3, KW-14, KW-4, KW-37, KW-38, KM-2, KM-3, KM-37, KM-38, KT-3, KN-1, KN-3, KN-5, Superwhite, and Gena Beige.

Countershading: CS-1, CS-2, and Beardcover BC-3, Hair Whitener HW-4

Shading: S-1, S-13, S-14, S-4, S-6, S-8

Cheekcolor: Genacolor Rose and Genacolor Pink

Eyecolor Kit #1: 12 water-applied eyecolors in a plastic box

Pencil Kit #1: 10 haircolor pencils in a plastic box

Brush Kit #2: Two each: 1R, 3F, 4F, 7F, 10R, Eyebrow, and Eyelash
One each: 12F, Wig-cleaning brush

Lipcolors: CP-1, CP-3, CP-4, CP-5, CP-6, CP-14, LS-5, LS-12, DP, LS-16G, Gold Sparkle, Copper

Lipgloss: No-Color Gloss

Lipliner Pencils: Maroon, Dark Red, and Lake Red

Pencil Sharpener

Mascara: Black and Brown

Sponges and Puffs: 5 packs of polyurethane, 1 stipple; and 2 puffs

Powder: No-Color Transparent and PB Powders

Tools: Stainless steel spatula, dental college pliers, and tweezers

Special Material: Plastic Wax Molding Material, (Light) Scar Material, Matte Adhesive, Matte Plasticized Adhesive, Eyelash Adhesive, Matte Plastic Sealer, Tears and Perspiration, Foundation Thinner, PMA Molding Material (Light), Color Process Blood (Types A and C), Prosthetic Adhesive (A and B), Scar and Blister Making Material

Appliance Foundations: KW-2, KM-2, KN-5.

THE FULL-CONCEPT KIT

This list is based on a full kit for both straight and character make-up use to be carried along with the Hair Kit. It expands the basic kit previously described with additional materials and tools and is a full working kit for a professional make-up artist.

CP Foundations: Shinto I to IV, Ivory, F-2, F-3, F-4, KW-23, KW-24, KW4M2, KW4M3, KT-1, KT-2, KT-4, K-3, KW-36, KN-2

Shading: S-2, S-3, S-7, S-9, S-10

Cheekcolor: Flame, Dark, Pink, Lilac, GC Plum

Special Shades: 1667, 6205, Green
Clown Kit: Red, Yellow, Blue, Black
Bruise Kit: Raspberry, Violet, Yellow, Black and the Old Age Spot Kit

Eyecolor Kit #3: 24 different shades in two plastic boxes

Pencils: Dark Silver Gray, Navy

Brush: Wig-cleaning brush

Lipcolors: CP-7, CP-9, CP-10, CP-11, CP-12, LS-17, LS-18, LS-19, LS-20, CP-4G, CP-11G, CP-12G

Tools: Nail file, aluminum tail comb, hair scissors, curved scissors

Plastic Wax Molding Material: Clear, KW-3, KT-3, KN-5, Violet

PMA Lace Adhesive, Prosthetic Adhesive Thinner, Blood Type B, Acetone

Appliance Foundations: Kits #1, #2, and others, or with single containers of these shades.

Other Items: Liquifresh, RCMA Lip Balm; Visine Eyedrops; Small Package of Aspirins; One Plastic Container Each of Q-Tips, Hair Clips, Bobby Pins, Straight Pins, and Rubber Bands; and a Single-edge Razor Blade

Dental Wax: Package each of Black and Red

False Lashes: One Each Black and Brown in Plastic Box

KIT TRICKS

1. Replace the regular low-density polyethylene stock bottles with linear high-density types. Especially suitable for lotions, acetone, alcohols, and so on.
2. Place about a dozen mascara remover pads in a regular 1-ounce foundation container for ease in carrying.
3. Remove sponges from glassine shipping envelopes, and place in plastic sandwich bags.
4. Use shipping cardboard boxes for holding foundations, lipcolors, and small-sized countershading, shading, cheekcolor, etc., containers.
5. Label tops of bottles for easy selection.

Although the full-concept kit will serve for most general applications and work, there are times when the kit must be adjusted for special occasions or specific assignments. For example, those make-up artists who are only doing commercial straight make-up might wish to remove some of the special materials and replace them with extra lipcolors and eyecolors. In addition, when it is known that only one person is to be made up (as in the case of politicians who hire a make-up artist to improve their appearance for camera or public appearances), one might transfer the known use materials to a small attaché case where a make-up cape, towel, and so forth may also be carried rather than carrying the normal hair kit.

There are other available types and varieties of make-up cases. However, these two are well adapted for weight, capacity, and long-term suitability.

FIGURE C.1   *Accordion case closed.*

FIGURE C.3   *RCMA Professional Case.*

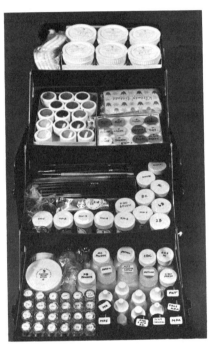

FIGURE C.2   *Accordion case filled.*

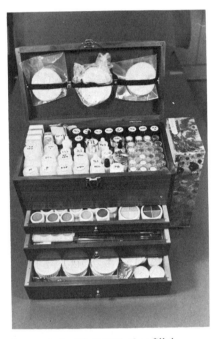

FIGURE C.4   *The RCMA Case filled.*

MAKE-UP ARTIST EXAMINATIONS

Qualification in a union representing make-up artists consists of being able to prove a certain number of days of employment in the field as well as to take an examination in practical make-up artistry before a union committee to demonstrate the applicant's ability. As the main production areas are New York City and Hollywood, both represented by different Locals of two different unions, IATSE and NABET, and all with different examination procedures, one must first select the work area in which he or she wishes to gain employment and the opportunities afforded by each. Intelligent business letters to each should be the first method of approach, asking for an application and/or an appointment with the business manager for an interview if feasible.

SCREENING COMMITTEES

Unions normally have screening committees that review applications before interviewing the prospects. It is to any Local's advantage to consider carefully such applications so that the best talent is made available for their ranks and to increase the artistic potential of the Local. However, much depends upon the progressive attitude of the Business Manager (whose opinion is always given on these matters) as to how unknown or new applicants are handled. It has always proven, in the long run, a serious disservice to itself for any unionized group to seriously restrict membership at any time, even in slow periods of work, as talent, like time, does not rest or wait as they will *make* opportunity. If any applicant feels that unfair treatment or undue favoritism was exhibited in the screening procedure, one does have access to the National Labor Relations Board (who have often ruled in favor of the individuals when a narrow attitude of employment is afforded by the local in question).

EXAMINING COMMITTEE

There are many union members who refuse to be on the Examining Committee because it often takes much volunteer time for the work entailed. However, it is the most important committee function of any Local, and great care should be taken with its membership. All examiners, without exception, should either have taken such an examination

or have performed all the work entailed in its procedures. It is enormously unfair for any applicant to take an examination before Examining Committee members who have not done and possibly could not do every phase of the examination during a work day themselves.

The Examining Committee should consist of three make-up artist members in good standing (who are not union officers, paid, or craft representatives), with two alternates selected to fill in when a regular member cannot attend an examination for one reason or another. This Examining Committee need not be rotated on a fixed periodic limit if it operates properly, although the membership of the Local should have the privilege of asking for a new committee to be formed if they feel that the present one is not operating properly.

One of the most difficult problems of an examiner is to be completely fair in judging an applicant's work. Examiners cannot inflict personality problems (either their own or the applicant's) into the procedure of talent judgment and must, in all instances, judge the completed work of an applicant with proper perspective and fairness. The main question should always be: "Can the applicant's work fully represent the art and craft of the Local in a job on the very next day if he or she is allowed to pass?" Only "Yes" should suffice.

REQUIREMENTS FOR APPLICANTS

After filling out the application for the union and requesting an examination, the applicant must appear before the Screening Committee. The applicants should be ready to show pictures of their work, proof of their employment requirements, and maybe show what their make-up kit looks like. Completeness of these essentials should be judged along with the personality and appearance of the applicant. Just having the tools of the trade does not make a professional make-up artist, but it does show a basic step toward this end.

Once the applicants have been screened and are ready to take an examination, then a date should be set up at which at least two and not more than six applicants are to be examined at the same time. The frequency of such examinations should be at least every six months when applicants are available.

On the day of the examination, applicants must present themselves ready to work, with two models, one male and one female, furnished at their expense and selection. A tip for applicants: A very attractive female with few, if any, facial problems and a male with some character lines in the face, no facial hair, and a normal haircut are best. It is also best to select Caucasian models as more changes can be made on their faces for the examination procedures. Applicants must have a full make-up kit and the hair goods necessary for the examination as well as any appliances that may be required. They must have paid all the fees necessary to the Local and otherwise be in good standing with the union's requirements. It is the strict responsibility of the union to provide a proper space, lighting, chair, and mirror for each applicant. It is extremely unfair to expect applicants to work in inadequate conditions when they are asked to show their work to enter the union. Union members have the right to complain if the producer does not furnish proper make-up rooms, so why shouldn't the applicants have the same privilege?

PAYMENTS BY APPLICANTS FOR EXAMINATION

Although some Locals do not pay Examiners, it is wrong for any applicant or Local to expect that a make-up artist examiner should give up a day or more of time to serve on the Examining Committee or to expect the Local to pay the Examiners to serve. Such expense should be borne by the applicants. A fee of at least $100 should be required, with at least half this amount going to the examiners and the remainder to the Local for administrative work and securing a proper place for the examination. The fee should be an individual one and not be returnable in case of failure in the examination. Once again, applicants will think twice before requesting an examination if they must bear its cost and will have the tendency to prepare themselves fully. It also places the Local under the responsibility to provide adequate examination premises and conditions. An applicant who fails the examination should have to wait at least 90 to 180 days before being allowed to take another.

SCORING THE EXAMINATION

Although most applicants for any form of examination will be subject to apprehension and nervousness, it is only in the *work completed* that an examiner may judge the talent of the applicant. Whatever system of point grading is employed, the percentage rating of a passing grade should not be less than 80 percent. If the applicant fails to complete any project or part of the examination in the required time, no points should be allowed and, if done, only for one project or part of the examination. These circumstances must be agreed upon by all examiners present.

No applicant should be informed as to the progress or marks of the examination until it is completed. Telling an applicant that he or she is passing or failing at any time during the examination is unfair.

CATEGORIES WITHIN A LOCAL

Some Locals may set up certain categorical groups such as department heads, charge make-up artists, assistant make-up artists, and so on, employing seniority of membership or status, work ability, or area of work (film, television, or stage), and may require an examination to rise to a higher category within the Local's work structure.

Such categories should not be harmful or restrictive to the talent advancement of any member, and they should be carefully administered and designed to provide fairness and opportunity potential. In today's similarity between the make-up requirements of all mediums, any examination should be as strict as another and standards not lowered in any manner or for any medium.

PERIOD OF EXAMINATION

The suggested examination (which is designed for one full day) may be extended to two or even three days of time, with all elective projects required as well as additional hair and prosthetic work, if it is believed that such a competitive level of demonstration of ability is necessary. This is based, of course, on the needs and requirements of an individual Local, but the decision should be the norm and not used solely to make one particular examination more difficult than another. Due to considerably more character work being performed in the California area of production, the extended examination time is the case, while in New York City, both unions require only a one-day examination at this time. No examination should, however, consist of less than the stated requirements and projects.

EXAMINERS' MARKING PROCEDURE

All three examiners must mark independently and not compare individual scores until the examination is fully completed. A scoring card should be made for each applicant and the final score for each be an average of the three examiners' marks. Applicants

SUGGESTED TYPICAL EXAMINATION

Time: 8:30 A.M. to 5:30 P.M. with a 1-hour lunch break.

APPLICANTS GRADED ON:	POINTS	TIME (Minutes)
Attitude and Conduct	2	
Appearance	1	
Make-up Kit	2	10
Oral Exam: At least three questions from each examiner	5	20
Written Exam: A series of 10 questions (selected from a standard list of about 50)	10	30
Set-up Period for Materials and Examiners Marking Written Exam		20
Practical Exam		
Straight Beauty Make-up on a Woman	10	45
Straight Make-up on a Man	5	25
Fashion Make-up on a Woman (including false lashes)	5	45
Lunch Break		60
Age a Man 20 Years (include hair graying but no appliances)	10	30
Lay a Beard and Mustache on a Man	10	30
Apply Eyebags or Other Aging Prosthesis and Make-up	5	30
Apply a Prosthetic Nose and Make-up	5	30
Note: The last three exercises can be combined in one make-up.		
Apply Old Age Stipple on Half a Face	5	45
Exercises: Required		
Apply cuts, bruises, tattoo, scars, burns, tears, and sweat	5	30
Attach a men's toupee, lace beard, or sideburns	5	30
Exercises: Elective	15	60
Attach a Bald Cap and Make-up		
Attach an Appliance to Show a Bullet Hit and Blood Flowing		
Apply Oriental Eyelids and Make-up		

should have the right only to total scores, and such should be posted in the Local's office within three days. As most examiners know within an hour or so what the final scores are, there should be little reason to make an applicant wait two or three weeks for the marks. Examiners' score cards must be filed with the Local after being signed by the person who scored the card.

NOTIFICATION OF APPLICANTS

Those who pass the examination should then follow the union's procedure for membership, while those who fail should either ask to be placed on the list for the next examination or seriously re-assess their desire to be a professional make-up artist.

To make the examination more comprehensive, the three electives can be made required, with 5 points given for each exercise and the time extended an additional hour. If this is done, it should be standard and constant and not done for just a certain or single group of applicants.

As can be totalled, the score available is 100 points, and at least 80 points are required for a passing grade. Written, oral, and kit account should go for 20 points, straight make-up for 20 points, and 60 points for character make-up.

* * * *

Mr. Kehoe's qualifications to discuss these procedures are based on his 25 years of membership in the New York City IATSE and having been on the Examining Committees for over ten years, in addition to heading and writing their Apprentice Training Program. As well, he formulated the first examination procedures for the New York NABET Local as well as holding a card in that union under various categories for 20 years. His original professional book on make-up, published over 25 years ago, was the bible of study for the majority of union members all over the world.